An Insider's Guide

Edward Eves

VISTA IBÉRICA PUBLICAÇÕES

First published in 1993
2nd edition 1994
3rd edition 1996

Text copyright: © Edward Eves 1996
Illustrations copyright: © Brian Harris 1996

Published by Vista Ibérica Publicações
Len Port - Peter Daughtrey
N.I.P.C. 900398086.

Address: Largo 5 de Outubro, 28,
8400 Lagoa, Portugal.
Tel/Fax: 351 082 52370.

UK Distributors: M K Book Services
7 East Street - Newtown - Huntingdon PE18 6RZ
Tel/Fax: 0480 431703

Printed by Tipografia Peres, S.A.
Rua das Fontaínhas, Lote 2
Venda Nova - Amadora

All rights reserved. No part of this publication may be reproduced or transmitted in any form or by any means without permission in writing from the publishers.

Every reasonable care has been taken in presenting the information in this book, but no responsibility can be taken for any problems or claims arising from any inaccuracies.

ISBN: 972-8044-18-6
Dep. Legal N.º 100238/96

ACKNOWLEDGEMENTS

This edition of the BureauJungle Book would have been much the poorer without help and advice generously given by a number of experts. Our heartfelt thanks go to the following contributors in their specialist fields:

Building	Des Taylor and Angus McLean
Computers	Chip Howlett and Steve Reid
Education	Peter Maddison
Gardening	Geri van Bergeijk
Guns	Ken West
Heating	Ralph Broad
House management	Anna Rose
Law	Dra Carmen de Andrade e Silva
Medical insurance	Margaret Norris
Motoring regulations	Andre Claeys
Pools	Des Taylor
Television	Hugh Cocks and Ron Palmer-Hall
Veterinary care	Doctors David Hogger and Ian McLaren

To the above list must be added the flow of information in the form of letters and conversations from the membership of AFPOP during the years that the writer was Editor of the *Update* newsletter.

CONTENTS

Foreword	6	79	House Letting
Introduction	7	83	House Moving
Accounts	11	86	Identity Cards
Banking	13	87	Insurance
Births	18	97	Interior Decor
Bombeiros	20	105	Languages
Building	23	107	Lawyers
Businesses	29	110	Marriages
Computers	31	113	Medical
Consulates	37	122	Motoring
Deaths	39	147	Offshore Companies
Education	43	160	Pastimes
Electricity	47	155	Pets & Vets
Employees	52	161	Police
Financial Services	56	163	Pools
Gardening	60	168	Post
Guns	66	172	Porperty
Health & Beauty	69	181	Residency
Heating	74	188	Restaurants & Food

CONTENTS

Security	195	221	Travel
Taxes	199	226	Water
Telephones	208	233	Wills
Television	214	237	Wine
Timeshare	217	245	Services Directory

FOREWORD

By 1988 when Edward Eves came to live in Portugal, he had spent eight years with the Rootes motor group, 14 years designing and building cameras in his own advertising and portrait studio, and more than 30 years as a technical writer and editor for leading motoring and aviation magazines in Britain.

From 1955 to 1966 he covered every Formula One Grand Prix, and every major rally and sports car race in Europe. In 1964 he founded the Thursday Club. It is still going and all the top UK engine designers are members. He did not miss a Monte Carlo rally between 1955 and 1975, or a Le Mans 24-hour race from 1956 to 1980. All the while he was test driving and reporting on a wide spectrum of rare, high-performance cars - more than 200 models in all - including many Mercedes and Mercedes-Benz Grand Prix cars.

He collected, restored and flew vintage aircraft, amassing 28 different types in his logbook, sometimes flying his own planes to car races and twice competing in the King's Cup air race. There was even time for writing books, four of them, including two on Rolls-Royce cars.

After a heart attack in 1988, Ted foresook the roar of engines and the smell of printer's ink in the UK and opted for a quiet life in the fragrant countryside of the Algarve.

Having thrown away the last of a long line of burnt-out typewriters, he soon found himself as the unpaid editor of *Update,* the newsletter of the ever-expanding AFPOP organisation. As such he was constantly ferreting around for information about new laws and keeping abreast of other developments of special interest to expatriates in Portugal. When the idea for this book first came up in 1993, he was the obvious person to ask to write it. His state-of-the art IBM and Microsoft set-up has been overheating and belching smoke ever since.

While every reasonable care has been taken in presenting the information in this third edition, like the others, it is not intended as a substitute for professional specialist help. The intention is simply to offer pointers and establish guidelines to make life all the more enjoyable in an ever-changing Portugal.

Len Port - Peter Daughtrey
Vista Ibérica Publicações

INTRODUCTION

Flicking through the pages of this book one could easily come away with the impression that here is a country riddled with bureaucracy, greed and corruption. But is any other nation, your own included, very different? A lot of the unfortunate things that go on here have been imported from northern Europe. The urge to make the quick buck is not the prerogative of people born in lands where the sun shines incessantly and the olive trees grow.

This book is meant to ease the way for you, to make an already enjoyable country more so. Don't be put off by the warnings in some chapters. This is usually the worst that can happen. The nitty-gritty of life in Portugal, the bureaucracy and autocracy of the Napoleonic Code Civile, has its parallel in many other EU countries. Put into perspective, it is only a very small part of the wider, colourful spectrum of living in this fair and pleasant land.

Looking back at our own reasons for retiring here, we recall visions of sunshine, clear air, a gentle pace of life, a white house in the hills away from the sea, a few like-minded British friends, some good wine at affordable prices. All this we have found and much more. In common with many other immigrants, our circle of friends of all nationalities is wider, far wider, than if we had stayed in our own country. If you like interesting people you will find them here.

An unforeseen fulfillment was that for six and a half years we were able to contribute our writing skills voluntarily to try and make life a little easier for other immigrants through the regular newsletter of the Association of Foreign Property Owners in Portugal. We like to think that the *Update* newsletter was a significant factor in building AFPOP into the influencial organisation it is today. Early in 1995, for personal reasons, we relinquished the editorship and production of *Update*. This has allowed us to concentrate our efforts on this book, whose object is to bring together and explain in plain English to the whole foreign community, the pleasures and pitfalls of living in Portugal.

Portugal may be part of the Iberian Peninsula, but it is a very special part. Cross the border at Vila Formosa and you leave a wooded, hilly countryside ripe with history and enter a land of semi-arid plains. It is as if a great hand had smoothed out Spain like a tablecloth and left the folds, the hillocks and the hummocks over the border in Portugal, much to its advantage scenically and strategically.

In an area little more than a third of the United Kingdom, this long narrow country contains an enormous variety of scenery and climate, from the sub-tropical Algarve to the ski-slopes of Malhão da Estrela in Beira Alta. It is steeped in history and rich in beautiful buildings and precious objects. What is sad is that so many people from Northern Europe emigrate to the Algarve, with its beautiful weather and untidy building sites, only to vegetate, never moving further north than Alzejur or making only the occasional trip to Lisbon to shop rather than explore that beautiful, historic city. What even these people cannot avoid if they travel by road, is the unforgettable panorama of the capital as they cross the great bridge over the Tagus.

In Lisbon there are exciting - we mean that - museums full of artefacts which helped to shape the modern world. There are other equally exciting places to see and enjoy elsewhere in Portugal. Coimbra has the most beautiful library in Europe. Sintra is emotive with its wooded hills and royal palaces. Or go to Caramulo where you can take the waters and have a look at one of the better motor museums in Europe.

And don't underestimate the people. They have been described, unkindly, as proud but devious. We prefer to regard them otherwise. If you are British you might find a parallel with Wales and the Welsh tribes. They were pushed by foreign invaders into the left-hand side of the country. One feels that the same thing happened to the Portuguese people in the Iberian peninsula. They have the same sturdy independence, and maybe the Welsh proclivity to sing finds an echo in *fado*. Certainly they are very different from their opposite numbers east of the border and we find them more agreeable, if less ambitious.

What is very evident is a strong artistic tendency. Our maid Isabel, a simple countrywoman, will re-arrange ornaments or place flowers, always to better effect. And if a builder is making alterations to profiles of walls or buildings, it is always better to give him a rough idea of what you want, or even leave him to his own devices, rather than making a detailed sketch. Portuguese craftsmen have an inherent eye for line. Just take a look at some of the unspoilt villages and the way the buildings blend into each other. No architect had a hand in this.

There are so many aspects of Portugal to write about, and so little time or space to do it in. A number of good writers have been inspired to write about the country. Marion Kaplan, Susan Thackeray, Rose Macaulay and Sarah Bradford have all written fascinating stuff about the history of the country and the character of its people. Rosemary de Rougemont discusses the economics of living here.

In this 1996 issue of the BureauJungle Book we have added two more chapters: one on renting out your property, the other on protecting it from human predators. Both of these offer guidance in two important but opposite facets of life in Portugal. With these new chapters together with those added to the last edition, you will find yourself, having penetrated the bureau-jungle, all set to decorate your villa, install satellite television and generally settle down for a long and happy sojourn in Portugal. As before, we like to think that this handbook will be complementary to existing literature because it is an ongoing thing by virtue of new information which is coming in all the time.

Once again we have to thank Dra Carmen de Andrade e Silva for her unstinting and ever cheerful help in updating the legal sections.Other helpers have made a lesser but still essential contribution. They are listed on page 3.

As in the last edition there is a certain amount of advertising. It is hoped this will help readers to find what they are looking for. It also helps to subsidise the free copy of the book to each of AFPOP's full members. For easier reference, the advertising is contained in the editorial pages. This does not mean that we, as the author, necessarily endorse the goods or services offered. Nor, as you will see, have we allowed commercial considerations to influence our opinions in any way.

Have fun, enjoy Portugal.

Edward Eves

ACCOUNTS

Do you need an accountant?

Retired people living as residents in Portugal on their pensions will scarcely need the services of an accountant. If they are members of AFPOP they can have Anglicised forms to guide them in completing the standard Portuguese income tax form. Or if they are paying tax on their overseas income they can follow the procedure outlined in the chapter on Taxes.

Business accounts

If you have a business in Portugal you will need a Portuguese accountant to prepare your accounts for presentation to the *Finanças*. In the case of an unlimited company, *sociedade anónima com responsabilidade ilimitada,* there is a legal requirement for an official chartered accountant. In *quota* companies this is a requirement only if you have more than a set number of staff, or an income above a set amount. In reality everyone should use an accountant, even for the smallest business.

Small businesses employ local accountants to comply with all the legal requirements regarding bookkeeping and records. They prepare and submit the IVA returns every quarter and prepare a tax statement at the year end. They will also organise the regular payment of *caixa,* and those fiddly little taxes that must not be forgotten about.

Corporation accounts

So far as corporations are concerned, we are indebted to Blackstone Franks for the following information. The rules are somewhat different here.

- ❏ Accounts are prepared to a standard format.
- ❏ Depreciation rates are laid down by law and are on a straight line basis.
- ❏ A lower rate may be used so long as it is not less than the legal rate.
- ❏ Depreciation can be increased by 50% if equipment is being used by more than one shift in a factory.
- ❏ Appropriations from profits may be put into reserve for fixed assets and are deductible if they are used within three years.

ACCOUNTS

> ❏ There is no adjustment of profits for tax purposes.
> ❏ Consolidated accounts are not prepared. A holding company only takes into its accounts dividends actually received.

Foreign income

If your main income is derived from investments in your own country and they have to be consolidated into a Portuguese account which attracts IRS, there are a number of foreign accountants with a foot in both camps.

They can be of great assistance, but in some cases their fees are considerable. Before engaging their services it is as well to establish, in writing, exactly what they are going to do for you and what their fees will be.

BANKING

Time is money

Following the 1974 revolution, Portuguese banks were nationalised, resulting in bad service and bad loans. The more liberal governments which followed the immediate post-revolutionary ones returned the banks to the private sector in 1985 and the situation is now improving daily. However, one relic of the old regime does not make for efficiency: bank staff still have the same fireproof employment they had in the heady days of nationalisation. It is almost impossible to sack them and although salaries are low, they can retire on full pay after long service.

The first thing a new arrival notices is the enormous amount of pen-pushing and double checking that goes on in banks here. No doubt that will diminish now that private banking and computers have arrived. Fortunately, we no longer have the situation at the foreign exchange counter where the number of every dollar bill has to be recorded.

The real concern of residents is the length of time required to have money transferred. Most residents have a friendly bank manager who will credit a cheque immediately rather than having it transferred through the international system, which is costly. Although you don't get the most advantageous exchange rate, the "friendly" method is good for you and good public relations for the bank. It used to be for free but with falling interest rates, a charge is now made. It is still good value.

If you plan to bring in large amounts of money, it pays to do so in winter. During the summer, exchange rates seem to be artificially low to take full advantage of the tourist season.

With Portuguese overnight interest rates what they are, one has to take a sidelong glance at the banks' yarn that foreign cheques travel by post from the provinces to the central clearing bank in Lisbon, and then to the clearing bank in the country of origin, with credits the same route back.

Conventional foreign exchange transactions are a sore point with many expatriates and visitors. Home country banks are ever generous to themselves when transferring money from one country to another. Here telegraphic transfers from Portugal by the "Swift" procedure are charged at 8,000$ by NovaRede, and 3,000$ plus 0.25% of the sum transferred with a minimum of

BANKING

2,000$ by BPA.

Travellers cheques are coming in for harsh treatment. British banks are warning their customers that Portuguese banks are charging up to 2,000$ for each travellers cheque over an above the Government tax of 0.9%. Their advice is to take large denomination cheques or to go to an American Express office where it will be done for free with the exception of the Government tax. This does not only apply to British travellers cheques. This type of cheque from any country attracts the same treatment.

Another way of transferring money from one country to another is the IBOS inter-bank computer link. This is supported initially by six banks: the Royal Bank of Scotland in the UK, BCI in Portugal, Banco Santander in Spain, Credit Commercial de France in France, Kredietbank and Credit General in Belgium. Charges in sterling are as follows when moving money from the Bank of Scotland:

❏ Outward transfers	0.2% with a minimum charge of £7 and maximum of £18.
❏ Standing orders	£3 flat rate.

The other banks have their own scales of charges.

Royal Bank of Scotland have offshore presence in Gibraltar, Jersey and the Isle of Man, while BCI, which is a subsidiary of the Scottish bank, has an offshore presence in Madeira and Nassau. In all dealings with offshore tax havens one has to bear in mind that, as in other countries, the Portuguese *Finanças* appears to have complete access to all bank records within their own country.

Current accounts

One can immediately write Portuguese cheques on a friendly transfer but be warned: what you have done in effect is fixed yourself a short term overdraft. That foreign cheque of yours will not become real money in your account until it has been cleared. This can take three weeks. If you were near to your limit and immediately went on a cheque-writing spree, you would find when you received your statement a bevy of D's, indicating debtor, on the right-hand side. Your cheques will be honoured, but you could incur swinging charges called *juros*, which are anything

BANKING

but just . It is banking practice here to enter debits before credits so that even if you are credited on the same day with more than you are debited, your account will show you to be overdrawn on that day and the computer could decide to impose a *juro*. An acquaintance, inadvertently overdrawing to the tune of 50,000$ for two days, was charged 6,000$ by one of the leading banks.

Tourist accounts are now a thing of the past. Thanks to the EU, foreigners can now have current accounts. Some banks pay interest on these accounts so long as they have your *Número de Contribuinte*. Provided you keep about 250,000$ in your account you will be paid about 2.5% interest. At the top of the scale, should you regularly keep in excess of 1,000 contos in your current account, you will be paid more depending on interest rates. Whatever you are paid will be subject to deduction of tax at the rate of 20%. Bank charges vary from bank to bank and between customers and non-customers.

Dud cheques

If a foreign cheque for a substantial amount bounces, you can be charged up to 20 % in interest and fees when you come to repair the damage.

Should you be presented with a dud cheque for a significant amount, like selling your car, take it back to your bank and ask them to put their red stamp (*carimbo vermelho*) on it. Promptly, that is within five days, take it to the GNR in your *Câmara* area. If you do this, the GNR will be prepared to go and talk to the person who issued the cheque. If this doesn't work, then you have to contact your lawyer. It should be pointed out that to issue a dud cheque is a criminal offence which can be cause for the issuer to be blacklisted by the Banco de Portugal and have his cheque facilities withdrawn. Nevertheless, many rebounding cheques are issued; the supermarket checkouts have long lists of culprits. If one of your cheques is returned to you, it should be handed to your bank.

It should also be born in mind that you cannot post-date cheques. If a bank is presented with one, it will pay it immediately. And the banks do not hold themselves liable to check signatures. If you lose your cheque book, the finder can have a cheque-writing spree at your expense if you don't put a stop on all cheques at once.

BANKING

Borrowing from the bank

If you apply for an overdraft for a specific amount and it is credited to your account, you will be charged interest on the whole amount from "day one" whether you have spent the money or not. The bank sees it as a loan rather than permission to go into debit.

An interesting and much used banking device available to companies doing business with each other is the *Letra*. This is arranged between the two companies and their banks whereby, with approval of the customer's bank, a supplier can have credited to his bank account an agreed sum which his customer will pay back to his bank at the end of a fixed period of one, two or three months. The supplier has the full use of the money immediately, the customer is expected to pay it back to the bank at the end of the fixed period.

If at the end of the period it is inconvenient for the customer to pay all, he can pay back 10% of the original amount if it is for a month, or 25% if it is for three months, and fix a fresh *Letra* for the remainder for the same amount of time as the initial period. If at the end of this second *Letra* he doesn't choose to pay back all of the balance, he can pay another 10% or 25% of the original amount and arrange a third *Letra*. In all, a three-month Letra can be renewed three times and a monthly *Letra* nine times. The interest charges are high and there is stamp duty to be paid.

Personal banking

Many of the expatriates who read these pages are retired and like to take care of all eventualities. It is wise to ensure that a surviving spouse has money in the bank to draw on in the event of a bereavement, bearing in mind the length of time it takes to settle an estate. One needs to ensure with the bank that the survivor has access to the whole of the balance and not just part of it. Some couples hand each other a signed, blank cheque to cover this eventuality.

One way, naturally, is to have a current joint account. It is important to keep a good balance in this because if one of the account holders should die, the survivor does not automatically have access to the whole of the balance. Although it may be distressing or even technically illegal, upon the death of a partner people have been known to immediately withdraw the whole bank balance before the death has been officially notified.

BANKING

Offshore Private Banking

Deposit Accounts in Escudos and other major curencies
Current Accounts * Offshore Funds
Bond and Share Dealing and Custody
Managed Portfolios

Reliability and tradition in the Algarve

HAMBROS BANK
(GIBRALTAR) LIMITED

Contact Wendy Haden da Conceição, Apartado 119,
Rua Dr João Batista Ramos Faísca 15/17, Boliqueime,
8100 Loulé, Tel. (089) 360266 Fax. (089) 360347
Licensed by the Financial Service Commission Gibraltàr
Nº. 00033B

Our range of financial services is backed by a Rock solid reputation

Whether you are looking for an excellent return from a savings account or a loan to help buy a home in Portugal, at Abbey National Gibraltar Ltd. we are here to help. Our wide range of deposit accounts gives you the benefit of high interest automatically paid gross, along with the added tax advantage of an offshore base. We also offer a choice of terms, both variable and fixed rate, as well as accounts in Sterling or Escudos, whichever is more convenient for your own needs.

Our mortgages cover Portugal and with help from our advisors you can get into your dream home as quickly and painlessly as possible.

For help and advice in Portugal, please contact our Portuguese Office on EN125 - Edifício Cor de Rosa, R/c Esq. - Quatro Estradas - 8125 Quarteira or phone 351 89 397900.

ABBEY NATIONAL
(GIBRALTAR) LIMITED

The habit of a lifetime

Licensed by the Financial Services Commission to carry out Financial Services Business. Licence Number PSC00044-B.
Abbey National (Gibraltar) Ltd. will require a charge over the property. A life assurance policy may also be required. All loans subject to status and not available to persons under 18. Written quotations available on request.
YOUR HOME IS AT RISK IF YOU DO NOT KEEP UP REPAYMENTS ON A MORTGAGE OR OTHER LOAN SECURED ON IT

BIRTHS

Registering a birth

Maybe to encourage the birthrate, registering the birth of a child is just about the cheapest encounter you're likely to have with the bureaucracy.

Two documents are required when registering a birth. One is a simple birth registration which is performed at the *Conservatória de Registo Civil* in the same way that you would register a property. The other is the *cédula* (the word means schedule) acquired in the same place. This is a personal log book in which all the major events in a person's life are recorded, including marriage, children born of the marriage, and death. Most of these events can also be added to the birth certificate in the *Conservatória*. Notarised copies are only valid for three months. And since this period is enshrined in Portuguese law, it also goes for notarised copies of foreigners' birth certificates. It can be important, and frustrating, when people outside the EU are applying for residential visas.

Birth Certificates

When a child is born in Portugal a medical certificate of birth is produced by the hospital in which it is born. This states the sex of the child and the date and time it was born.

The next stage is to obtain the *cédula*. If the child is to be given a commonly used Portuguese name there is no problem here. The hospital certificate is taken along to the *Conservatória de Registo Civil,* the appropriate form is filled in, a small fee is paid and the birth certificate will eventually materialise.

If the child is to be given a non-Portuguese name like William or Friedhelm and at least one of the parents is foreign, it is essential, before filling in the form for the *cédula,* to go to the appropriate consulate and obtain a certificate stating that the name is one recognised by the authorities in the country in question.

Nationality

A child born of foreign parents in Potuguese territory may take Portuguese nationality if the parents so wish, provided the parents have held a valid residence permit for at least six years if their nationality is of a country where Portuguese is the official

BIRTHS

language, or 10 years if the official language is not Portuguese.

If a non-Portuguese father wishes his child to become a citizen of his own country, he must go as quickly as possible to his consulate with the *cédula* in his hand, and register the child with them.

The certificate of birth from the hospital is taken to the *Registo Civil* for the details to be recorded and for a *cédula* to be promulgated.

BOMBEIROS

BOMBEIROS

Join the Bombeiros Voluntários

If you need an ambulance, or have a fire in your home raging out of control, or the forest around you becomes an inferno, the public service which will come to your help with remarkable alacrity is the *Bombeiros*, literally the "Pumpers". Their full name is the *Associação dos Bombeiros Voluntários*.

In most of our native countries the fire brigade and ambulance services are paid for out of the rates and we take them for granted. Here in Portugal the men who run these services are bands of volunteers whose wages are paid for by private subscription. Exactly how is something of a mystery. On the one hand we have the *bombeiros* of Silves going on strike because the *Câmara* would not replace the worn-out tyres on their fire engines. On the other hand we see the Portimão *brigada* driving a splendid ambulance bearing German customs plates, which is clearly on loan from an auspicous manufacturer in Stuttgart. What is patent is that somehow *bombeiros* make ends meet. They get a lot of public support, and deserve it.

For as little as 50 escudos per annum - most of us would want to make it 1,000 escudos - one can become a member of the *Associação dos Bombeiros Voluntários* of your particular area and thereby make not only a positive contribution to the local community, but also make the acquaintance of a very worthy and brave set of people who, perish the thought, you may badly need one day.

They are unlikely to tip you off the stretcher or stop for a drink on the way to your fire if you are not a member, but it would be nice to feel that you were a contributor in such an emergency.

Seriously, joining an *Associação* is not only self-satisfying but virtually a social requirement. It also provides a rare opportunity to get to know worthwhile members of the local community. We are sure they are equally keen to get to know you.

There is the thought that if every expatriate family in the Algarve were to put one *conto* per head into the *bombeiros'* kitty, they would probably have the best fire and ambulance service in Portugal.

Go along to your local *bombeiros* station, make their acquaintance and join. Many of them speak English or French.

BOMBEIROS

You will need:

- ❏ Two passport-size photographs. One for your membership card, one for their records.
- ❏ An entry form which their secretary will provide.
- ❏ Money for your subscription.

They will give you a membership card. Equally important, they will also give you the best local telephone number to ring to get them in a hurry.

BUT REMEMBER, 115 WILL ALWAYS GET THEM ANYWHERE.

BUILDING

A new house from scratch

It is not difficult to understand why so many people prefer to build a house from scratch rather than buying an existing one. Most of us dream of planning and building a house in the sun. But, especially in the Algarve, there are already too many houses and at least half of them are for sale. So before you decide to build, it is well worth having a good look to see if there is anything that meets your requirements.

Bear in mind that lots of people before you have had a yen for a home with a view of the mountains or sea. It is highly likely that they have found that best viewpoint way ahead of you and built a house on it. An established house will have an established garden; moreover, it will be well settled on its foundations. If a properly qualified, independent surveyor who is not a friend of the vendor passes it as sound, all you really have to worry about is the plumbing.

However, if you are determined to build, it pays to take precautions. There are few building inspectors here in Portugal and it is not unknown for them to be on friendly terms with local builders. We know of one development in the Algarve where a fast-talking Portuguese builder/developer was putting up houses which showed every indication of bringing a whole development of individual homes into disrepute because of poor construction.

BUILDING

The result was that owners were investing large sums of money in property which, in a few years time, could well be unsaleable because of defects like a pool sliding down the hillside. It is highly likely that there are similar cases elsewhere, especially in the southern region.

AFPOP has drawn up the following recommendations to protect their members. They are typically thorough and well worth following.

Prior to the contract

If you are using an architect, see other work that he has done, including completed houses.

- ❏ Obtain a detailed quotation of his services for:
  Sketch designs.
  Complete drawings and specifications for *Câmara* submission.
  Engineering drawings and calculations.
  Provision of drawings and specifications for builder's quotations.
  Site supervision.
  Quotations are usually based on the superficial area of the house.
- ❏ Some builders offer a design service. In such cases use the same approach as for an architect. Never commit yourself to anything which gives such a builder a contract to design and build; limit any arrangement to an agreement that he will be one of the people asked to quote at stage 4.
- ❏ Obtain three quotes for the actual building. Make sure that you have seen examples of each builder's work and have talked to the owners. Make sure that the builder you choose is a registered builder, i.e. has an *alvará*. He should have been in business for at least five years, have a reasonable office set-up and should have a good command of your own language, both written and spoken.
- ❏ Make sure that the specification covers everything, every power socket and light point, insulation, weather proofing, plumbing (material of pipes) etc. Both you and the builder must know exactly what is included in the building.
- ❏ The quotation should include the stage payments required by the builder.
  Never pay a large deposit to start work or make payments in excess of the value of work done.

BUILDING

> Payments should relate to easily recognised stages in the construction, and it is better to make twenty payments of 5 % than five payments of 20 %.
> ❏ The quotation should also contain a building program, and possibly a penalty clause for delay and a bonus for early completion.

Contract

❏ The contract should include the drawings, specifications and the accepted quotation.
❏ The contract should state that the builder is responsible for obtaining connection of mains services and the issue of the habitation certificate when building is complete.
The completion of the building must clearly be shown as the date of receipt of the habitation certificate. The final payment, which should be a large one, must not be made until this is to hand.
It is worthwhile even after this to hold back 2½ % for a six month defect period.
❏ The contract must state that no alteration can be made except in writing signed by both parties. If you initiate an alteration, any cost or time implication must be contained in the written agreement (confirmed in writing).
❏ The contract should define a process of arbitration in the case of a dispute.

Construction

❏ If you are employing your architect for site supervision, it should be made clear in your contract with him that this should be a weekly visit and he should submit a short report and photographs indicating the progress of the works. He must have a copy of the contract with the builder so that he can advise you on stage payments.
The builder must be advised in his contract that you are employing a supervising officer for this purpose.
❏ If you are not using an architect, you should employ a qualified engineer to act as supervising officer. This will be money well spent.

BUILDING

- If you are a resident and feel that you can do your own weekly visits, it will still be money well spent to employ an engineer to accompany you on a monthly basis; a trained eye can see so much more.
- You or your supervising officer will want to see and approve samples of the materials used: bricks, sand, woodwork etc. etc.
- The majority of owners and builders are honest people who just want to see the job done and paid for.

  Most disputes arise from misundertandings. Most of these could be avoided by attention to detail in the drawings, specifications, quotation and contract. Time spent then is time saved at the end.

Beware ...

The foregoing is an ideal situation, but remember the Roman *quis custodiet custodies,* "who shall guard the guardians". We sadly lack a ruling body in the estate and building business with real teeth. One has to play it very much by ear when building a new home. For example, the aforementioned builder/developer speaks very good English and is very convincing, but builds bad houses. His rival on the site, who is a an excellent builder, speaks no English. It is a sad thing to have to say, but in the south particularly there are a good many people in the building and associated professions whom one cannot trust implicitly; and this refers every bit as much to the immigrants as it does to the Portuguese professionals, many of whom are excellent craftsmen with a wonderful eye for shape and line.

Licences

Decree Law 445/91 of 20 November 1991 approves licensing rules for private buildings. These cases can now be authorised by the *Câmara Municipal* or by the central administration (the Government).

Private individuals can now request previous information *(pedidos de informação prévia)* on their projects, thus eliminating risk and costs. This does not jeopardise the time scale.

This decree law creates the *Certificado de Conformidade* for certain types of licence to improve the quality of the projects. It avoids the intervention of the *Câmara's* technical department and reduces by 50 % the intervention of the *Câmara* as a whole.

BUILDING

New legal instruments are created to ensure that the work is carried out by the applicant. Third parties can now carry out work themselves if there are damages resulting from an applicant's non-activity.

There are now very heavy sanctions against illegal building. Decree Law 35/93 of 7 October 1993 refers to building licences issued before the enforcement of Municipal Direction Plans (PDM's). It means that no building permission is valid until it has been verified under these new regulations unless you can prove you have already started and not suspended building before the relevant PDM has been approved. The same applies for development (*loteamentos*) and tourist enterprise approvals.

Project management

Portuguese law requires builders to be responsible for minor defects for the first year and for structural defects during the first five years after handing over the property.

Unfortunately, unlike most states in the EU, Portugal does not require architects and builders to carry insurance against design or construction faults. As a result, few of them go in for this desirable commodity, relying on personal charm, fast talking or sheer disregard for the law to avoid claims. It's a lucky, or rich, man who succeeds in recouping any losses under the civil law.

The main reason for this state of affairs is that the mortgage industry in Portugal is in its infancy. There is, therefore, no national builders' association to set standards which the builder and architect must comply with before a building society will grant a mortgage.

One way round this is for the client to have his own insurance. This works out at approximately 5% of the cost of construction. The alternative is to employ a project manager who will charge about the same, but may well save more than that through his experienced management.

A project manager's qualifications are somewhat different from those required of a building surveyor. Ideally, he should be a qualified structural engineer or experienced architect, speaking your own language, who will attend to such details as the choice of site, review of the architect's drawings (many Portuguese architects are disinterested in detail) and see the construction right

BUILDING

through to the granting of the *Licença de Habitação*. This is a very desirable arrangement if you are not resident in Portugal or are unfamiliar with building methods.

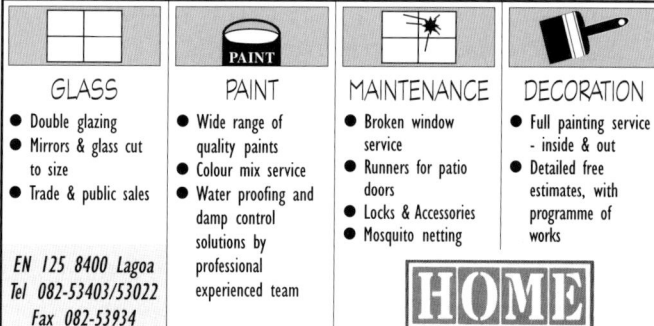

GLASS	PAINT	MAINTENANCE	DECORATION
• Double glazing • Mirrors & glass cut to size • Trade & public sales EN 125 8400 Lagoa Tel 082-53403/53022 Fax 082-53934	• Wide range of quality paints • Colour mix service • Water proofing and damp control solutions by professional experienced team	• Broken window service • Runners for patio doors • Locks & Accessories • Mosquito netting HOME	• Full painting service - inside & out • Detailed free estimates, with programme of works

Eur. Ing. DES TAYLOR

Chartered Engineer

CONSTRUCTION CONSULTANT

* Surveys of villas for sale

* Design, preparation of specifications and contracts for new villas

* Supervision of Construction * Arbitration... etc.

Tel (082) 69296, Fax (082) 764969

POWER TOOL RENTAL
Lightweight tower scaffolding
High power pressure washers
Generator 4 k.v.a.
Concrete mixers and chainsaws
Various Hilti power tools
We are always expanding our stock!
Call for our price and stock list!
Tel: 082 342764 Fax: 082-52105

BUSINESSES

Setting up

If it is your aim to earn an honest penny while you enjoy the delights of living in Portugal - it can be enjoyable despite the bureaucracy - you will probably have settled your options before you read this. For those who have not made any decisions on what kind of business to set up, the options are broadly as follows. To deal with them in more detail is beyond the scope of this book and would certainly require more pages than there are in it.

> - You can seek employment with a local, national or international company.
> - You can exercise your professional skills as an individual in, say, photography, writing, drawing or some kind of craftsmanship; not doctoring or dentistry which require registration with their respective professional associations.
> - You can set up a retail or wholesale business, with employees, as an individual or with a partner.
> - With a partner or partners, you can form a private company, *sociedade de quotas,* with limited liability. Each member is in effect a partner holding a share of the capital. This share, the *quota*, is transferred by deed. There are no share certificates and you need a minimum of two shareholders.
> - You can form a full-blown public company, a *sociedade anónima com responsabilidade ilimitada*. The law calls for a minimum of five shareholders. The board of directors is elected by the shareholders in the usual way. At the same time, the General Meeting elects a supervisory board, the fiscal board, to keep an eye on the directors. NB: The term *ilimitada* means that personal capital can be called on in case of debt.

Decree laws in 1993 called for notaries, to get approval for the names of new companies within 48 hours, as distinct from the lawyers or their clients having to do the work. This has so far proved impractical because of the cost to the state of equipping every notary with a fax machine. There is now talk of privatising the notarial offices!

The first option is a lot easier now that Portugal has passed

BUSINESSES

laws allowing citizens of EU countries, and their families, to have residence permits as a matter of course. For non-EU citizens the situation has not changed. For both categories, work permits are still required.

The second option requires you to register as self-employed with the Ministry of Social Security and with the income tax office. Thereafter you can roll up your sleeves and get going.

Setting up your own business with employees could call for a knowledge of the Portuguese language. That is unless your first employee is hired as an interpreter. Under the old law, the first six employees had to be Portuguese. Maybe now that Portugal is a full member of the EU, these can be EU citizens. You will need to keep proper accounts and abide by the strict Portuguese employment laws.

Non-residents wishing to set up a Portuguese company no longer need permission from the Institute of Foreign Investment to import capital like in the old days. However, all shareholders are now required to sign a declaration, which is filed with the notary, that they were not previously shareholders or administrators of any other Portuguese company which still has fiscal debts outstanding.

The fourth and fifth options call for the services of a good company lawyer. In this respect take a recommendation from a compatriot who has done it ahead of you. If you don't have one in your immediate circle, the ever-present AFPOP could be of assistance.

When forming a company, or even if you are self-employed, you will need an accountant to handle the forms. Different forms are required for each activity, but they are equally difficult to fill in, especially if you are a foreigner.

When it comes to finding premises in which to pursue your business, you will need one or more of the following:

- ❏ A rental deed for the premises, four walls, a floor and a roof.
- ❏ A *trespasse* (lease) if you are buying a business.
- ❏ A *trespasse* and a rental deed if you are buying a business and taking over rented premises.

COMPUTERS

Personal computers

It has taken a little time for personal computers to arrive in Portugal. But now there are computer shops in most of the main town, usually with the owner's son hovering in the background ever ready to demonstrate his skill with Windows. Machines still tend to cost more here than in Northern Europe, mainly because they are sold through dealers rather than by direct marketing. The plus side of this is technical back up from the dealer which doesn't always come with the direct method of buying.

One practical disadvantage of buying a computer in Portugal, if you are not Portuguese, is that the hardware and software manuals, and the screen messages, are in Portuguese. Moreover, if you are American or British, the keyboard will have many letters and symbols in the "wrong" places. US/English keyboards are hard to come by. As a result, a few dealers whose customers are expatriates are prepared to source equipment from outside Portugal. It is also possible to buy custom-built machines assembled from selected components by expatriate experts.

The most prevalent basic operating system for computers here in Portugal is MS-DOS (Microsoft disc operating system) with Windows or Windows 95 superimposed on it. A few die-hard PC owners, mainly small businesses, stick with MS-DOS on its own because they are running only one or two well-tried programs, which contain all their data, and are happy with the software. However, the new intake has to have the latest and best and the main trend among single users is to buy equipment with Windows or Windows 95 and CD-ROM. They are slick and quick and most new software is written for these high-powered machines which require so much memory that a world shortage and price hike of memory chips is forecast.

Be that as it may, when buying a computer and if you intend to run Windows 95, there are a few basics worth observing.

If the PC is IBM compatible make sure:
- ❏ It has at least a 486DX2/4 or Pentium processor, at least 8 megabytes of RAM and a 540 megabyte hard disc.
- ❏ The latest version of MS-DOS is installed, version 6 or higher.

31

COMPUTERS

- It is easy to fit extra RAM chips and there is room for expansion up to, say, 32 megabytes.
- It is designed to run on 220-250 volts.
- It has a SVGA colour monitor, or better.
- The case is big enough. (A small, streamlined box looks good but it is likely to be under-ventilated in this climate. And there may be no room for extra drives, or RAM, or extra "cards" to allow you to use CD-ROM).
- The fan is reasonably quiet. (You may have to live with that noise for hours on end).
- Any installed software is in a language that the person who is going to use the equipment understands.

It is possible to buy what appear to be high-spec machines from hypermarkets at attractive prices. These are Portuguese-language machines and you need to make sure that they will accept extra RAM. One we looked at had only 2 Mb of RAM. Buying RAM to make this up to 8Mb at current Portuguese prices would cost 75,000$ more, thus absorbing any price saving.

When budgeting for a PC allow for the cost of some kind of emergency power supply, or at least a "spike" protector to preserve your equipment from sudden fluctuations in current voltage. The Portuguese power supply, in the Algarve at least, has its ups and downs and may disappear altogether at the first sign of rain. It is worth knowing that if you can prove your equipment has suffered damage as a result of supply surges, you can claim compensation from the EDP. However there have been cases of visitors from America bringing 110v machines to Portugal and plugging them straight into the Portuguese 220 volt supply with devastating results. The EDP doesn't pay for that. Current transformers are available from dealers. Also, if you have a modem which is permanently plugged into the telephone system, there should be some kind of lightning protection in the line between the 'phone plug and the computer.

The pace of computer progress during the last few years has been fantastic. Specifications have gone up and prices have come down almost monthly. As of now, we seem to have reached some kind of plateau. Unless you insist on the latest developments whether you need them or not, the above equipment should be

COMPUTERS

adequate to handle most Windows requirements for some time to come. That is so long as you steer clear of computer buffs and computer magazines. It is worth bearing in mind that the majority of PC computers world-wide do not even have Windows installed and there are many people getting all they want out of computers which are four or five years old. You don't need a Ferrari to go shopping.

Looking ahead, it is obvious that the increasing use of CD-ROM will call for vast increases in data storage and that "floppies" of the current 1.4 Mb capacity are rapidly becoming out of date. The magazine boffins are advising their readers to go in for hard discs of at least one gigabyte capacity (a gigabyte is 1,000 megabytes).

One feels that home computers are at a cross roads. If you simply want the aforementioned working tool with one of the excellent 'office' suites of software which give you a word processor, spreadsheet and database, plus a modem for access to the Internet, last years model will see you through. If you are looking for a working tool, the moral seems to be not to specify CD-ROM unless you are desperate to play games or want to have access to reference discs such as the Complete Oxford Dictionary. The alternative is a multimedia machine with games, music, not very good video, plus the foregoing, but be prepared to dig deep and continue digging to keep up with trends and improvements.

The Internet

This is the buzz word at the moment and threatens to be a way of life with many owners of PCs. It should be emphasised that the Internet is in itself it is not a commercial organisation. Basically it is a number of international computer networks, including government establishments, universities, libraries and learned establishments, commercial organisations, not to mention every variety of computer guru, linked by the world telephone system. Gaining access to all this information is where the cost comes in.

The Internet is used for communication and its proponents claim that E-mail is much more efficient and economical than fax. The Internet is also a massive information source with the possibility of accessing practically everything you want to know. FTP is for the scholar or writer, Gopher is for the humanist. Most

COMPUTERS

people will go for the World Wide Web which has been described as a virtual World Fair.

The Web is seen as THE up-and-coming advertising medium, with the reservation that you have to advertise through the normal newspaper and journal channels that you are doing it. With the Internet, computer-shopping at last becomes a reality. American retailers have been on the Net for some time and you can shop at British high street names, Barclays Bank, Sainsburys and Argos for example, and pay by credit card. There was anxiety about this but a program is available (Netscape) in which card numbers are scrambled on admission to the Internet and unscrambled at their destination.

However, you don't get anything for nothing in this world and to access the Internet you have to go to a service provider and pay a connection fee. There are many of them in the more developed countries and the user benefits accordingly. Three small Internet service providers have recently been established in Portugal. The most prominent of these is Telepac, S.A. jointly owned by Telecom Portugal and Marconi. Others are Comnexo, who use British Telecom lines, and a Portuguese universities' network.

Telepac have already established PoP's (Point of Presence in the jargon) in most areas of Portugal. They make an initial registration charge and each month will send you a retrospective account with a minimum charge which entitles you to 15 hours on the Internet. Thereafter you are charged in five hour tranches. There is also a deal going with one of the banks giving almost unlimited access for the under-thirties. As elsewhere, over an above this you will be charged by for the telephone time between your location and the location of the service provider. Thus, you can be in contact with the world for the cost of a local call. The costs (1996) work out something like this:

- ❏ Software for E-mail, file transfer and world-wide access about 18,500$.
- ❏ Exploratory software for exploring the 'Web. If you intend shopping by the Internet, a highly recommended one is Netscape Navigator which includes encription of credit card numbers. Cost about 15,000$.

COMPUTERS

- A suitable modem. They are rated at the speed at which they transmit information. A V32 is OK, a V34 is twice as fast. Expect to pay about 50,000$-60,000$ for a Telecom Portugal approved V34, half of that for a V32. Telepac can handle the time-saving and thus cost effective V34 modem transmissions.
- Telepac joining charge 1,600$ plus IVA.
- Minimum Telepac connection time per month 15 hrs charged at 2,500$ plus IVA whether you use it or not.
- Call charges from your office or home to the nearest service provider. For example, if you were calling the Portimão provider from Lagoa, which is a regional call, your phone bill for the 15 hours, if you used all of it, would amount to approximately 18,000$ at daytime rates. In the evening, or if your call is a local one, the charged would of course be less.

If you are a computer buff you will most likely be able to fend for yourself if you want access to the Internet. CD's are available telling you how to do it. Otherwise there are commercial organisations who will take you in hand, modify your computer, set up an account for you with Telepac, supply the software and teach you how to use it, at a total cost of about 134,000$ at the time of writing.

With all this information floating around in mega quantities there is bound to be a downside to the Internet. One manifestation of this is the availability of software to protect your children form being subjected to the hard pornography which has inevitably found its way into the Net. And not surprisingly, that section of the community which lives on the back of the rest is looking hard at this medium as a means of making itself richer. Be warned also that while your computer is switched on and plugged into the telephone system it is wide open to hackers (if they feel that you're a worthwhile quarry) and computer viruses of every degree of perniciousness.

There are those who see the Internet as being one of the most important steps forward in information exchange since moveable type. On the reverse of the coin it is not difficult to see that in its ability to invade privacy and transgress national, religious and cultural boundaries it has enormous, one could say frightening, potential for good or otherwise.

COMPUTERS

As a final thought, when Internet users are connected to the Net they are disconnected from their friends. There are many members of the expat community who waited literally years to have a telephone; to them it is an essential social contact. There's nothing more frustrating than trying to call a number which is permanently engaged.

Your **COMPUTER** Shop
LERENS Informática, Lda
Centro Comercial Carlota, Lj 22-23, Rua da Liberdade
8400 Lagoa ■ Tel (082) 342138 ■ Fax (082) 342135

Computer Solutions - Technical Support
Supplies and Accessories
Printers - Software - Spare Parts - Scanners
Fax/Modems - Multimedia - Network - UPS - Hard Disk

Computécnica - Porches
Repairs - Upgrades - Sales

082-381 053

Nederlands
English
Deutsch

More than 10 years of experience
YOUR SPECIALISTS FOR ALL HARDWARE SOLUTIONS

CONSULATES

Help is at hand

For you and me the consulate of our own country can be of great assistance, much more so than the embassy whose main concern is with matters of state. Consulates deal with the nitty-gritty matters of individuals.

If we are visitors to a foreign country and encounter a problem, our consulate may be the best place to head for. Extreme situations, like being thrown into the cooler, may not allow us to go to the consulate. In such cases, the consul or another representative of the consulate will come to us.

Even if you are not in trouble but intend to spend some considerable time in Portugal, you are well advised to go along to your nearest consulate and register with them. It may be of great benefit in times of personal emergency.

Consulates are a source of information on all sorts of subjects and their role includes giving guidance and practical help to citizens not merely visiting, but living abroad. For example, they can arrange the issue of passports, contact relatives and friends if need be and advise on transferring funds.

What they cannot do is give away money. But if you are robbed or find yourself destitute in some other way, they will bend over backwards to help obtain funds from your bank or elsewhere. This money has to be guaranteed to the consulate's satisfaction. Once that is done, they will make the money available to you immediately.

If you do happen to find yourself in prison, incidentally, consulates can be very helpful. The consul or a member of his staff will visit you within 48 hours of their being advised of your predicament. They will provide you with a form which when completed, will enable you to contact family and friends.

Should you perish, consulates are adept at helping to make arrangements to repatriate your remains on instructions from the next of kin.

On the next page is a list of consulates in Portugal, with their telephone numbers in the Algarve, Lisbon and Oporto.

CONSULATES

Consulate phone numbers

Austria	(082) 416202	(01) 3874162	(02) 2084757
Australia	In extreme emergency, contact UK consulate		
Belgium	(089) 803219	(01) 549145	(02) 2005956
Brazil	(089) 396719	(01) 3473565	-
Canada	(089) 803757	(01) 3474892	-
Denmark	(082) 22031	(01) 545099	(02) 695071
Finland	(089) 394085	(01) 607551	(02) 6102396
France	(089) 313731	(01) 608121	(02) 6173777
Germany	(089) 803181	(01) 3523961	(02) 6102336
Greece	-	(01) 3016991	(02) 698968
Iceland	(082) 413311	(01) 3955224	(02) 307966
Ireland	-	(01) 3961569	-
Italy	(081) 44274	(01) 546846	-
Japan	-	(01)3523485	-
Mexico	(082) 762814	(01) 3862683	-
Morocco	(089) 702449	(01) 3979193	(02) 2008877
Netherlands	(089) 20903	(01) 3961163	(02) 2004867
New Zealand	In extreme emergency, contact UK consulate		
Norway	(089) 823505	(01) 3015344	-
South Africa	-	(01) 3535041	-
Spain	(081) 44888	(01) 3472381	(02) 563915
Sweden	(082) 413311	(01) 3955224	(02) 307966
Switzerland	-	(01) 3973121	-
Turkey	-	(01) 3014275	-
UK	(082) 417800	(01) 3924000	(02) 6184789.
US	-	(01) 726660	-

DEATHS

Long before the inevitable

Even if the likelihood of your falling victim to a fatal illness or accident seems remote, it is wise to have a basic contingency plan, all the more so when you are living in a foreign country. You will not be able to supervise the arrangements after you are dead, so lay the groundwork now.

- Make sure your passport contains the name of your next of kin. If in the event of an emergency your next of kin may be difficult to locate for whatever reason, include in your passport a permanently-based family representative such as a doctor or lawyer.
- Register with your local consulate. Make sure the information on file under your name is updated as appropriate. For example, your consulate should be informed of a change of your next of kin, or changes of address.
- Leave clear instructions with your next of kin and/or your consulate on what you wish to be done with your remains, i.e. buried or cremated, and in which country.
- Separate Wills (see under that heading) should be made and notarised to cover assets in Portugal and assets elsewhere.

When it happens

When someone dies and it falls upon you to take charge of immediate arrangements, the following steps are recommended:

- If a person dies at home, notify the deceased's regular doctor without delay. Wait for the doctor to arrive and examine the body.
- If the regular doctor is unavailable, notify any other doctor.
- If you are unable to contact any doctor, contract a firm of undertakers (see Services directory under "Funeral services"). They will arrange to transfer the body to a hospital. A doctor there will probably order an autopsy to determine the cause of death.
- Whether the death occurs at home or in hospital, notify the deceased's closest relatives and/or their local consulate.
- If you are the next of kin or if it is otherwise appropriate, determine the deceased's funeral wishes and then contact a firm of undertakers if you have not already done so.

DEATHS

Documentation

In due course, it may be necessary for the next of kin to check that the following paperwork is in order, but a good funeral director will organise it all on your behalf.

- Death certificate. (To probate Wills, you will need extra copies including, perhaps, a notarised translated copy).
- Document certifying that the body is free from infectious or contageous disease.
- Certificate giving permission to transfer the body for burial or cremation.

Funerals

In Portugal the arrangements for disposing of the remains of loved ones are somewhat at variance with those in more temperate, northern climates. The reasons are cultural, religious and climatic. Mediterranean and Moorish influences still persist. Religious beliefs do not encourage cremation. And this is a hot climate with few temperature controlled mortuaries.

There are four ways of disposing of remains:

- Burial in a non-permanent grave.
- Burial in a permanent grave or wall tomb which has to be purchased at the time or in advance.
- Cremation.
- Repatriation using specialist services.

Burial

Burial in a non-permanent grave entails the distressing procedure of exhuming the remains in three to five years time.

To keep anguish to a minimum, the initial procedure is to add chemicals to the body at the graveside to aid decomposition. This calls for the lead coffin lining to be pierced or opened up.

Watching this harrowing procedure can be avoided by arranging for the coffin to be brought to the church or cemetery chapel with all the preparation gone through and the coffin ready

DEATHS

to be lowered into the grave.

Alternately, the chaplain will conduct the service in church, leave the congregation, and go alone to the cemetery to note the grave number and witness the burial.

At this stage, after the interment, many families lose interest and in due course the remains are put on one side by the cemetery staff. If relatives wish their departed to be permanently interred, it is the widow's or widower's privilege to arrange to collect the bones, wash them, place them in a linen bag and put them in a second coffin. This is placed in a wall tomb, or catacomb, purchased by the family. This gruesome procedure can be carried out for you by one of the funeral services.

Bear in mind that there is no official notification that remains are to be disinterred. It is necessary to visit the cemetery at regular intervals and look at disinterment lists.

A characteristic of Portuguese funerals is the lack of respect sometimes shown to the deceased. The coffin is likely to be handled roughly by a gang of "bearers" dressed in dishevelled shirts and old jeans. Their dress and behaviour can sometimes be improved by speaking to the funeral director beforehand.

Burial in a permanent grave

A great deal of the foregoing can be avoided if a burial plot or wall tomb can be purchased in advance. The availability of such a location may have a bearing on where remains are interred. It is becoming more difficult to find such a place despite the fact that many parishes, *freguesias*, are dedicating new burial grounds. In Lisbon there is, of course, the British Cemetery. But space is becoming very limited; only parishioners of the Anglican churches in Lisbon, the United Church of Scotland in Lisbon, and St Vincent's Anglican Church in the Algarve may be buried there. It is administered by the Chaplain of St George's Anglican Church in Rua S. Jorge. His address: Rua da Estrela, 4.

Cremation

The Catholic Church in Portugal does not encourage cremation, consequently there is only one crematorium in the whole of Portugal. It is in Lisbon. It is countenanced for various reasons, one of which is to dispose of hospital remains. There is no chapel

DEATHS

at the crematorium, but services can be held in one of the Anglican churches; or a memorial service can be held in the parish of the deceased with or without the ashes being present.

If cremation is contemplated, it is important to refuse the offer of any funeral organisation in your locality until you have contacted the cremation agents. Some local morticians prepare the body and the coffin in a way which makes cremation difficult, calling for a second coffin and consequent extra expense.

The agency running the crematorium is entitled *Barata*. Their charges include the cost of the urn containing the ashes and scattering them in the garden of the Alto de S. João in Lisbon. There is an extra charge if you wish to dispose of the ashes elsewhere, because of a legal requirement regarding movement of remains. Address: Agência Funerária Barata, Rua Saraiva de Carvalho, 200, 1200 Lisboa, Tel. (01) 3961113 or (01) 3965027.

Repatriation

Specialists in the repatriation of remains operate 24-hour, seven day a week services which are said to be impeccable and to relieve the bereaved of much anxiety and distress. Naturally there are charges for this. They are covered by some medical insurances.

Should it be intended to repatriate remains, proceed as with a cremation and refuse all offers from undertakers. This is important because the more "progressive" morticians maintain watchers at the hospitals and may easily know before you do when a relative has died. The first intimation you may have is a knock on your door and a gentleman with his hat in his hand offering his services.

If a foreign resident dies, the appropriate consulate should be notified immediately. The Swedish Consul tells us that she has arranged the repatriation of a number of her compatriots using the services of a Swedish specialist undertaker. No doubt the other consulates will do the same.

In addition to this, British consulates in Portugal will accept a sealed envelope containing your wishes regarding disposal of your remains, as will the Chaplain of St Vincent's Anglican Church in the Algarve. This can save next of kin anguished decisions.

EDUCATION

Which school ?

If you have children of school age there are several options across the whole educational spectrum. They range from Portuguese state schools to what is virtually a British public school on Portuguese soil, not to mention an American co-educational establishment for children up to 17 years. And, of course, there are the Portuguese universities.

State schools

Right at the beginning of a child's education there are the *infantários* and *pré-primárias*. These are State kindergartens for children of three to six years.

While the kindergarten schools are not compulsory, the next stage of schooling is. Portuguese state schools are improving all the time with help from the EU. They make sense for children of expatriates if it is intended that the child will spend the rest of his or her life in Portugal. Many *estrangeiro* children now attend them with satisfactory results.

One of the snags, we are told, is lack of supervision when teaching is not in progress. In the Algarve this, combined with widespread teacher absenteeism, can result in children roaming the streets unsupervised. There have also been reports of drug abuse and bullying. Presumably this means that bullying is not kept under control due to lack of supervision. After all, school bullying has been with us since schools began. As for drugs, this is an insidious evil which pervades the whole educational establishment worldwide. However, one feels that the above are some of the reasons for both expatriates and Portuguese parents turning towards private education.

Permission from the Ministry of Education in Lisbon is required for foreign children to attend a State school, and potential pupils are expected to speak some Portuguese. An advantage is that they quickly become fluent in what is still an important commercial language, spoken by some 140 million people worldwide.

Portuguese State Schools have three grades:
Escola Primária   6 - 10 years
Escola Preparatória   10 - 12 years

EDUCATION

Escola Secundária (Liceu)   13-15 years

By law, children should spend a minimum total of nine years at the above three schools. If you wish to send them on to university, they spend a further three years at the *liceu* preparing for their entrance exams.

Private schools

There is a good selection of private educational establishments in Portugal, both Portuguese and international. Most of the latter are listed in the International Schools Directory of the European Council of International Schools, ECIS for short, and nearly all use English as the language of instruction.

This publication gives a page to each school, listing information about the school and its staff. At the back is a geographical index, including non-ECIS members, giving the name of the head, and the age and number of pupils. Since the information is supplied by the schools themselves, you're unlikely to read much that is critical on those pages. Nevertheless, it is a starting point when looking for a school.

The questions you have to ask yourself when looking for a school are:

- ❏ How long has it been in existence? Does it look as if it will last?
- ❏ How well financed is it?
- ❏ Do the owners of the school own the freehold, or is it on a lease? How long is the lease?

  In our view, having to move children from a school which has "gone bust" is a big setback to their education.
- ❏ What are the qualifications of the headmaster and staff?

  In the northern countries the choice of a headmaster is a very selective process. Here it can be more perfunctory. In Portugal information about this person and the school staff may call for access to that lusty growth, the grapevine telegraph. Take a cynical view of the information that comes out of it. Get as many opinions as possible. Many people have extreme views about education.
- ❏ How easy is it to get to from your home?

  If the school has its own bus service, check how near to your home the nearest pick-up point is. A twice daily duty run along the Marginal or the EN125, especially in summer, is not our idea of fun. And there is a danger factor.

EDUCATION

- ❏ Does it have facilities for scientific education, e.g. a science laboratory or computer instruction?
- ❏ Are the staff full-time? Do they have degree qualifications? Are they backed up by an administrative secretariat?

In the opinion of Peter Maddison, headmaster of the International School at Porches, there is only a need for two international schools for secondary education in the Algarve, with an extra primary school at the eastern and western extremities. He further reckons that there is room for only one sixth-form establishment.

However, this could change as the Portuguese economy improves. There is a definite trend among Portuguese parents to educate their children in international schools. Take the example of the auspicious St Julian's School at Carcavelos where half the pupils are Portuguese being educated to a Portuguese curriculum.

English Primary School
4 - 11 years inclusive

Barlavento English School

♦ All nationalities welcome

♦ Excellent facilities including large gym with stage, computer room, and sports field

Near Lagos, north of EN 125, between Quatro Estradas & Espiche
Postal address: Rua Silva Lopes, 28 - 2º Fr - 8600 Lagos
Tel. (082) 789 206   After school hours: (082) 760 202

EDUCATION

INTERNATIONAL SCHOOL OF THE ALGARVE

ESTABLISHED 1972 - EC15 REG. MEMBER

British and Portuguese Sections.
Experienced, qualified teachers.
Kindergarten to 16+.
IGCSE (Cambridge board).
Family boarding.
Buses from Lagos, Faro, Messines.
Extensive learning and sports facilities.

Apartado 80, 8400 Lagoa.
Tel: 082 342547, Fax: 082 53787

VILAMOURA INTERNATIONAL SCHOOL

The school caters for children from Kindergarten up to and including A level.

Buses are provided from a wide area including Olhão, Albufeira, Loulé, Faro, Quinta do Lago, Vale do Lobo, Quarteira, Vilamoura e Guia.

Both International and Portuguese sections

Please contact the school for further details
Tel: 089-366585/360603, Fax: 089-360388

ELECTRICITY

The supply of electricity, and the administration of it, is one of the facilities where liberal EU funding appears to be finding its way to the right place. New coal-fired power stations are being built (one of them in a most unlikely place in the far north) and *Electricidade de Portugal* offices are becoming fully computerised with trained staff. What is most important in a country riddled with obdurate bureaucracy is the cheerfulness and helpfulness of the staff, a change of attitude which must come from the top.

In addition to the charge per unit of electricity, the universal Kw/hr, the average consumer will find the following charges added to his bill:

> ❏ *Potência*, a supply charge which depends on the type of supply, two or three-phase.
> ❏ An exploration charge (*Taxa RS*).
> ❏ Value added tax (*IVA*) on the total.

Having said all that, there is still much leeway to be made up. Billing is a case in point. Once an account is in a person's name, should he sell his house, the new owner is going to have to move mountains to get the account into his own name.

Bills

It is not unusual for EDP consumers - nationals and foreigners alike - to get a big shock in the shape of an extortionate electricity bill. At the root of this is a shortage of meter readers. As a result, many bills are estimated on the basis of past usage.

ELECTRICITY

Thus, if the former resident of one's home was miserly with his electricity, you could very well be getting very small bills; but when, in the fullness of time, EDP get round to reading your meter, you could be in for a hefty invoice as they take up the slack. On the other hand, if your predecessor was profligate with his power and you are miserly with yours, you could well be receiving far bigger bills than you deserve. One thing for sure: if that big bill arrives in your postbox you will have to raise a bank loan and pay up, and argue afterwards.

Meter reading

EDP have gone public on this and point out that they have around 4,500,000 clients and therefore 4,500,000 meters. These have to be read periodically. But people are not always at home and in any case EDP do not have enough meter-readers. It is estimated that half of these meters are not read at all.

Consequently, EDP are encouraging consumers to read their own meters. If, over a number of months, customers can arrive at the average number of units they use per month, the company will feed this figure into their computer and bill the client accordingly. Here is what they have to say:

- ❑ When EDP send you a bill based on *estimativa,* the amount may not coincide with the real figure. The difference, either way, will be corrected on the next reading of the meter by their staff. But sometimes you might feel that the difference is so great that you prefer not to wait for the next visit of the "electricity man". In that case it is best to go to any EDP counter, taking with you your meter readings. The correction will usually be effected immediately.
  OR you can ring 0500-1150 (a freephone number) and do it by telephone. But this must be done prior to the last day for payment of the bill.
- ❑ You can also telephone EDP every month on 0500-1140 and give them your meter reading and your client number. This is shown on every bill on the top right-hand corner.
- ❑ The other method is the "EDP agreed account" (*conta certa EDP*). For this you have to fill in an EDP direct debit form and take it to your bank. Basing your calculations on what you paid the previous year for electricity, you can agree with the EDP a fixed monthly

ELECTRICITY

amount which will not vary throughout the year. The bill is then sent to your bank and your account is debited with this amount. At the end of the year your meter is read and corrections are made. Should you owe large sums of money to EDP, you have up to three months to pay. Probably the first notice of this will be anguished telephone calls from the bank telling you you're overdrawn. It does seem that corrections are made without notice. Should EDP owe you money, they will pay you back immediately in one lump sum by crediting it to your bank account.

Meter location

Eventually it is hoped to overcome the shortage of meter-readers. Looking forward to that time, the EDP have issued guidelines for the location of meters in new property and for a change of position in old buildings. Here they are:

- On all new houses the meter must be sited so that it can be read by EDP meter-readers without having to gain access to the building.
- Owners of all new buildings are being "asked" by EDP to resite their meters, if necessary, to comply with the above requirement.
- The availability of a resident or domestic servant in the house does not serve as an alternative to having the meter "outside".
- Provided that the owner of the building has constructed the necessary receptacle to receive the meter, EDP, at their expense, will disconnect the meter and re-install it in the new location.
- There is no intention at this time to disconnect power supplies to users who do not comply with this request.

Recording units used

In case you have never read a meter before, the recording section of the dial is similar to the mileage indicator on your car speedometer. The kilometres on your speedometer (the mileage read-out is properly called the odometer) are units of electricity on the EDP meter. It is just as easy to record the readings as when you're calculating your mileage on a journey for your expense account. Don't bother with the last figure on the counter; this is tenths of a unit. A unit of electricity, incidentally, is the amount

49

ELECTRICITY

of power you would use if you left a 1,000 watt fire on for an hour, or a 100 watt light bulb for ten hours.

Take the readings to your local EDP head office where you should find people whose job it is to feed the information into the EDP computer. Your bill will then be adjusted accordingly and, if you have overpaid grossly, you should either get money back or have free electricity for a few months.

Night tariff

It was good news for heavy users of electricity when EDP introduced a night tariff as of 1 January 1993. It is now possible to have one's meter changed to a computerised device which switches over to a cheap rate for seven hours each night, 17 hours on Saturdays and all day Sunday. Alternatively, one can have 10 hours cheap rate every day of the week.

To achieve this, simply go along to your main EDP office and seek out one of the staff members operating the computers who speaks your language. You must take your last electricity bill giving details of your account to enable the operator to find your records. He or she will arrange for a new meter to be fitted and possibly for you to be credited with a refund.

This service is available to any consumer using more than 270 units per year. The only condition is that EDP require your main switchboard to be of the latest type, with circuit breakers instead of fuses, and an earth trip.

Changing the name of an account

To achieve this you will require the following:

❏ *Contribuição Autárquica Modelo* 15, a form which is obtainable from your local EDP office. This is a form for representations to the suppliers of water, energy and telecommunications, therefore it would probably also stand in good stead for changing your name on water and phone bills. On this form you will have to state:

- ❏ Your address
- ❏ Location ID code as on bill
- ❏ Type of occupancy
- ❏ Names of the proprietors, and their address

ELECTRICITY

❑ Comments.
> A list of electrical equipment.
> A certificate from an electrician stating that the installation is in good order.
> Receipted electricity bill.
> Your *contribuinte* number.
> Identity card or passport.
> *Fiscal* stamp.

EMPLOYEES

Workers' rights

After the Revolution of 25 April 1974 the various governments which followed had strong Communist/Socialist sympathies and they enacted legislation giving workers rights which were the envy of workers in most capitalist countries. These are being slowly revised but some of the main principles remain. The employment law as it stands is a mix of statutory law and contract law.

Working hours are limited to eight hours a day and 48 hours a week. At present there is a statutory requirement to give workers one day a week off, but there are moves to increase this to two.

There is a further requirement for a mid-day break of not less than one and not more than two hours. And each working period should last not longer than four hours.

The statutes also decree a minimum monthly wage for industrial workers. A lesser figure is published for domestic staff and farm workers.

Overtime may only be worked with the permission of the Ministry of Labour. It is paid at the rate of 50% extra for the first hour and 75% for ensuing hours. Work on an employee's day off or on public holidays calls for double pay.

Holiday entitlement is 20 working days or 2½ days per month per year. At this juncture we come up against the fourteen month year. With this annual holiday, whether it be for three or four weeks, goes one month's holiday pay. This is the thirteenth month. When December comes, a further month's pay is required as a Christmas bonus; that is the fourteenth month.

The actuality is sometimes a little different. In the present economic climate many workers in Portuguese-owned firms are being paid only half of their contract rate, or often not at all.

They continue to go to work for fear of missing the day when there is a pay out. The effect of this on the unemployment statistics can be imagined.

The same goes for many public service workers and professionals. A much publicised example is that of the hospital doctors who are owed vast sums of money in overtime.

EMPLOYEES

Domestic staff and social security

Domestic workers and gardeners employed by expatriate residents are relatively better off than those in industry and public service due to the simple fact that their foreign employers have never latched on to the idea of not paying wages.

Domestic employees who work full-time for a single household are regularly paid and the fourteen month year is usually just one of their perks.

There are also a growing number of maids and gardeners who work for several employees during the course of a working week. They have no work contract and therefore cannot easily claim the fourteen month year. They have to rely on their various employers to give them a donation when they take their annual holiday, and another at Christmas. In our experience they do equally well.

In the main these are simple, honest people who, because of the elitist policies of the old Salazar regime, can often neither read nor write. It is up to us, their employers, to make sure that one of our number looks after the formalities of making their social security payments, usually referred to as *caixa*.

This sounds more difficult than it is. In our case we give our maid a paper with the amount of tax per hour her other employers must pay. She collects it from them over the month and hands it over to us.

We fill in the form, drive down to the local office of the *Segurança Social,* and hand over the form and a cheque. The form filling is described in detail below because it is the most usual formality most residents have to deal with.

Incidentally, you may find that your maid is not paying *caixa*. If this is the case you should see to it that she does. To achieve this, take her to the *Junta de Freguesia* of your district neighbourhood to obtain the necessary application form.

With this in her hand she then has to go to the *Casa do Povo* in the same conurbation as the *Junta de Freguesia* - it may be in the same building - where the staff will help her to fill out the form. You may be called on to vouch for her.

Eventually she will be posted a *concertina* of the forms from the *Ministério do Emprego e de Segurança Social* and bring them to you. The form has to be filled in by you, the employer, and

EMPLOYEES

taken for payment to the local office of the *Segurança Social*. Thereafter you can obtain further supplies of the form, which is Cont. No 277900428-9, from the same office.

Caixa forms

The procedure for filling in the form is as follows:

- ❏ Make a start by recording the employee's date of birth, taken from her identity card. There's a row of seven squares, top right, *Data Nasc*. It is expressed as, for example, 0512993.
- ❏ Move over to the left and put a cross in the square box labelled *Remuneração horária* (third down on the left) to indicate that she is an hourly paid worker.
- ❏ Just to the right of this is a vertical box marked *No. Horas*. Write over it (it's the wrong shape to get the number in it) the total number of hours she works per month for all of her employers.
- ❏ The next box to the right is a long horizontal one, also marked *Remuneração horária*. It is the right shape and obviously intended for money because it has a $ sign in front of it. Write in this the minimum national hourly rate established by decree, NOT what you actually pay her. If you don't know what it is ask AFPOP if you're a member, or friend who employs a maid. The national hourly rate changes upwards once or twice a year. The ladies behind the social security office counter will notify you of this.
- ❏ Alongside the *Remuneração horária* box is a short dotted line. Write somewhere near it the hourly rate multiplied by the monthly hours.
- ❏ Beneath the hourly rate box is a further box marked *Contribuição horária*. This is for your own share of the contribution. At the moment the national rate for domestic staff is 166$ per hour. Of this you or your group of employers will be expected to pay 30%, say 50$. Record this figure in the box. Then multiply this by the number of hours worked in the month and inscribe it on the third line down of a big box headed *Contribuições*. Then write it again two lines below, opposite the words *Total a Depositar*.
- ❏ Move over to the top right-hand corner of the form where there is space to write in Portuguese the month and year you're paying for.
- ❏ Underneath that write again your **Contribuições** (6) in figures.

EMPLOYEES

- Below that, alongside the words *Extenso,* spell out the sum in Portuguese.
- You will be expected to pay by cheque. There are small spaces on the form for the cheque number and the initials of the bank. Since you have now had a lesson in small handwriting you are fully qualified to make out the cheque to the *Instituto de Gestão Financeira da Segurança Social*. Nothing less will do and there is just enough space for it.

  Then write on the back of it your maid's *No. Beneficiário*. That brings a nod of approval from the clerk, or a black look if you haven't done it.
- Right at the bottom of the form are spaces for your full name, your address, and your signature.

  This is your monthly chore and is part of the old world charm of living in Portugal. Take the result by hand each month to the local office of the *Segurança Social*. Or it can be posted to the regional office of the SS and paid quarterly. If you attend personally, this must be done before the 15th of the month. It pays to go the week before unless you're British and enjoy standing in queues.

  Your maid may ask you to hand over to her the carbon copies of the forms. They are, in fact, your property, proof that you have made the payments. Hold on to them and supply photocopies if she insists.

  Gardeners come under a separate heading, being classed as industrial workers. There is a different official form to be filled in for them.

It is Portuguese law if you employ staff on any kind, and plain common sense so far as you are concerned if you live at any distance from other dwellings, to have available a good first aid kit. The contents are defined in law according to the employees activities. Specialist companies make up these kits and will supply them off the shelf.

FINANCIAL SERVICES

The money tree

It follows that if any responsible person retires to Portugal he has some kind of income from resources either in Portugal or elsewhere. The usual source of income is a pension, maybe two. If two, one usually comes from a government, the other from a company worked with for a number of years. This income may be backed up by interest, or returns of some kind, derived from savings accumulated over a working lifetime.

Two other varieties of immigrant should be taken into account, though they are of lesser interest to the financial community: those who come here on a shoestring and work for their living, and the very well-endowed who most probably have accumulated their wealth by managing money wisely. The latter could probably tell the financial advisers a thing or two.

A few year ago, the main class of immigrant, the modest chap with a couple of pensions and some savings, was sitting pretty. Interest rates were high and he could live comfortably without having to worry unduly about his financial situation. When bank interest rates started to plummet at the beginning of the nineties, there was an immediate reaction to look around for another source which would bring income back to the old level.

The alternatives to the banks are building societies, diving into the stock market with the help of a good stockbroker, or using a financial service. Building societies are fine, but they tend to be a little too near to the tax collector in your home country. Not many of us have the skills to work the stock market. Thus, the scene was set for the rise of financial services. They had existed before, but suddenly they were in far greater demand.

One thing is certain: under the general heading of "financial services" we have to include banks and building societies. All of them are in the business of making money out of your money and giving you a cut of the proceeds. Where financial services and merchant banks scored was that they tended to be more supple and agile than the mainland big banks.

The big banks offset this by forming offshore subsidiaries. All of them can give you conservative, or adventurous advice depending on your whim or fancy.

You pay for the privilege of moving into trust funds and the

FINANCIAL SERVICES

like, and out of the shelter of a low interest account with a mainland bank, or one of its subsidiaries. In many cases you do not have instant access to your money. Most likely there is a financial penalty if you want to move it elsewhere. And there are sevice charges, minute fractions of a percentage which are in effect an additional interest charge, compounding month by month.

On the bright side, the returns can be exciting, but when one is in a stormy sea you will have your ups and downs. The further out you go the greater the ups and the deeper the downs.

If you are tempted to move your savings out of safe, but monotonously low, banking rates, into investment funds do, please, keep enough back in the safe haven of a bank to tide you over the times when the financial market takes one of its regular dives. When this happens you should be free to sit on the fence, cancel your investment income and wait until the market takes an upturn.

Here are some ground rules:

> ❏ Look hard at the background of a financial services company before committing yourself. How long have they been in business? What are their financial resources? Size up their representative.
> ❏ Be very wary of any return greater than 2% over the bank rate
> ❏ How quickly can you withdraw your capital?
> ❏ What are the penalties if you want to withdraw it shortly after investment?
> ❏ What are the penalties if you withdraw it after one or two years? It varies.
> ❏ Can you stop your withdrawals if, say, the bid price of your bond fund drops so low that you are giving away funds to obtain income?

In AFPOP we have two financial advisers. Both of them are employed by financial establishments of integrity whose business is to make money out of your money. However, in fairness to them their impartiality has to be somewhat restricted. One would be naive to expect them ever to give advice which went against the interests of their employers.

That is by the way. Their advice is sound and they do warn against high risk income plans. But, in the end, any decision is yours. It is a true adage that a fool and his pence are soon parted.

FINANCIAL SERVICES

There is an acute possibility when the market is buoyant and seemingly set to continue to do so, that the aforementioned fool will throw caution to the winds and go for the high income earning plans. There is a simple basic rule here: high income means high risk and low income means low risk.

As an example of what can happen, take the bond market. At the time of writing, with only promises of better things to come to live on, there are a good many Algarve residents who are currently regretting having fallen for high earning, bond-based income plan structures at the end of 1993. Even the "award winning teams" who are meant to be managing them do not seem to be able to make much of the current situation.

We are assured on all sides, however, that historically the bond market has always had its ups and downs, but that the ups have always been bigger than the downs. Investors have to be patient. Incidentally, we have always been curious about those "award winning" teams who manage our money. Are they, like footballers, changing sides occasionally in exchange for a large transfer fee?

A financial adviser, however good he is, cannot predict the market with certainty. At a presentation two or three years ago, one of the best-known of the Iberian financial gurus stated that the lowest the British bank rate could go was 7.5%! However, your adviser or financial service should be able to give you a true picture of the past history of the type of stock you are proposing to invest in. If he is worthy of his salt, he should also repeat our advice: put a good sum on one side, in a bank deposit, as a financial buffer when the graph is taking a prolonged dip. But if you have gone for financial advice, your advisers are duty bound to offer you the big earners as well as the little, safe earners. It pays to play safe and keep more than a little in your pocket.

FINANCIAL SERVICES

100% GUARANTEED

- Professional expertise in relation to tax and investment planning
- The establishment of a personalised financial strategy
- Detailed objective solutions with realistic aims
- The establishment of real understanding and trust
- To act as a financial advisor and not as a salesman
- To provide high quality on-going services

THESE ARE GENUINE GUARANTEES

Do not be attracted by exaggerated claims where promises made may not be kept.

We promise, in an honest and impartial manner to provide an objective assessment of your requirements and to leave you to decide what action, if any, you may need to take to benefit from any recommendations we put to you.

An initial report will be prepared for your consideration without cost or obligation on your part.

Contact your local Blackstone Franks Partner:

David Rennie

Almancil Office
Av. Duarte Pacheco, 226
8135 Almancil

Tel: 089 / 397 707
Fax: 089 / 395 249

Blackstone Franks

GARDENING

Establishing a garden

It is impossible in a few words to cover the whole gamut of gardening in Portugal, especially when one's sole experience is in the Mediterranean-type climate of the Algarve. Consequently these rough notes concentrate on starting a garden in the southern region. We hope they will be of assistance to established home owners, and to those avid gardeners who are about to buy property in the area.

Hobby gardening really arrived in the Algarve with the influx of large numbers of expatriates, many of them retired and yearning to create gardens. As a result, garden centres with proprietors of all nationalities have sprung up everywhere to satisfy requirements for trees, plants, fertilisers, potting compound and so on. The prices have gone up too.

Purists maintain that it is wrong to propagate anything but native Portuguese flowers and shrubs. Not everyone will go along with this. It is now possible to purchase plants indigenous to the south coasts of France, Italy and Spain. They are a delight in any garden and perfectly adapted to the climate and scenery in Portugal. Many of these plants have been developed over many years by devoted gardening experts. It seems wrong that we should be denied the fruits of their labours. Bear in mind that until 30 years ago the Algarve had few of the great gardens, or gardening traditions of the French and Italian Rivieras, or of Lisbon for that matter.

What you plant in your garden is up to you. What is for sure is that your plants will need three elements to keep them alive: soil, sun and water. Sun we have plenty of, too much for some plants. Soil is a variable. Water is generally in short supply, and expensive if you're running off the mains.

Soil preparation

Taking an overall view of soil types one finds black acid soil in the rain shadows of the Monchique mountain. Moving south this changes to the large area of clay-like, alkaline, cinnamon-coloured soil located roughly between the Arade and Bensafrim rivers, i.e. between Lagos and Portimão. All along the coast the soil tends to be mainly sand for one or two kilometres inland, even

GARDENING

more in the Almancil-Vale de Lobo area, where it is relished by the pine trees. North of the EN125 there is a large fertile area extending east from the Rio Arade to Faro and beyond.

Most of the Algarve soil is reasonably fertile if you work at it. After all vines, fig, almond and olive trees grow in the stony, cinnamon-coloured "earthenware" soil in the area south of Monchique without any artificial watering at all. Most of the Algarve is well adapted to citrus fruits too. They do very well if given a little water and fed with manure, either natural or artificial. As a rule most native plants will survive without water once they are established, but they really come to life and thrive if watered regularly.

Nearer to the house one looks for more decorative plants and the soil needs to be treated to support them. Some very handsome aloes and agaves grow in the native soil, but more exotic plants need soil treatment. Left to its own devices but regularly tilled, the cinnamon soil can be akin to dust in dry weather and turn to concrete when it dries out after rain or watering. Great improvements can be made by treating it with peat, humus and natural fertiliser (*estrume*), or blaukorn artificial fertiliser. One of the snags, even with well rotted *estrume,* is the crop of weeds it leaves in its wake.

It goes without saying that one cannot drastically change the nature of soil in a garden, except at enormous expense. However, the above treatment should result in decent growing soil around the house. Rotted down compost effectively breaks up some of the clay soils, but it is hard to come by because of the climatic difficulty of maintaining a compost heap. These dry out quickly, and have to be watered once or twice daily to keep them going. Chopped bark is now becoming available. This is a good soil-improver, and an effective top-dressing for flower beds or decorative urns containing shrubs.

We have a personal penchant for a layer of medium-fine stone gravel laid on the surface of the soil in large flower pots and small, walled beds. It keeps the soil moist and cool by reflecting the sun's heat, and prevents mud splashes on the walls of the bed when hand-watering with a hose. If a plant needs a special soil type it is best to plant it in one of those nice earthenware pots which are to be found everywhere. The soil can vary so much between one quite

GARDENING

small area and another that it is essential to seek expert advice if you have problems. The expert does not have to be a professional.

Salt

One thing to beware of is excessive salt in soil in areas near to the sea. Look out for excessive salt for four kilometres or so inland from the west coast, maybe lesser amounts on the south coast. And one should be very choosy about sand. Don't help yourself to the left-overs from a building project. It is most likely to be sea sand and full of salt. Go either to a river bed a few miles inland, above the tidal section, or buy treated sand. There is a new sand desalination plant near Silves in the Algarve.

Another source of salt may become a problem in the future. Boreholes near to the coast are beginning to produce brackish water as a result of excessive extraction from the water table. If you live near the sea and use a borehole solely for watering, check it for salt. The treatment for salty soil is large amounts of gypsum, one part to two of soil. Chopped bark, peat and river sand are also a help. Plants that are tolerant to salt are the acacias, most of the aloe family, pampas grass, ice plants, European olives, pomegranates, and the false acacia (robinias).

Watering

There are various ways of getting water to your plants. All of them call for the watering to be done in the cool part of the day, either very early morning or late evening. The two commonest:

1. The most primitive, and probably the best, is with a hand-held garden hose played into a shallow, circular depression round the base of the plant. This way you know how much water each plant is getting and you can give it more or less according to the plant's requirements. Essential equipment is a pistol-type nozzle on your hosepipe. It makes watering so much more precise, and saves a great deal of water when moving from plant to plant. It's fine for a small garden with a few fruit trees.

2. A popular choice is an irrigation system with mains and branches using black plastic pipe of graded sizes ending up with strategically placed, mini-spray nozzles. The nozzles are available in different sizes to give a specific volume of water per hour. This is labour-saving and effective, but the system needs

GARDENING

regular inspection to make sure that the jets are not blocked. A water filter helps. A kitchen timer is useful to remind you when to turn off the irrigation if it is of the manual type.

Professional growers, and some wealthy home owners have adopted computerised irrigation This will give a large variety of plants the correct amount of water at the right time. It is used in association with micro-bore irrigation utilising small diameter, plastic pipe. It is particularly useful in a nursery when a lot of pot plants have to be watered. It demands an effectively filtered water supply and, of course, the cost has to be considered.

Some gardeners who adopt the number 2 method bury their main pipes to prevent the water lying in them getting too hot. Should you do this, make sure that they are at least 30cm (12in.) deep, otherwise they will be very susceptible to gardeners' mattocks. Our personal preference is to keep them above ground, reasoning that by the time the water has soaked down to the roots of the plants its temperature will have stabilised.

On the subject of fine sprays, it strikes one that there is some loss by evaporation between the water leaving the nozzle and hitting the ground. Also when it lies on the warm earth before soaking in. Many gardeners draw their water supply from boreholes. What they do not always appreciate is that underground water is communal property and one should be provident with it. There are ecologists who would regard lawns in the southern region as anti-social and golf courses an ecological disaster because of their water requirements.

Insecticides and fungicides

Pests and plant diseases are another subject which is too big for this small book. There are sprays for all the regular plant diseases, and most insects. If you are doubtful about what is affecting your plant or tree, take a sample leaf to your local purveyor of insecticides. He will then hand you a suitable antidote. On this score you will find Portuguese gardeners are extremely liberal with dangerous fungicides and insecticides, and not exactly careful about the storage of them.

Poolside plants

There are many species of plant that will not thrive in pool

GARDENING

areas because of fumes from the chlorine. Succulents and cacti are a case in point. But you can plant juniper, geraniums, begonia, non-variegated ivy and myrtle, palms, gazanias and agapanthus to name a few. It has been said that the backwash from cleaning the pool filter affects plants. Maybe some, but not all. Our fruit trees seem to have no objection to it. Beware of leaf-shedding plants or bushes near a pool, or you will be forever cleaning the skimmer filter.

Gardeners

Many expatriates employ Portuguese gardeners to keep their gardens neat and trim. It has to be borne in mind that most of them are agriculturists, not horticulturists. The majority of these very likeable people are sturdy sons of the soil who will labour away all day, plying their mattock, cutting off the tops of the weeds and making the ground look tidy. Some have tips about fruit trees that you won't find in books. If you let them they will also grow a few vegetables for themselves in your garden.

Time was when it was usual to employ one of them full-time, with possibly the spouse working in the house. With the increase in the expatriate population there are not enough gardeners to go around. This, coupled with Portuguese inflation, causes many expatriates to employ a part-time gardener and maid, or maybe keep one and dispense with the other. Gardeners to beware of are the ones who like to spend a few hours in your garden and a few hours in your neighbour's. It's putting temptation in their way when they come to present you with the scrappy piece of paper that passes as a bill.

GARDENING

The Ultimate Barbecue

2 sizes.
With wooden trolley or "build in".
Lava rock grill for char-grill cooking.
Hot plate for griddle cooking.
Made from heavy weight cast iron.
Optional wok insert for stir-fry.
Optional barrel cooker lid for roasting.
Drip tray included, easy clean.
Australian product with 30 yrs experience.

GÁS
SUNSHINE BARBECUES

JORO, Lda - Tel (089) 393202 - Fax (089) 393201

Greenfingers & Q

Landscaping & Irrigation

Two long established and reliable businesses which combine to fulfil all your garden & landscape requirements.
Many contracts completed for large developments as well as hundreds of individual villa gardens.

Garden Centre

One of the best displays in the Algarve of garden and indoor plants, aquatic plants, ponds and exotic fish such as Koi - Japanese coloured Carp.

Q's Tel./Fax: 082 - 96217
Greenfingers Fax: 082 - 96207
Mobile: 0931 812 328

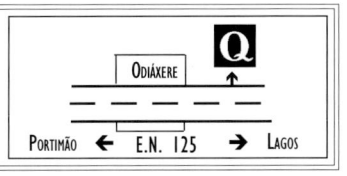

PORTIMÃO ← E.N. 125 → LAGOS · ODIÁXERE · Q

GUNS

GUN LAW

Some of us have owned firearms for sporting purposes in our home country. Now, with the possibility of hunting game ("shooting" to the Brits) once more becoming available in Portugal - the Government has established large game preserves in the Alentejo and elsewhere - the possibility of keeping a sporting gun here in Portugal becomes more interesting. Only residents of Portugal or foreigners holding a residential visa may apply for a gun licence. A further, more-difficult-to-obtain hunting licence, necessitating a written and practical examination, is required if you wish to shoot over the countryside generally. However, we understand, this hunting licence is not called for if you are paying to hunt on an organised outing in the game preserves.

Non-residents may apply for a temporary sporting licence covering a short period, for skeet shooting, for example, or attending an organised shoot. Here is the Portuguese law as it affects the possession of firearms.

Personal defence gun licence

Refers only to pistols of .22, .25 and .32mm calibre. Unless there is a valid reason acceptable to the police a licence for this purpose will not normally be granted. Licences are issued by your local *Câmara*. When granted they are available for from one to five years.

The fees, which were recently increased by 500% are now as follows:

| 1 year | 5,017$ | 2 years | 9,967$ | 3 years | 14,917$ |
| 4 years | 19,867$ | 5 years | 24,817$ | | |

Recreational gun licence

Refers to all firearms for target shooting and to shotguns and rifles for game shooting. Firearms used for game shooting must not be capable of holding more than three rounds fully loaded, Licences may be granted for from one to five years. Licence fees are:

| 1 year | 1,625$ | 2 years | 3,250$ | 3 years | 4,875$ |
| 4 years | 6,500$ | 5 years | 8,125$ | | |

GUNS

Obtaining a licence

- ❏ From your Consulate obtain a certificate showing that you have no criminal record. This is called the *Requerimento de Certificado de Registo Criminal*.
- ❏ When you have done this, obtain from your local *Câmara* the wording for the letter of application for the type of licence you require. You must then make out your letter of application using the exact words specified.
- ❏ Obtain from your bank a certified cheque for the amount of the fee. Cash is not accepted. The cheque should be made payable to: O Comandante, Polícia de Segurança Pública.
- ❏ Take the *Certificado de Registo Criminal*, the letter of application, your certified cheque and two copies of a recent photograph of yourself to your local *Câmara*, who will forward the whole lot to the PSP.
- ❏ If and when your licence is granted, the PSP will send it to the *Câmara* for issue. When you have received it you may purchase the gun. The gun must then be taken to the *Câmara* for them to register the details.

Warning

The *Câmara* may take up to 18 months to consider your application, and even then the answer may be a refusal. If you are refused you will have your fee returned, less a deduction for administrative purposes.

If you wish to bring firearms into Portugal, the PSP will not issue any licence in advance. You must surrender your weapons to Portuguese Customs and then make your application for a licence. If the Customs can produce your firearm after an 18-month wait, you are home and dry. It is not known what happens if the PSP refuse your licence because the Customs can only return your firearm upon production of the relevant licence.

We are indebted to Mr. Ken West, an international pistol shot, for the foregoing. The last section confirms that firearms brought into Portugal with your personal effects, and not registered before entering Customs, are ILLEGAL.

We understand that if you do not get a licence, you must apply to Customs for the return of the weapons the next time you are leaving the country.

GUNS

As before, competitors in international clay shooting events should obtain certificates from their national clay shooting organisation declaring that their guns are to be used in a specific competition.

Exceptions

Air rifles and pistols, archery equipment and cross-bows are exempt from any form of licensing.

The hunting season

The legal framework for hunting/shooting is contained in two Decree-laws, Law 30/86 dated 27 August 1986, and 274-A /88 dated 3 August 1988. These lay out Government policy on recreational hunting and the conditions under which it can be practised. Here are extracts:

Article 14 Law 30/86

❏ Shooting (the firing of weapons) is prohibited in all areas where hunting can constitute a danger to life, tranquility of persons, or constitutes a risk of damage to property.

❏ It is also prohibited to shoot without permission of the owner in walled-in land, gardens/orchards, gardens attached to property, along with any ground surrounding the above. (The dimensions of this area will be established by further legislation).

❏ It is prohibited to shoot without consent on any land which is completely surrounded by a perimeter fence or wall of a minimum height of 1.5metres, in the courtyards, parks or gardens attached to habitations, as well as on any land surrounding them to a depth of 250 metres.

The hunting/shooting season

Thursdays, Sundays and public holidays:
Mid August to Mid October   -   Birds only
Mid October to 31 December   -   All legal quarries
1 January to end of February -   Hunters with written permission may shoot birds in olive groves with more than 25 trees and in specially designated areas.

In the Algarve, more information can be obtained from Eng. Alberto Espirito Santo, Divisão de Caça, Delegação Florestal do Algarve, Rua Dr. Jerónimo Isório, 1 - 3/4°, 8000 Faro. Tel 089-822273. Fluent in English and Deutch.

HEALTH & BEAUTY

A couple of centuries ago, decaying British aristocrats were shipped out to Portugal by their doctors to die unobtrusively. It is recorded that they took an unconscionably long time doing this because of the climate and the ready supply of fresh fruit, particularly oranges. The situation has not changed. Portugal is the first part of Europe to receive the warm south-westerly winds from the Atlantic, clean and fresh from several thousand miles of ocean travel. The pure air, combined with an abundance of fresh fruit and vegetables, fish wriggling on the slab, and excellent meat and poultry, make this one of the healthiest countries in Europe to live in. Even the automobile has so failed to take its toll. For economic reasons the Portuguese car population is less than that of many other European countries. Pollution has yet to become a way of life.

Wholesome food

The more complex vitamins and minerals in the right quantities are only to be found in food. Doctors tell us that if we eat a balanced diet we take in all the vitamins we need.

Portuguese food is excellent in this respect. Buying in the market you will be offered only freshly grown vegetables and fruit, in season. If you eat plenty of this kind of fruit and fresh vegetables there should be no need for vitamin pills. Only in the new supermarkets, when a specific vegetable is out of season, will you find standardised, uniformly coloured, tasteless versions of it on the shelves. They come from the northern growers, and the fugitives from the north do not take too kindly to them.

Good, fresh meat is plentiful. Beef, lamb, goat-meat, pork, chicken and turkey are here in abundance. From the health aspect, turkey or chicken are to be preferred to the red meats which are high in cholesterol. Poultry is a favourite in the diet of both our hosts and ourselves.

No part of Portugal is far away from the coast, so there is a plentiful supply of all kinds of fish. The oilier kinds such as sardines, mackerel and *carapau* are important sources of vitamin D. It is a bourgeois affectation to ignore these shoal fish simply because they are cheap and plentiful. They are some of the best food you can buy at any price.

We are finding out more about the health aspect of

HEALTH & BEAUTY

vegetables and fruit all the time. The latest research indicates that *pimentos*, broccoli and carrots are anti-oxidants and important cancer deterrents. So are onions and garlic which are here in abundance. It may be a coincidence that the standard Portuguese salad consists of tomatoes, peppers and onions. We add grated carrot to ours. How about a new slogan: " A salad a day keeps cancer at bay"?

A most important health precaution is to ensure that all fruit and vegetables eaten with their skins are thoroughly washed before use. Portuguese agriculturists tend to be rather lavish with a wide range of lethal pesticides; the intake of these can drastically offset the health-giving qualities of what you're about to eat.

An interesting newcomer to the fruit menu during the last few years has been the New Zealand kiwi, fruit not bird. These are now grown in Portugal. One kiwi fruit is said to have more than the normal adult's daily requirement of vitamin C. While it is decorative and good to eat with most things, its acidity can affect the taste of wine and cream.

Last but not least, the ready availability of olive oil of all qualities gives us no excuse for not using it for almost every kind of cooking. It gets us away from detrimental animal fats and takes us into the realms of Mediterranean cooking. While it is not to everyone's taste for frying bacon and eggs, it makes a perfect starter for most stews or for frying omelettes. It also makes superb shortbread, replacing butter.

A wok is a useful health device because it allows one to fry vegetables with a minimum amount of oil quickly enough to seal in the flavour. It requires less than you would use in a salad dressing. Don't use olive oil for this, it can't stand the heat. Go for the readily available peanut oil, *óleo de amendoim*.

We eat too much fat. To reduce your fat intake:

- eat less fried food.
- trim the excess fat from meat.
- avoid spreading butter or margarine thickly on bread.
- use skimmed milk, *leite magro*, whenever possible.
- eat less cream and hard cheese.
- reduce the intake of cakes and pastries.

HEALTH & BEAUTY

Sun

"All sun-tanned men are handsome" the advertisements used to say. The ladies feel very much the same and fry themselves to a frazzle in the process. Cries for moderation fall on deaf ears. Be that as it may, sunshine is what most immigrants came here for. The locals are used to it and only come out of their cottages on a sunny day in search of warmth. It would be unheard of for any of the older generation of Portuguese to actually bathe in the sun.

The newcomers revel in it, sometimes to excess. In large quantities, sunlight can cause lethal melanoma although this seems to be less prevalent here than in the southern hemisphere. The fear of this cancer is transforming sun-worshipping Australia into a shirt manufacturers' paradise.

Many of the old hands in the Algarve seldom sunbathe. Others never get out of the habit. The latter have a saying that the "morning sun is the burning sun, afternoon sun is the browning sun." Sunlight in moderation is a main provider of vitamin D, by acting on a layer of fat beneath the skin. This fat contains dehydro-cholesterol which is converted into vitamin D by ultraviolet rays. Oily fish, like sardines and mackerel, egg yolks, liver and margarine are other sources. The main source of dietary vitamin D is meat.

To many ladies it is more important to have a sun-tanned face than one free of wrinkles. For the wrinklaphobics, our resident expert suggests that wrinkled skin can be avoided by wearing sunscreen all the time, possibly built into moisturiser cream. One thing is certain, once you have acquired a wrinkle it is there for keeps. Wrinklaphobics should also take a tip from the peach-skinned ladies of the British Raj and always wear a wide brimmed hat.

For men it also pays to wear a hat of some kind in the hot, sunny weather. Sunglasses are equally, if not more, important for both sexes as a protection against sunstroke.

With the summer sun comes heat in abundance and at this time it suits many people to take a salt pill daily to retain their body moisture.

HEALTH & BEAUTY

Alcohol

One has a sneaky feeling that as many people from the northern countries come here for the cheap alcohol as they do for the sunshine. If they do, there is again a case for moderation. It is being forced on those who drive. However, for non-drivers joy abounded when some messiah, we believe from the Bordeaux region, proclaimed that the reason his countrymen are so healthy is that they drink red wine He recommended half a bottle a day as a healthy dose, now one of his disciples has decreed that a whole bottle a day is not harmful. Naturally the red wine does not have to come from Bordeaux. Our local product is worth sniffing at. Any of the excellent Portuguese red wines will do.

Bear in mind that Portuguese wines are a little stronger than French wines, and that it does not pay to sink the whole bottle at one go. If you do drink more than the prescribed ration of any alcoholic drink, as many expats do, it is helpful to drink at least the equivalent amount of water afterwards, especially in the heat of summer.

In the hot weather, wine or any alcoholic drink may give a quick lift, but even in the short term it is dehydrating and counter-productive. It is best to keep to soft drinks when the thermometer knocks 38ºC in the shade. Hot tea, or cold tea with plenty of lemon is excellent. Coke, either breed, diluted with *água com gás* and loaded with ice and lemon is another alternative. Let the sun go down before you reach for the gin.

Water

This universal commodity is highly valued in Portugal and comes in many bottled varieties as well as from the tap. One could almost write a learned paper on the different kinds of water and their special properties from healing springs all over Portugal. Portuguese people are very choosy about their bottled water. They go into a bar as a matter of course and have a bottle of water, enjoying it just as much as the northerners enjoy a beer.

As one expert has very wisely stated, it is wasted effort for water authorities world-wide to strive to supply drinking-quality water in huge quantities when the proportion of it used for human consumption is minuscule. Much more is squandered

HEALTH & BEAUTY

on watering the garden or washing the car. Since the efforts of the water authorities appear to be universally unsuccessful, there is a strong case for purifying one's own. This can be done with a water softener to remove calcium, and with small filters which can be attached to a tap and are claimed to remove bacteria. From personal observation, the claims seem to be justified. Some people need the calcium and make do without a water softener, but keep the special filter.

HEATING

Heating your house

Read the travel brochures and one visualises the Algarve as a climatic paradise. But much depends on whether you're a summer visitor or a resident. The climate is similar to that of North Africa; when the sun disappears below the horizon the temperature drops due to lack of cloud cover. Summer is wonderful with temperatures in the 30 - 35°C bracket most of the time, but when you become a resident you quickly find that winter temperatures can drop as low as 5°C and you will feel an overcoat colder. Late autumn and early spring evenings are more pleasant with a fire in the room. Don't go away with the idea that when you come to live in Portugal you have said goodbye to heating bills.

Early Planning

With this in mind, if you are building a new house it is a wise move to have the building of chimneys properly supervised, and for the architect and builder to get the heating and cooling specialist in on the act at a very early stage. For example, if you had ideas about ducted hot air heating - not a bad idea because the ducts can also carry cold air in the summer - the ducts need to be built in during the early stages of construction rather than being added later. Likewise, solar heating panels can be designed into the structure with the header tank concealed in the ridge of a pitched roof if the decision is made early enough.

Unless you know exactly what you want, it is wise to seek out a firm of heating and cooling specialists who can offer all the options rather than just one. Bear in mind that a single-product man will always dwell on the benefits of his pet system and ignore the snags.

Wood

When considering heat sources, the cheapest option is wood, the native heating fuel in a land without coal mines. Hard, dry timber is readily available and one load will generously heat a home right through the heating season when burnt in one of the imported or locally-produced, enclosed, wood burners. Most homes, large and small, built in the last few years, use these

HEATING

very efficient units.

First cost of a properly designed wood burner with ducted air around the firebox is about 250,000$ and it will need a lined chimney if it is to give of its best. Snags are the amount of covered area required to store the wood - here again the architect can make provision if warned early enough - and the hassle of storing a supply of it in the living-room, handy for the fire.

Gas

The second fuel option is gas, which comes in 11kg or 45kg bottles and costs approximately 10$ to produce the heat equivalent of one unit of electricity. It is also available in large, permanent storage cylinders which you can locate in the garden. The petrol companies supply the gas and are not slow to jack up the price at regular intervals. In the last five years the price of an 11kg bottle has virtually doubled.

A few years ago Portugal acquired a bad reputation because of the large number of faulty water-heater installations and consequent carbon monoxide fatalities. However, new regulations put paid to that and heater installation seems to be one of the few aspects of building to be properly controlled by the authorities. Installations by licensed technicians are perfectly safe. It is certainly the cheapest method of heating water, but heaters need to be inspected and descaled at least every two years. Gas can be good for room heating in the cool winter and spring evenings now that it is possible to buy efficient room heaters in Portugal.

Electricity

The price of electricity increases annually. Currently it costs 18$20 per kW/h plus IVA with an extra charge for *potência*, which is the capacity of your meter. One effective way of getting value for your money is to install a heat pump. It operates by extracting heat from air and raising it to a useful temperature. A domestic fridge is a heat pump on a small scale only the heat extracted from the interior goes to waste. To get large amounts of heat from these devices they have to be large, and expensive. However, versions which will operate under-floor heating, or raise the temperature of swimming pools are commercially available.

HEATING

They can give you up to four times the amount of heat for every unit of electricity consumed. The first cost has to be set against the savings made.

In the south of the country there is a ready and constant supply of sunlight. In these areas solar heating is attractive and popular for water heating and warming swimming pools in the autumn and winter. Even two and a half hours of winter sun will give enough heat for showers, and the latest types are effective in grey sky conditions. There are built-in thermostatically or time-controlled immersion heaters if you get desperate. It might be said of them that they provide vast amounts of hot water when it is least needed, and not quite enough when it is. Nevertheless, they economise on fuel and are ecologically most desirable. When you have a solar heater there is that cosy feeling of getting something for nothing, which is inherent in all of us.

Checkpoints

Second-hand property:

> ❏ Location of chimneys. *Are* there any behind those fancy fireplaces, especially in apartments?
> ❏ Wooden beams in chimney structure.
> ❏ Steel reinforcing rods across and through chimneys preventing installation of chimney liners (very prevalent).
> ❏ Access for sweeping chimney.
> ❏ Facilities for gas storage.
> ❏ Properly installed, built-in gas system, and its condition.
> ❏ Conveniently located, properly earthed electric points.
> ❏ Covered storage for firewood.

New property (Heating with wood):

> ❏ If opting for an open fire, choose a nice, still day and test the chimney before moving into a new house. Note the remarks about chimney design. This goes for house chimneys and inbuilt barbecues.
> ❏ Install chimney liners if a wood-burner with doors which are closed to control the burning rate is chosen.

HEATING

- ❏ Build adequate secondary wood storage close to the main fire; at least one cubic metre capacity.
- ❏ Ensure easy access for yourself and delivery lorries to a capacious main wood storage. It should be able to take a full lorry load of wood, be well ventilated, well drained and dry.

New property (general):

- ❏ Have at least three, earthed electricity sockets in every room (except the bathroom, which should have a heater out of reach of anyone standing on the floor or in contact with plumbing).
- ❏ Demand a properly installed, copper-pipe gas system with outlets in the kitchen and main living-rooms.
- ❏ Adequate and secure storage for the largest gas bottles.
- ❏ Provision, including plumbing, for the installation of solar heating panels.
- ❏ Electric wiring in adequate ducts so that it can be replaced and repaired without having to knock holes in concrete walls.

"GEOFFREY, YOU DID CHECK FOR A CHIMNEY BEHIND THAT FANCY FIREPLACE DIDN'T YOU??"

HEATING

HIGH FUEL BILLS?

Algarve has approximately 3,400 hours of sunshine per year. Use that free solar energy with **Solahart** solar systems for * DOMESTIC HOT WATER * HOT AIR HEATING SYSTEMS *

FOGO MONTANHA — WOOD BURNING STOVES

STOVAX — FREE STANDING STOVES

GAS-BALANCED FLUE CONVECTOR HEATERS

ENVIRO FIRE — PELLET STOVES & FIREPLACE INSERTS

JORO Lda., Rua 5 de Outubro 200, 8135 Almancil Tel 089 393202 Fax 089 393201

THE INJECTOR
CENTRAL HEATING SYSTEM

Compact Boiler - Fits anywhere - No water mains connection - Complete with normal radiators - No Flue - Silent - No Maintenance - Low Installed Price - Very Low Running Cost - Ideal for Villas, Apartments and Commercial use.

For more details: Tel / Fax (082) 769790

FIREPLACE CENTRE
Centro de Lareiras

A RELIABLE RANGE of Woodburning Stoves & Gas Fires
- Underfloor Heating ■ Wall Heaters & Gas Convectors ■ Fireside Accessories & Natural Stone Surrounds including marble.

Included in our range are TOP NAMES from the UK, Holland, Belgium, Denmark, Norway, France & Portugal (**Agents for Fogo Montanha**)

VISIT OUR SHOWROOMS and talk to us the heating experts for advice on heating your home. FREE ESTIMATES.
EN 125 at Vale de Lousas, Alcantarilha.
Tel: 082 314188 / 322000   Fax: 082 322670

Nederlands ■ Deutsch English ■ spoken

HOUSE LETTING

Owner obligations

Having become the undisputed owner of a Portuguese property and not wishing to occupy it for the whole of the year, the idea of letting it for the periods you are away is an attractive one. Indeed you may have had this in mind when you acquired the property.

There are infinite variations on the letting theme, but there is only one set of rules, enshrined in Portuguese law (Decree Law 441), and one set of guidelines based on common sense and the experience of letting agents. The law requires the following precautions. It also requires local authorities to have inspectors and inspection teams to ensure that they are carried out. Fines can range from 5,000$ to 250,000$.

Registration. All properties let to tourists must be registered with the regional tourist authority.

Insurance. It is essential to have public liability insurance in case of accidents involving guests.

Pools. The depth in metres must be clearly marked at the shallow end, the middle and the deep end. If the pool is unsuitable for diving, a further sign should be displayed saying "Diving forbidden" in the language of the nationals who you are likely to be letting to.

Gas appliances. If there are gas appliances in the villa, an initial inspection must be carried out and a gas safety certificate must be signed annually thereafter by an approved local inspector. Gas water heaters within rented premises are now under deep suspicion and most letting agents demand an alternative method of water heating.

Fire. A fire extinguisher or a fire blanket must be installed in the kitchen, and smoke detectors at other strategic points.

Wood burning fires. Log burning fireplaces must have the chimney cleaned annually.

HOUSE LETTING

First-aid. An approved first-aid kit must be available on the premises.

To let your house you may need the services of two distinct categories of professional: a villa manager to ensure that your house is maintained in suitable condition for letting, and a letting agency to obtain clients.

Villa managers

If your villa is to be let while you are away, you will need someone to look after it. This is where the villa manager comes into the picture. Villa managers abound in the southern region. Some are friends, some do it for pin money, others are professional with varying degrees of competence. Choosing your villa manager is of paramount importance. Many home owners have learnt this lesson in the hard school of experience. Conscientious villa management is really not an activity for amateurs. Your villa manager should be expected to:

- ❏ Speak Portuguese or employ staff who can do so. This is of primary importance in hiring and supervising staff to clean and service the villas under their control, as well as liaising with local authorities.
- ❏ Have a good working knowledge of Portuguese law as applied to property.
- ❏ Have a through understanding of the appropriate sections of Portuguese social security law to be able to handle staff obligations.
- ❏ Pay taxes, staff wages and social security contributions at the appropriate time.
- ❏ Take responsibility for small repairs, present estimates for major work and make sure that work is done to a good standard and at a fair price.
- ❏ Submit monthly accounts of all outgoing payments with receipts.
- ❏ Ensure that all the legal requirements for letting as laid out above are adhered to.
- ❏ Prepare the house for each individual letting. This means making sure the previous occupants have moved out on time, that the house is thoroughly cleaned and in good working order prior to the newcomers arriving, and that there are basic cleaning materials and any food requirements in place.

HOUSE LETTING

- Provide an information sheet on the house and its contents, the telephone numbers of local doctors and dentists, other emergency telephone numbers and a map showing the area and the location of nearby restaurants with a rough guide to their prices.
- Provide clear instructions on how to change gas bottles, light the oven and operate the dishwasher, microwave, burglar alarm etc, as well as the location of the main stop-cock and fuse board.
- Have a good knowledge of the property and visit it regularly.
- Keep an inventory of the contents of the house and their condition.
- Charge tenants responsible for any significant breakages and arrange for repairs or replacements.

The last point above is where the manager's prompt "post-let" inspection is so important because the cost of the damage can be promptly collected. If this is not done it can take months to recover the damage, if at all.

There is also the instance of owners who let their property for only a few weeks in the year and live in them for the rest of the time. If they are wise they will make a personal check list of everything they wish to put into store (it could be in the garage) for this short period, and see that it is done.

British tour operators are not allowed by law to reveal the names and addresses of their clients. However, it is a nice gesture to place a visitors book in the house to obtain the comments of your guests.

Letting agencies

There are five main categories:

- International tour operators who provide accommodation as part of their package holidays.
- Agencies abroad who specialise in holiday lettings and have many properties on their books.
- Villa managers who work closely with an overseas agent, perhaps in the owner's country of origin.
- Villa managers who let property under their management on an ad hoc basis.
- Owners who act as agents themselves.

HOUSE LETTING

Categories one and two call for the services of a highly professional villa manager who is prepared, if necessary, to act tough on your behalf. If you are an owner who lets his home during short periods of absence only, the last three categories may be more appropriate. If so, the proviso with category 3 is that the letting agent should have visited the property and should chose the clients sympathetically.

Other responsibilities

Responsibility does not stop with the villa manager. An owner should not expect all the above services without making a contribution other than cash. He should make it his business to get to know the villa manager on friendly terms. Ideally the owner should spend at least a month per year in his house. A householder is bound to find shortcomings which the manager will not pick up because, without living in it, a manager cannot hope to know the house intimately. The owner also has the responsibility to pay running costs and his manager's fees on time, especially if the outgoings are substantial.

There is a further factor, which many people learn from experience and which a good manager will point out. A well cared for villa commands the respect of clients and will encourage them to return, while one which is neglected is very often treated with indifference.

Income derived from rentals in this country should, of course, be included in your annual tax return. This applies to non-resident property owners as well as those who spend more than 183 days here in any one year and are thus classified as resident for tax purposes. Non-residents must declare income from their Portuguese property to the Portuguese tax authorities even if they declare it in their country of residence. Double taxation treaties should ensure that the income is not taxed in both countries.

In Spain, owners of homes who live outside the country but derive income from their property are required to have a fiscal representative who will fill in their tax return and pay any dues. At the time of writing, a similar requirement is not enforced in Portugal although there is provision for it in the statute book and it is very likely to become the rule here. As we see it, a fiscal representative should be either an *advogado* or an accountant.

HOUSE MOVING

Open borders

A few years ago, moving home from another European country to Portugal was a major operation. Portugal was jealous of its frontiers and economy, and had no intention of letting foreigners bring loads of goods into Portugal in the guise of domestic furniture.

You could bring in your beds, chairs and tables so long as you listed them in detail and they were not too new. Any kind of electrical equipment had to be meticulously recorded, backed up with invoices to prove that you had owned the goods for at least six months prior to arrival in the country. Once your belongings had arrived they had to be unloaded under customs supervision. The strictness of this could be somewhat alleviated by the award of a bottle of Scotch; our man was a connoisseur and checked that it was malt.

This kind of house-move was a job for specialists with just one or two companies having a monopoly. They maintained offices here and in their base country, knew the *Alfândega* well, and charged accordingly. In the boom years, when immigrants in search of the sun were moving home in their hundreds, it was good business. Nowadays, for every family that arrives, two are likely to be repatriating themselves, so there is still business for the movers.

Thanks to the EU open borders policy things are now different. The time has gone when a company had to bear the cost of a senior person and an office staff, plus the expense of maintaining the goodwill of the *Alfândega*. One of the objectives of the EU was to simplify cross-border traffic and it has done so. Now it is easy for anyone with a 7-tonne truck, or a transit van, to set up in business as an international carrier. All that is required in the way of an office is a voice at the end of a telephone line.

However much the established companies resent this intrusion into their established activity, it is an inevitable development as the market opens up. These new companies, and they are not all one man and a van, should be seen as general carriers rather than furniture movers. Some will go out of business, others will establish a reputation for reliability at reduced cost and survive.

HOUSE MOVING

Certainly, with the relaxation of controls on the movement of goods, there is greater freedom of choice for you and me. It is now so much easier to source bulky household goods or furniture wherever you wish in the EU and have them delivered to Portugal. And it is now possible for established residents to bring in the personal item which previously would not have been contemplated because of the expense of customs formalities.

Having earlier mentioned customs, the *Alfândega*, do not imagine for one moment that there is no customs presence. The Algarve is one of the main European entry points for drugs. For this reason there are regular checks on the roads leading to and from the border crossings, especially late at night.

The practicalities

If you are moving home you will naturally go to the experts. If so do not try to pack anything fragile yourself, especially glass and porcelain, let the agents unpack it when your goods and chattels arrive in Portugal. Stand by with a paper and pencil to record any breakages. It is unwise to leave any fragile goods

HOUSE MOVING

unpacked and to be dealt with later. If you read the small print, you have only a very short time to put in a claim.

If you are moving house to Portugal, the price will be arranged as an overall contract. For transporting individual items of goods from the Algarve to the UK, for example, the going rate with the established specialists is currently £80 per cu. metre delivered to their depot in England. There will be a further delivery charge to your home. The non-establishment carriers charge about £50-£60 per cu.metre and some of them deliver door-to-door. That is the measure of the competition. Your choice will be conditioned by the value and fragility of the goods you are despatching. The rule is not to accept anyone who cannot offer insurance backed by a known company. For the record, three tea-chests constitute a cubic metre.

IDENTITY CARDS

How to get one

Every Portuguese citizen possesses two documents, a *cédula*, a 'book of life', and a *bilhete de identidade*. The latter contains a photograph of the person concerned and a print of his right index finger.

Once having received your *autorização de residência,* you count as a Portuguese citizen. You now need to equip yourself with a *bilhete de identidade.*

The first move is a visit to the *Registo Civil* of the *Conservatória* to obtain the appropriate form. The next one is to your local *Serviços de Estrangeiros* office where you will be given a list of requirements. They should be as follows:

> ❏ A declaration from your consulate stating that you are registered there.
> ❏ A *certificado de residência* from your local *Junta de Freguesia* to show that you have lived in your present abode for more than three months. Supporting evidence can be letters directed to you at the address and/or a statement from a Portuguese neighbour.
> ❏ A photocopy of your *autorização de residência.*
> ❏ Two passport-size photographs in colour.
> ❏ An 80 escudos *fiscal* stamp.

Having acquired all these things and filled in the form, you return to where you started, the office of the *Registo Civil.* Here your height will be measured and recorded, and your fingerprint taken. You will then be given a receipt and told to return in 30 days to collect your *bilhete*; it could be longer.

If you intend to live in Portugal, the identity card is an essential document. Apart from the fact that it is a legal necessity, without it you cannot acquire a Portuguese driving licence. It also enables you to leave your passport safely at home. And it is of assistance when cashing cheques, paying bills and for a whole variety of purposes.

INSURANCE

Home insurance

The insurance market in Portugal has opened up considerably in the last few years as a result of government controls being taken off. There is now much greater market competitiveness. Previously, the large insurance companies and their agents dominated the business and set the rates.

It is now possible for insurance brokers to operate. You can save yourself a lot of money and protect yourself against unforeseen risks by using the services of a broker. It certainly pays off to shop around rather than accepting the first offer without question. AFPOP has a broker who specialises in members' problems and gives substantial discounts to members.

Buildings

The value to insure for under the "building" heading should be sufficient to cover the cost of rebuilding the villa or apartment, plus swimming pools, outbuildings, garages, storehouses and adjoining buildings; everything structural. Don't forget that walls, gates and fences form part of the property.

Exclude from your calculations the value of the land and any value of the property which comes from the view or the location. In other words, insure for the replacement cost, not the market value, of your home.

- ❏ A guideline to valuation is available in the official government listings which state the current building cost per square metre for various parts of Portugal. Remember to update it annually.
- ❏ If the property is rented and is insured by the owner and not by the tenant, any improvements or betterments should be added to the policy together with their value.
- ❏ Landslip or subsidence is often not included in a policy. Check to see that yours does include this provision.
- ❏ If a swimming pool is part of the property, make sure that it, and its terracing, are included. A pool has a relatively fragile concrete skin. Landslip or subsidence can crack it like an eggshell.

INSURANCE

Contents

The value to insure for on a householder's policy under this heading should be the replacement cost, with new items, of the personal and domestic effects of the insured and any other contents of the dwelling. The principle should be new for old.

Normally, insurers require one to list high-value items and their serial numbers. It is a sound idea to do this even if not requested. High-value items are those which individually have a value which is over 5 % of the total sum insured or, when combined, represent more than 30 % of that sum. Some insurers also impose a monetary limit on non-specified items. It is therefore a good plan to include a list of possessions which do not meet the 5 % criterion but are still valuable, such as:

- ❑ Photographic equipment; cameras, lenses and expensive flash equipment. Note the numbers of the cameras and each individual lens. The numbers are on the camera bodies and on the front of the lens mountings.
- ❑ Television sets, hi-fis, videos, satellite receivers and suchlike. Serial numbers are usually on a small plate on the back or underneath the equipment.
- ❑ Power tools.
- ❑ Jewellery will not have a serial number, but it can be photographed at short range with modern cameras. Valuable watches usually have serial numbers lightly engraved on the back or inside the back of the case. In the latter event get a watchmaker to check it for you.
- ❑ Original paintings and drawings. Photograph them and have them valued.

It's a bore looking for the serial numbers of electrical equipment, especially videos and hi-fis which usually live with their backs to the wall. A flashlamp and a make-up mirror are a help here, plus the ability to read numbers in reverse. But it is essential to record this information on your list. After all, it only has to be done once. Update this list regularly as you add items or dispose of others. And keep receipts of everything you buy, or have bought.

Negatives of any photographs of valuable items should be

INSURANCE

stored away from the house. An interesting example of proof of ownership was in a case of a valuable fur coat. No receipt was available but an old photograph of the owner wearing the garment at a social occasion was sufficient proof.

Under insurance

Failure to update the value of the building or its contents leaves one open to the application of the "average" factor. In other words, if the insurers decide you are under-insured by, say, 10 %, they will reduce the payment of any claim by that amount. Or in the case of a specified item, they will only pay the declared value and not the current value. Some companies automatically include an inflation-linked increase and adjust the annual premium accordingly.

House break-ins

Normally, insurance companies will only meet claims when there has been forced entry. To prove this it is necessary to produce a *certidão* from the GNR. It is also advisable to have photographs of any broken locks or windows. Check that your policy covers break-ins using a false key. Often the GNR will not visit the scene; but the insurance companies will still require a GNR certificate issued less than 60 days after reporting the incident.

Portuguese house insurance does not normally cover breakages. If you want this cover it will increase the premium substantially, and you will be called on to pay substantial excesses.

Public liability

Most house policies cover the policy holder, his family and domestic employees against public liability, but with rather modest limits. Make sure that this cover is for at least 50,000,000$. Employees should be covered by a separate policy.

Employees

Even if a maid or gardener is retired and drawing retirement benefits from the Government but is still working for you even

INSURANCE

for a few hours a week, you are liable in the event of an accident arising from the employment. Your insurance company will need to know the number of hours a week your employee is working for you and will issue a policy based on the minumum official wage rate for the particular type of employment.

Deep-freeze

Some policies will pay the loss of the contents of a deep freezer due to stoppage of the freezer by an insured peril under the policy. For example, a serious fire could cut off the power to the freezer for a number of days.

Damage to freezer contents due to a power failure can sometimes be claimed from the EDP.

Travel

There may be coverage for world-wide travel in your household policy. Check with your agent.

Coverage normally falls into three categories: Portugal, Europe and world-wide. Portugal costs least and world-wide most.

Insurers will want full details of any high value articles you take with you. Such items are:

- Cameras, camcorders, tape recorders, portable computers, binoculars and the like. Keep a record of the model, make and serial numbers. This can come from your household list. Put them there if they're not already recorded.
- Jewellery; a receipt or valuation certificate will be required.

In-flight coverage

Some policies differentiate between scheduled and "common carrier" flights offering lower limits, or even exclusion in the case of chartered air services. (If you pay for the latter by credit card there is usually some cover included).

A world-wide all-risks policy can also cover home contents in your absence. In the event of a loss, for any reason, arrangements should be made for the police to be notified immediately and the insurers as soon as possible.

INSURANCE

The premium for an all-risks policy is generally about ten times that of a householder's policy. Consequently, it is a good idea to define the period of coverage and to ensure that there is no duplication of coverage, say, with your householder policy.

Guests' holiday insurance

Items brought over by guests on holiday are not usually covered under your householder policy. It is best to warn visitors to take out their own insurance.

Normally they would do this with their travel agent and be covered not only for personal effects and illness, but also for cancellation or curtailment of flights.

If travelling by car, make sure there is coverage for items left unattended in the vehicle.

Choosing a company

We recommend that if you do not speak Portuguese well, you should ensure that the insurers you choose are able to provide you with a service in your own language. It can be critically important when filling a claim.

It is a good deal simpler when negotiating claims to have a broker or a company located in Portugal rather than offshore.

Claims

These will be processed much more quickly if they are typed in Portuguese. However, check first with your insurance company. In the case of British insurance companies and brokers, English-language claim forms are available and claims can be submitted in English.

INSURANCE

Car insurance

Four types are available:

- ❏ Third party, minimum obligation
- ❏ Third Party, fire and theft
- ❏ Fully comprehensive.
- ❏ Unlimited cover.

Third party, minimum obligation

This is exactly what it says. It insures you against claims from a third party in an accident. That is all the law calls for.

Third party, fire, and theft

Third party, fire and theft is more protective. It is relatively expensive from the established companies, many of which are British, because the rates are based on the UK experience where, currently, there is a fashion for young drivers to steal cars, strip them of their radios, and then set fire to them. This custom hasn't permeated to Portugal as yet, but if you insure with these companies they charge as if it had.

Fully comprehensive

This is not all the name suggests. It covers only collision, overturning, fire and theft, not necessarily injury to passengers unless you have specified otherwise. It is usually valid only inside Portugal.

Request a territorial extension *(extensão territorial)* if you wish to motor outside Portugal and retain full cover. Failing this, once you leave Portugal with your car the cover is reduced to Third Party only, and then only up to the minimum required in each country.

When applying for fully comprehensive insurance don't be surprised if one of the insurance company staff asks to see and inspect your car for damage before accepting the cover. If the car is damaged in any way, they will almost certainly refuse comprehensive cover until the damage is repaired.

In our experience only one insurer in Portugal includes territorial extension as a matter of course.

INSURANCE

Unlimited cover

If you ask for the fourth type of policy, providing unlimited cover in Portugal, it should be applicable outside Portugal. Check with your insurer.

General

Check which countries are included on the green insurance slip (green card) which comes with your insurance papers. (Note that "X" typed over a country means that it is included, not excluded). This green card should be signed by you in the space marked *"assinatura"* and carried with you in your car at all times.

Don't overlook passenger coverage. Liability for bodily injury to passengers in a car is included in Portuguese policies so long as they are not related to the driver (to the third degree) or employed by the driver.

It is recommended that car-owners take out an occupants' policy *(ocupantes)* which can also cover bodily injury and medical costs for the driver. This occupants' policy functions even when the driver is the innocent party, i.e. not liable.

Claims

In the case of damage to your car with no third party involvement, check with your insurer to decide whether it will be to your financial advantage to make a claim. Remember that with comprehensive policies there will always be an excess, usually 2 %, which will have to be met by you. Then there will most likely be an increase in future premiums and the loss of your no-claim bonus which can generally take four years to win back.

No-claim bonuses are transferable from one company to another whether they are located inside or outside Portugal. All that is necessary is a certificate from the previous company. We know of one company which offers as much as 50 % no-claim bonus.

It is worth knowing that in Portugal, so far as the insurers are concerned, there is no restriction on who drives the car.

Windscreen coverage is not automatic. It may require a separate policy or special mention in the main policy.

INSURANCE

Car contents

Movable private property left in a car cannot be covered under a motor policy (see household policies). However, fixed items such as car radios, CD or cassette players and their speakers can be covered at an additional premium. The insurers will want full details and serial numbers.

Likewise insurers will want the values of extras such as spotlights, logos and aerials (not forgetting fancy wheels).

Car value

The correct value to set on a car is its *"valor venal"*. This is generally accepted to be its "market buying price", its replacement cost to the insured. Your insurance company should have lists of values for you to refer to.

This value will normally decrease annually and you should inform your insurance company of the reduced value when you re-insure your car each year. This should be done one month before the renewal date. Insurers also require 30 days notice if you wish to change companies.

In case of accident

In the event of an accident causing injury to a third party, you are strongly advised to allow the insurance companies to resolve all matters between themselves.

Do not become personally involved in any way. Taking a sympathetic attitude, and maybe visiting an injured party in hospital or at home, puts you on the spot for all sorts of claims from families and friends of the injured party.

Leave everything for the insurance companies to settle.

Unlike the UK, there is no knock-for-knock system in Portugal. If the other person involved in the accident can be shown to be to blame, your claim against him will be paid in full by his insurance company and your no claim bonus will remain intact.

INSURANCE

Medal
GESTÃO E MEDIAÇÃO DE SEGUROS, LDA

WE PROVIDE COMPREHENSIVE
BROKING SERVICE FOR ALL CLASSES
OF INSURANCE

Rua do Colégio, 46 - 1° C
8500 Portimão
Tel. (082) 417662/3
Fax. (082) 417667

Lloyd & Whyte
(Insurance Brokers)

Special Motor Schemes ● Multi Risk Household
Healthcare Schemes ● Travel ● Marine ● Commercial

Head Office: Av. Dr. Mateus Teixeira de Azevedo, Lote 3 R/C
8800 TAVIRA. TEL: (081) 32 58 42 FAX: (081) 32 58 79
Brendon (Personal Insurance) Services

INSURANCE

General Accident
PORTUGAL BRANCH

SPECIALISING IN THE ALGARVE REGION IN
ALL TYPES OF PERSONAL INSURANCE

* HOME - BUILDING AND CONTENTS
* YACHT AND MOTOR BOAT
* MOTOR VEHICLE

SPECIAL ATTRACTIVE TERMS FOR OVER 50'S ON PRIVATE MOTOR

COMPREHENSIVE COMBINED COVER AVAILABLE
FOR SMALL / MEDIUM BUSINESS ENTERPRISES

Portugal Head Office: Rua de Malaca, 30, 4150 Porto. Tel. 02-6104388
Lisbon Branch: Rua Ivens, 26 - 2º Dto, 1200 Lisboa. Tel. 01-3460712
ALGARVE REGION: LLOYD & WHYTE (INSURANCE BROKERS) LTD
AV. DR. MATEUS TEIXEIRA AZEVEDO, LOTE 3 R/C Dtº, 8800 TAVIRA
Tel. 081-32 58 42   Fax 081-32 58 79

INTERIOR DECOR

Inside your home

When you move to Portugal, your home is likely to become very much more the centre of your social life than it was in your homeland. There is a natural tendency for expatriates to form groups and to get together. If you are one of these sociable types you may soon find yourself doing more house entertaining than ever before. In this context, your home becomes the showcase of your own personality. Consequently you want it to look good.

Furniture

Many expatriates bring with them the contents of their former homes, and consequently their own national style of furnishing, and adapt it to their new surroundings. Other newcomers appreciate the opportunity to start afresh. Some of the latter may be natural, inborn, interior designers. For those who are not but are sufficiently well-heeled, there are professional interior designers who will do everything for you from the original design work to providing the furniture and furnishings.

If you do it yourself, it does implant your own personality on your home. One can take a lead from designers of Mediterranean homes in other European countries. If you run out of ideas, there is inspiration to be found in house-design magazines. The Portuguese version of *House and Garden*, shows off the work of good Portuguese designers who make the most of traditional materials. Other sources of inspiration are the Italian magazines *Domus* and *Casa*, and various French interior design magazines.

The style of furnishing and decor you choose may be conditioned by the region in which you live. In northern Portugal the style will tend to be more formal, in the south there are a number of trends. Typical of the newer Algarve villas is the colonial approach, with well-proportioned, elegant furniture set out in light and airy interiors. Alternatively, there is the farmhouse style: white walls, rustic furniture and splashes of intense colour. The immigrants have made their own rustic styles. Portuguese middle-class homes do not give a good lead. They tend to be over ornate and Victorian.

Sadly, there is no real rustic style. Two-tier social policies have seen to that. If there is a rural style it would most likely

INTERIOR DECOR

be found in the big *quintas*, but foreigners seldom find their way into these precincts. It is a sad commentary on Portugal's past that while the exteriors of cottages and *quintas* are charming, the interiors are most times crude beyond belief.

Earlier we mentioned elegant furniture. It is available in Oporto and Lisbon, and at specialist stores in the Algarve. One needs to shop around. So far as Portuguese made furniture is concerned, we were told that it is cheaper to buy furniture in the north rather than in the south, and there is a bigger choice. We investigated and didn't find it so, but if you do, do not forget to add on the cost of transport.

Antiques are a great embellishment to a home; they are best brought with you from abroad. A few years ago there were a few real treasures to be picked up at country sales in the north of the country. International dealers quickly got wind of this. There was not a lot to be had and now the cupboard is almost bare. Don't expect to find bargains easily. Many of the items one sees in dealers' shops here are overpriced and tiresome. If you choose carefully, antiques can be a good investment and add character to your home, but, as in all things, you have to know what you are doing. If you bring your own with you, they all bring back memories and are comforting to live with.

Establishments selling second-hand furniture and bric-a-brac are a new trend. Before the expatriate invasion they did not exist. Portuguese people like to buy new and use it until the only home for it is the scrap heap. There is now a significant section of the population of the Algarve which tires of its possessions more easily. For them, one or two used furniture stores have emerged. They will buy the furniture you are bored with and provide you with something different which is not necessarily new.

If you need a piece of furniture copied, or something made to your own design, there are good joiners in every community. If you look carefully you will find craftsmen whose work is the equal of anything you would find in your own country, and much more readily available. As a measure of the available talent, a friend had a small period settee copied; set alongside the original it is difficult to decide which is which. Generally, Portuguese joiners and cabinet-makers are innate craftsmen and will work to quite simple drawings. There are also expatriate craftsmen who will

INTERIOR DECOR

do good work. We know of one ex-Battle of Britain pilot who produces beautiful Chippendale reproduction mirrors.

Furniture and soft furnishings

There are interesting furnishing materials to be had here in Portugal, be they for curtains, upholstery or loose covers, but one has to look around for them. High quality materials are usually only to be found in specialist stores in the main towns, or on the shelves of furnishing experts. In the latter case, the stockist expects to get the job of making it up for you. Some of these are expatriates and will understand your requirements and work to them. In this case the charge is likely to range from expensive to very expensive, but the quality will be good. Here again, you have to look around workrooms, examine work in progress and talk to friends who have used the same professional. Find someone you can trust and stay with them. These same experts usually offer an advisory service and will give you anything from a mix and match service to full interior design.

If you speak good Portuguese you may be able to find good local craftsmen and women who will do the job for you. There are also excellent upholsterers and trimmers, but be prepared to give precise instructions. One cannot expect craftsmen to change from their traditional methods without instruction.

When you make your choice of soft furnishings, bear in mind that the sun will bleach and rot most materials. It is essential that curtains should be lined and that the linings should be sun-proof.

There are now available window films, thin plastic sheets incorporating filters, which can be applied to the inner surfaces of windows. It is claimed they keep out some of the more damaging of the sun's rays. It is also claimed that as well as doing this they keep in the warmth in winter and make the glass more burglar-proof. It is best to try it on a small window first.

Beds and bedding

You spend about one third of your life in bed, consequently it is an important piece of furniture. Maybe for this reason you are likely to have brought your favourite bed with you from your home country. We didn't and were pleasantly surprised at the quality of Portuguese beds. They are firm, but once you are acclimatised to

INTERIOR DECOR

them they are wonderfully comfortable.

Don't be taken in by the fancy orthopaedic beds which are currently the rage in Portugal. At the risk of being accused of trying to teach grandma to suck eggs, go for a good pocket-spring mattress, if possible on a sprung base. Solid base beds are available and are good for people with back problems, as well as being cheaper to buy. A friend suggests that they are improved by putting a thin feather mattress or a feather duvet on top of the mattress. We would settle for a couple of thick woollen blankets under the bottom sheet.

And don't kid yourself you do not need an electric blanket in Portugal. Even in the Algarve the winter nights are cold. This is a cold climate with a hot sun. If you use duvets, a Tog-rating of 9 is the minimum in winter. On cold nights we supplement ours with a good quality Alentejo blanket, the coarse woven, multi-coloured type, laid on top of the duvet.

Kitchens

It is usually one's lady wife or partner who has the final say in the purchase of a house. Mainly for this reason it is usually accepted that the cost of a good-looking fitted kitchen is more than offset by the extra value it puts on your home, and the ease with which you sell it when the time comes. The amount of money you spend on the conversion will depend on whether your intention is long-term or short-term occupation. If you have no intention of selling the house in the foreseeable future, you can be more extravagant in your choice of fittings than you would be if the ultimate object is to sell the property.

There are a number of importers of most of the well known brands of kitchen equipment. They are sold alongside staid but sound Portuguese brands. The dimensions of all the units are to international standards. As an old-hand at fitted kitchens, our main impressions are that while the appearance has improved and the working tops are far more durable, the quality of construction is generally less good than it was 30 years ago. But, of course, there must be exceptions.

The general design is little changed. The deep cupboards are still at a grovelling height beneath the work tops. The shallow cupboards are up above whereas they should be at eye level. If

INTERIOR DECOR

your new house is at the design stage, why not have deep, eye-level cupboards with the backs let into the wall. Portuguese builders are very adaptable. Put the shallow cupboards underneath the work tops. You might even be able to arrange this in an existing house if the wall is not load-bearing.

When a new kitchen is being installed, ask the installer to ensure that the skirting panels are easily removable, and replaceable, so that you can regularly spray against ants and other insects. When choosing a manufacturer take a hard look at hinges, drawers and drawer handles. The runners should be all metal and allow the drawer to pull out at least two-thirds of its depth. The sturdiness and bracketry of the shelves in the lower cupboards, which often become overloaded , should also be examined. In the end your time may have been wasted. Fitted kitchens are very much a status symbol so far as the ladies are concerned. It's the name that counts, and what the girl next door has got.

Fitted kitchens are not the only possibility. In our book, the kitchen should be bigger than the dining-room, not a mere galley. If you have the space, or make it at the design stage, why not a farmhouse-type kitchen. Local craftsmen could make long cupboards with lots of shelves. There could be a spice cupboard and solid wooden work tables. Saucepans could hang on the walls, there could be space for your dream cooker under a big brick hood, rather than one tailored to fit into a standard unit. The hood could lead fumes into one of those nice chimney pots. The fridge-freezer could be king size. One could live graciously in a kitchen like that.

Doing it yourself

Should you be a do-it-yourself person you will quickly discover that supplies of raw materials are difficult to come by. There are fixtures, screws, wall-plugs, hooks and door catches galore. All kinds of glues and potions are readily available at very affordable prices. But Portugal does not seem to have got around to cut-to-size timber. Straight pine for shelving is hard to find, but there is an abundance of hardwood planking and a likeable, light-coloured, semi-hardwood which is used by builders for concrete shuttering. Our favourite material for

INTERIOR DECOR

light shelving is blockboard, **not chipboard**. Cut it into strips of the right width, or find a friend with a power saw to do it for you. Cap the raw edge with hardwood moulding, which is readily available from kitchen cabinet suppliers.

Finding the right piece of timber for a major project can be something of an adventure, especially in the south where first-class timber is often badly stacked away from the shade, and writhes and curls in the hot sun. If you own, or can borrow, a big power saw, an effective way to acquire timber is to find a likely-looking timber yard, take a friend along and physically go through the stacks of wood until you find what you want. It takes time, but normally no one will mind you being there so long as you put wood back where you found it. Put a piece of chalk in your pocket before you set off. When you eventually find the right thickness of wood, it will probably be too long and too wide. Don't expect someone to cut it up for you. In any case, you will be charged for the whole piece. Mark it clearly and ostentatiously with your chalk to make sure the right piece is delivered. Show it to the foreman, who will price it. You then pay up and ask for it to be delivered to your home where you can cut it to size.

There is some fine hardwood to be had at the right price if you look around. To prove it we have a chestnut (we reckon) barbecue table 5cm thick, 2.7m long and straight as a die.

Paint and decoration

"White is always right, cream is merely specious", cried *House and Garden* magazine in the fifties. It is still a first option in many expatriate homes, although coloured walls are back in vogue as more colours become available and computerised mixers have come on to the scene.

One of the main problems in the Algarve is damp, fungus and flaking. There are two reasons: the widespread use of sea sand in the universal concrete rendering, causing cracks and damp patches, and the practice of painting newly-built walls, inside and out, with non-porous paint.

It was once pointed out that about four tons of water go into the production of the average house. Ideally this should be allowed to dry out completely. It can do so only if you leave the walls unpainted throughout a hot summer, unthinkable if you are

INTERIOR DECOR

living in the house. If you can bear the cost, it is a good plan to paint the whole house with porous paint in the spring and then repaint with a non-porous paint, on the exterior walls at least, in September or October. The alternative, for the interior, is to use a special primer which soaks into the rendering, forming a barrier which prevents salt rising to the surface. This, apparently, can be followed by any type of paint.

What usually happens is that the average builder, in the southern region at least, will paint the whole house with non-porous paint just as soon as the building is finished. He then leaves the consequences to you.

If existing wall paint is flaking off because of underlying salt, a stabiliser is available which will give a firm foundation for new paint. Black patches of fungus on walls are another problem with modern villas. This can be corrected by washing them down with well diluted bleach, *lixívia*. If you use this, wear eye protection, rubber gloves and a waterproof apron. You may prefer to go for one of the proprietary anti-fungus mixtures.

The foregoing prevalent wall conditions do not give wallpaper much of a chance. If you do prefer to have colour patterns on your walls, maybe the best solution would be fabric panels on light wooden frames, hanging on a dark painted wall.

Finally, let a word be said in favour of the traditional wall paint: "calc", slaked lime, whitewash, call it what you will. It is whiter than white, lasts for years in situations where it is not subject to rubbing, and it is porous, allowing walls to breath. Ideal for outhouses and the rubble walls of country cottages, its only sins are that it is non-washable and rubs off on your clothes if you brush up against it after it is freshly applied. Its main social failing is that a thousand escudos will buy you enough to paint a house.

Floor coverings

Traditionally, floors in the living quarters of Portuguese houses are paved with either tiles or polished marble, with rugs large and small to give a feeling of warmth. One likes to imagine that it is a throwback to the days of the Moors. The floors of modern villas follow this pattern, for both *azulejos* and marble are natural Portuguese materials and very suitable in most ways for the climate. Small rugs should be underlaid with

INTERIOR DECOR

rubberised non-slip netting.

The fad for wall-to-wall carpeting has been upon us for several years. It is comforting and, to many people, socially desirable. However, we have a personal aversion to the thought of sticking carpets to those lovely floors as the only means of making them truly wall-to-wall.

Some homes in the rural areas and elsewhere have floors tiled with *ladrilhos*. These are very practical and non-slip, hence their use around swimming pools. If you have these, it is possible to use those nice, Alentejo, hand-woven, slip rugs which can be "bought right" from the tourist shops in the off-season. There is a scuff-proof varnish available which makes these tiles waterproof without making them slippery.

---

setere — *Argos* Distributor
YOUR BRITISH STORE

Your favourite British brands.
TESCO foods ◆ ARGOS catalogue.
Household & Electrical goods ◆ Linens, etc.
Make a visit, you will immediately feel at home.
Apartado 919 - 8125 Vilamoura
Tel: (089) 328370 / 380865   Fax: 328375

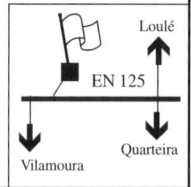

Loulé — EN 125 — Quarteira — Vilamoura

NEW KITCHEN! TALK TO THE SPECIALISTS

8 quality brands eg: Symphony, Contessa, Wellmann, Tielsa, Combistar, Wellpack, Funciona * 240 model doors in more than 100 designs and colours * Cheap "flatpacks" for DIY *

* Full range of bathroom models and more than 200 tile samples *

* Own trained staff to fit your kitchen * 100% reliability and Guarantee *

COME AND SEE FOR YOURSELF AT OUR SHOWROOMS IN VALE DE LOUSAS, ON THE EN 125 JUST EAST OF PORCHES.

IMPORTECO Lda.
Tel. 082 314287 Fax. 082 314369

LANGUAGES

Learning Portuguese

Portuguese is not an easy language to learn, but expatriate wives find it easier to learn than men do. It also appears to help if you have a knowledge of French. Hearing Portuguese spoken from a distance one can easily mistake it for French.

We feel that living in say, Lisbon, or one of the northern cities one would pick up the language more quickly than in the Algarve unless one attended a language school. Well-educated Portuguese or *Lisboetas* would, and do, have a quiet giggle if we Algarveans address them in the version of Portuguese we have picked up in the course of communicating with our home-helps and gardeners.

If you wish to spend your life, or even part of it, in Portugal, you should seriously consider learning the language properly. It makes everyday life so much simpler. Moreover, it is a matter of common courtesy to our hosts to do so. That having been said, many of those who are a little longer in the tooth than the others, find the utmost difficulty in learning any language other than their own.

Certainly the opportunities to learn Portuguese are everywhere. In all the main centres there are language schools which will give tuition to individuals, which means one or two people, to small groups of three to four persons or to larger groups of five to eight or more.

In Lisbon, or Coimbra there is a wider choice because of the universities. If you are young and really determined, we understand that the Lisbon branch of the Cambridge School of Languages runs a crash course of four and a half weeks with a money back guarantee. We were told by one of the victims that the course was 18 hours a day, six days a week, one to one with five rotating tutors. He came out at the other end weak and exhausted, but speaking fluent Portuguese, whereas he had gone in fit and healthy, and speaking none at all.

A less stressful alternative is to do it yourself with the help of tapes and manuals. Naturally, Linguaphone and Hugo offer these, as does the BBC. The latter, "Teach yourself Portuguese," consists of two tape cassettes and a manual. It gives one an excellent start; the one criticism would be that the early

LANGUAGES

lessons on the tape are spoken too quickly for beginners.

At the bottom of the list, but very effective, is to get yourself a Portuguese grammar, an exercise book and a Portuguese friend, preferably of the opposite sex (if you're in a position to do so). There is nothing like having to write something down to fix it in your mind.

---

* Language Courses *
Portuguese for Foreigners
English, French, German.
* Computer Courses *

**centro de linguas intergarbe, lda.
praceta bartolomeu dias, lote 7 esq. - 2° A,
8200 albufeira - tel. (089) 514469**

---

interlingua
instituto de linguas
language institute

RECOGNIZED BY THE MINISTRY OF EDUCATION SINCE 1979

PORTUGUESE FOR FOREIGNERS - German - French - Spanish
TRANSLATION SERVICE (Member of the Portuguese Association of Translators)
FREE LENDING LIBRARY (near the Tourist Office)

Portimão - Largo 1° de Dezembro, 28
Tel. (082) 416030 Tel./Fax (082) 27690
Lagoa - Tv. Elias Garcia, 1 - 2° Tel. (082) 341491

LAWYERS

On choosing a lawyer

If one intends to buy a house, start a business, make a will, discard a wife or husband, or start a business, the services of a reliable *advogado*, a lawyer, are essential in Portugal. Finding one you can rely on is not as easy as it should be.

One factor which sometimes causes immigrants large financial losses is that most of them have been brought up in societies where lawyers, architects, estate agents and the like are generally highly-qualified, well-esteemed professionals, men and women who will put their clients' interests before their own, people everyone can trust.

Without fully realising it, newcomers to Portugal, and to the Algarve in particular, are thrust into an environment where ethics are, to put it mildly, different. In this country, politicians and local administrators can be charged with corruption and still stay in office. Here the qualifications of many "professionals" of all nationalities are often perfunctory and sometimes non-existent.

From experience we know there are very good *advogados* in Portugal. But we are equally well aware that there are those in the profession who combine charm of manner with a blend of laxity and greed which would disqualify them for life or even put them behind bars in many EU countries. It is sad to have to say this about a profession which most of us have been brought up to trust implicitly, but there is no point in hiding our heads in the sand.

The only ray of hope is that the situation has reached the point where the Portuguese Bar Association, the *Ordem dos Advogados*, is taking a hand in the game and suspending the worst offenders. AFPOP are working with them to refurbish the tarnished image of the legal profession, especially in the southern region.

Nevertheless, for the time being when buying a property, for example, it is essential to check your lawyer every inch of the way, from the promissory contract onwards.

Main points to bear in mind

D[ra] Carmen de Andrade e Silva, gives the following advice about choosing a legal representative.

LAWYERS

- ❏ Check that the lawyer is registered either with your local consulate or with an appropriate chamber of commerce such as the Anglo-Portuguese Chamber of Commerce. Here again, AFPOP can help you. The problems of the Association's many members are all documented, and most of their sad and inevitably expensive encounters with the vagaries of Portuguese law offer salutary lessons.
- ❏ Always ask for an estimate of the costs and fees involved with the work being envisaged prior to confirming instructions to work on your behalf. Such estimates should always be given in writing, never verbally at a meeting or on the telephone. Make sure that terms of payment are included in written estimates.
- ❏ Lawyers are free to charge whatever they like, but for conveyancing they will generally charge on a percentage basis. The normal range is between 1% and 3 %, plus disbursements, depending on the price of the property and the lawyer's own estimation of the value of his services to a client.
- ❏ Lawyers will normally ask for money on account and generally this should never exceed 1% of the value of the transaction or sale price. Never, but never, offer to pay for all services in advance.
- ❏ If you are selling a property as a non-resident, sale proceeds are paid over to you either by way of a banker's draft made payable to yourself, or by direct transfer to your bank account.
  If sale proceeds are to be paid over to you via your lawyer's account, make sure that any discounts for fees and disbursements are agreed between you beforehand, in writing.
- ❏ On non-conveyancing matters it is usual for lawyers to charge on a time basis. Again, the normal rules for written estimates apply.
- ❏ We take the liberty of repeating the advice given in the chapter about buying property:
  > Do not allow one and the same *advogado* to act for you and the vendor.
  > Try to avoid using an *advogado* who is on the staff of an estate agent.
  > Refuse any offer by an agent to take care of the whole transaction for you.

LAWYERS

recourse to the Portuguese Bar Association, which is currently engaged in a campaign to improve the image of the profession. Their address:

>Exmo. Senhor
>Bastonário da Ordem dos Advogados,
>Largo de São Domingos, No. 14 - 2º Andar,
>1200 Lisboa.

Your complaint, preferably in Portuguese, must be made by you directly. For obvious reasons, it cannot be made through your own or anyone else's *advogado*.

WILLIAM ODDY, SAMPSON & CO.
ENGLISH SOLICITORS
PORTUGAL

ALMANCIL OFFICE
RUA 5 DE OUTUBRO Nº 174, 8135 ALMANCIL
TEL: 351 89 395556 /399131/399181, FAX : 351 89 395710

IN ASSOCIATION WITH GIBSONS SOLICITORS
74~78 ROCHDALE ROAD, ROYTON, OLDHAM OL2 6QJ
TEL: 0161 6205067 FAX: 0161 6243096

Carmen Andrade e Silva Neville Smith of Rego, Smith & Ferreira

1 Southernhay West - 3rd Floor
Exeter, England
Tel / Fax 0044 1647 24161

Offices in Portugal

Edifício Varandas da Luz, 1ºL
Praia da Luz, 8600 Lagos
Tel: 082 789805 Fax: 082 789 203

MARRIAGES

Getting married in Portugal

Portugal is not the place for a hasty marriage. Under Portuguese law one party must have been in Portugal for at least 30 days before notice of the intended marriage can be given. Having given that notice, the formalities may take several weeks to complete.

A foreigner wishing to marry in Portugal requires a *Certificado de Capacidade Matrimonial,* a "certificate of no impediment" from his consulate, stating that he is legally free to marry, before he can give notice of his impending nuptials to the Portuguese authorities. In the case of British subjects, he or she must live in the consular district for a minimum of 21 days before a notice of marriage will be accepted by a consul. After that, the notice of marriage must be exhibited in the consulate for a further 21 days before the certificate of no impediment will be granted.

The civil ceremony is the most important one and must be carried out before any form of church service. In the latter case, there are ample facilities for Roman Catholic rituals but few for the Protestant religion. The Anglican churches in Lisbon, Porto and Estoril, and the Scottish Church in Lisbon are not licenced for marriages but a religious ceremony can be arranged after the civil formality.

The Portuguese *Conservatória dos Registos Centrais* requires the following documents:

- ❏ Proof of residence. A Portuguese identity card if a foreign citizen is permanently resident here. A temporary resident should produce a valid passport.
- ❏ A birth certificate. In the case of foreign citizens, this should be a notarised copy issued not more than six months previously in a foreign country. If issued in Portugal, Madeira or the Azores it should be not more than three months old.
- ❏ A certificate of no impediment. It must be in the Portuguese language. The procedure for obtaining it is detailed above. It is valid for only three months from the date of issue. If it is in English and obtained from a British consulate outside Portugal, it can be exchanged for one in Portuguese at any of the British consulates in Portugal.

MARRIAGES

> NB In the case of a foreign citizen who has lived outside Portugal during the previous 12 months, the Portuguese authorities are, in exceptional circumstances, entitled to ask the person concerned to produce two persons who know him or her well enough to vouch for identity and good character.
> - Minors. The written consent of both parents is called for.
> - Previous marriages. Documentary evidence of the termination of any former marriage must be produced. This should be in the form of a decree absolute stating the reason for divorce, or a death certificate. These papers are dispatched to one of the Portuguese Appeal Courts at Lisbon, Coimbra, Oporto or Évora. Eventually, permission to re-marry will be given by the *Tribunal de Relação*.

Authentication of documents

Documents issued in the UK must be validated at the Foreign and Commonwealth Office in London. An exception to this is in the case of papers bearing an official seal issued at St Catherine's House.

All documents must be translated into Portuguese. This can be done in Portugal. If done outside Portugal, the translation must be certified by a Portuguese consular officer. Translators recognised by the Portuguese Consulate-General in London are Messrs. H. de Venna and John Venn in Gresham House, Old Broad Street, London EC2.

A copy of the Portuguese marriage certificate, with a certified translation into English, may be transmitted by a British consulate to the Registrar General, General Register Office, London, for record. Doing this has no effect on the validity or otherwise of the marriage.

Note that after the marriage ceremony all your Portuguese documentation will need to be renewed.

Nationality

A British woman no longer automatically becomes a Portuguese national if she marries a Portuguese man. Nor does a Portuguese spouse automatically acquire British nationality when marrying a British citizen.

Foreigners who marry Portuguese are eligible for

MARRIAGES

Portuguese nationality and may request it at the civil ceremony, or at a later date from the *Conservatória dos Registos Centrais*.

Portuguese spouses of British citizens can apply for British citizenship only after three years permanent legal residence in the UK.

Marriage in Gibraltar

For British subjects living in the Algarve or Alentejo, it is an easy drive to Gibraltar where they can be married by special licence. By so doing they avoid a great deal of bureaucracy and acquire a British marriage certificate. They will need the following documents:

- ❏ An affidavit sworn in front of your nearest British consul in Portugal giving names, addresses and dates of birth. If minors are getting wed, there must be written consent from parents or guardians.
- ❏ If either or both parties have been previously married, original or notarised copies of the decree(s) absolute must be available.
- ❏ A widow or widower will need to be able to produce a copy of their partner's death certificate and their previous marriage certificate. When all the above are to hand, they must be sent with the appropriate fee - the British Consul will tell you what this is - to the Registrar of Marriages, 30b Town Range, Gibraltar, where a Governor's special licence will be issued. You will need to take two witnesses with you to Gibraltar to assist in the ceremony.

MEDICAL

Hospitals

You will find a State hospital with 24-hour doctor attendance and operating facilities for casualties in most main towns in Portugal. Some specialist facilities are available in the main regional centres. The best facilities are in Lisbon, Faro and Oporto. There is much talk of new national hospitals in the regions, in the Algarve especially, but plans tend to get little further than protracted discussions about location.

An unfortunate side effect of the plans for new hospitals is to stultify development and modernisation of the existing ones.

To fall in with EU requirements, any new hospital has to be registered. This calls for stringent checks on eleven different parameters of the infrastructure, as distinct from medical equipment. These include fire precautions, sterilised air for the operating theatres, large lifts and full facilities for wheelchairs. Many of the older hospitals cannot comply with these new regulations but will have to be kept open because of the bed situation.

Private hospitals

With the increase in the immigrant population and the improved economic situation as a result of membership of the EU, there are plans for a number of private hospitals funded from outside the country and staffed partly with immigrant doctors. In these one would expect better standards of nursing care; but it is unlikely, in common with the situation in the UK, that they will have facilities for major specialist operations.

The oldest established private hospital in Lisbon is the British Hospital, founded in the 17th century as a hospice for British seamen. Three other private establishments in the capital are the Red Cross and Cuf hospitals and the Hospital Particular de Lisboa. In Oporto there is the Diagnóstico Médico Integral; in the Algarve the Casa de Saúde Santa Maria de Faro and the new Hospital Particular do Algarve, which includes a specialist eye unit. The standards and prices of treatment at all these hospitals differ considerably, as do their reputations among independent doctors and patients. As illustrated by the closure in February 1996 of Oporto's most modern hospital of any

MEDICAL

kind, the debt-ridden Clínica Particular do Porto, private as well as state-run hospitals have their problems.

State hospital problems

The real problem, lack of finance, is no secret. The Government owes millions of escudos in overtime to doctors who are so incensed by literally years of inactivity that they are prepared to abandon their Hippocratic oath and go on strike. As a result, special 24-hour clinics set up for tourists are manned only 12 hours a day; and the overnight staffing of hospitals is in doubt. The situation is exacerbated by the fact that nurses are restricted in what they are allowed to do unless instructed by a doctor; some are not even allowed to apply a plaster to a minor wound without supervision. We hear of instances where patients are having to travel 50 miles to a main hospital for treatment of minor wounds. (One feels that they might have to hurry in case the wound heals before they get there!)

Centros de Saúde

These Health Centres are to be found in every town. They are staffed by well qualified nurses - who can do much more than just sticking on a plaster - with a doctor on call.

The real purpose of the *Centros de Saúde* is to take the load off the casualty departments of the hospitals and they are equipped accordingly. Typical of the services and problems they can deal with:

- ❏ Give injections
- ❏ Cuts and abrasions from domestic and car accidents
- ❏ Snake bites
- ❏ Burns
- ❏ Jellyfish stings
- ❏ Syringing ears
- ❏ Medical certificates for driving licences (up to 60 yrs).

In the main tourist areas, during the high season, most *Centros de Saúde* are meant to have a doctor in attendance. Special blue and white signs are erected at the entrances to towns directing you to them.

MEDICAL

You will probably find it easier to get prompt emergency attention at a *Centro de Saúde* than going to a hospital. There is a national propensity to crowd hospital casualty departments with ailments as minimal as colds, sprains or nose-bleeds, to the detriment of real emergencies.

Doctors and clinics

Although the hospital and nursing system leaves a good deal to be desired, there is very little wrong with the quality of Portuguese doctors and surgeons.

Moreover, their numbers have been reinforced by immigrant doctors of various nationalities, and by an influx of doctors and specialists from the old Portuguese colonies, who are very well qualified.

"Clinic" is the euphemistic name for what is called in the UK a group practice. They are usually operated by groups of doctors with the clinic bearing the name of the organising practitioner. There are no beds. Expatriates usually attend as private patients and pay a consulting fee.

If you have transferred your allegiance from your national health service to the Portuguese *Segurança Social*, you can have attention at reduced charges. This also applies to medicines obtained on prescription.

Talking to doctors one discovers that the fees paid out to doctors by the *Segurança Social* are woefully inadequate and do not even include car expenses in a country area. Thus private patients are subsidising the service. It may be some consolation to those of us who pay privately that we are making it possible for the more enlightened doctors to give better treatment to their more impoverished nationals than they could otherwise afford to.

Incidentally, even the poorest Portuguese people have to pay something for their drugs. When they are prescribed three pills a day, it is not unknown for them to take only one to eke out the supply.

MEDICAL

Social security

British nationals who take up residence in Portugal are subject to the following rules if they wish to have assistance from the British National Health Service:

- ❏ If you have a home in the UK, even if you give up ordinary residence there, which is possible, you are entitled to hospital treatment in the UK.
- ❏ If you do not have a home in the UK and are ordinarily non-resident there, you are not entitled to treatment under the NHS even if you continue to pay contributions.
- ❏ The payment of voluntary contributions to the NHS while you are abroad does not maintain your right to the facilities of the NHS.
- ❏ If you have a residence in the UK, even if you have never paid a penny into the NHS, you are entitled to treatment in NHS hospitals.
- ❏ If you are ordinarily non-resident in the UK and require emergency treatment, you can have it free of charge while you are there.
- ❏ Voluntary Class 3 contributions maintain your National Insurance record for pensions purposes.

British citizens who wish to be treated under the Portuguese medical system can take advantage of a Protocol of Medical Insurance between Portugal and the UK dated 1992. Simply go to the office of the *Segurança Social*, (where you pay *Caixa*), and fill in a *Requerimento de Assistência Médica,* at the same time producing your passport or identity card as proof of identity. This applies whether or not you are resident in Portugal. This procedure appears to replace the old system calling for a form *Modelo* E121.

Hospital charges

For those under pensionable age, here are approximately the hospital charges if you are a beneficiary:

- ❏ Overnight stay, per day from 5.535$ to 22.000$
- ❏ Intensive care units, per day 61.820$
- ❏ Outpatients, per day (Psychiatry) 4100$
  (Others) 13.695$

MEDICAL

- Consultations from 11.500$ to 13.695$
  (Does not include extra examinations)
- *Urgência* consultations from 4.190$ to 6.600$
- Consultations at home 3.025$

Drugs

Doctors will give you a prescription which you can take to the nearest *farmácia* to be dispensed. You will be expected to pay:

- Full price if you are not a member of the Social Security scheme (*Segurança Social*)
- Reduced price if you are a Social Security member under pensionable age
- Nothing if you are over pensionable age and a member of the *Segurança Social*. (65 men, 60 women). Otherwise you pay full price. The *Credencial Pensionaria* does not help.

As a general rule drugs are more readily obtainable without a prescription than they are in the UK.

Health insurance

It is a condition of being given a residential visa that you should have some kind of adequate health insurance. Transferring to the *Segurança Social* fulfils this requirement. Or you can go for a *Credencial Pensionaria* described in the Residency section of this book. You can also patronise one of the private insurance schemes from which you can get a Portuguese-language letter certifying that you have health insurance.

It is up to you which one you go for. It depends on your means and your age. Some private schemes will accept over-70's. Over 75 you've had it unless you have been in a scheme for a number of years.

Read the small print on private schemes very carefully. Some insurances say that they will return you to your country of domicile. If you are a resident here, that means Portugal, which is possibly what you're trying to avoid.

MEDICAL

Choosing an insurer

Set up a hypothetical situation. Imagine being taken ill in the middle of the night, maybe with a heart attack, maybe with thrombosis. You would desperately like to get back to your homeland. Go to the insurer and ask them what they would do about it. Would they:

> ❏ Pay for the air fare without you having to pay and then claim the money back?
> ❏ Pay for an ambulance to the airport?
> ❏ Provide a doctor or nurse on the 'plane to look after you?
> ❏ Pay all expenses without question?
> ❏ Expect you to pay medical expenses and then claim? If the latter, how long would they take to settle claims?

Wherever you are
Whatever your age
Whatever your nationality

BUPA International

Will care for your health

Algarve Adviser: Doreen Eves - Tel/Fax 082 471 169
BUPA is approved by the Serviço de Estrangeiros

AIRES

ALGARVE INTERNATIONAL REFRACTIVE EYE SURGERY CENTRE

Our certified international eye surgeons specialize in Excimer Laser corrections of short- and longsightedness. Special programmes for AFPOP members and senior citizens.

VISÃO AIRES Centro de Oftalmologia, Lda
Hospital Particular do Algarve - Est. de Alvor - 8500 Portimão

Tel.: (082) 458 764   **Fax: (082) 458 765**

MEDICAL

New, Purpose-Built International Private Hospital

The first purpose-designed, built and newly equipped private hospital in Southern Portugal. Facilities for:

- In-patients ■ Permanent emergency department
- Maternity unit ■ Two operating theatres
- Full medical check-ups ■ CAT scan
- Pathology unit ■ Physiatric and Rehabilitation clinic
- Hemodialysis unit ■ Specialist pain clinic
- Stroke clinic ■ Specialist eye unit

HOSPITAL PARTICULAR DO ALGARVE

Cruz da Bota
(AlvorFérias)
Estrada de Alvor
8500 Portimão-Algarve
Tel.: (082) 420 4200
Fax: (082) 420 4204

NICHOLAS COLE DENTAL SURGEON

MASTER OF SCIENCE IN RESTORATIVE DENTISTRY
ADVANCED COSMETIC TECHNIQUES

SPECIAL INTEREST IN ANXIOUS PATIENTS

EMERGENCIES 24 HOURS

Largo Miguel Bombarda, 3 - 8400 Lagoa   Tel: (082) 341482

Alex Wilson

Dental Surgeon
Rua da Barroca 48, Lagos
(082) 763496

CHILDRENS
ORTHODONTICS
& COSMETICS

RUA DA BARROCA 48
PAY CAR PARK
AVENIDA DOS DESCOBRIMENTOS

MEDICAL

DR. JOHN PIPER M.B., B.S., F.R.C.S.
SPECIALIST SURGEON

(GENERAL, UROLOGICAL, GYNAECOLOGICAL
AND PLASTIC SURGERY)

CONSULTATIONS
Praia da Luz (LUZDOC), Lagoa, Albufeira and Faro.

MAJOR OPERATIONS
Hospital da Cruz Vermelha - Lisboa.

PROCEDURES UNDER LOCAL ANAESTHETIC
at Lagoa Surgery.

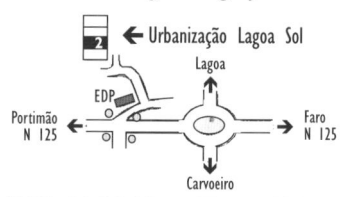

Tel : (082) 34 20 13   Fax : (082) 34 28 13

IMD - International Medical Department
Pereira e Moura, Lda

- ◆ International Assistance Service
- ◆ Medical Check-Ups
- ◆ Repatriation
- ◆ Admission to Private Hospital
- ◆ Housecalls
- ◆ Medical Consultant for Insurance Companies & Hotels

Linked with most International Insurance and assistance companies

Office: Vilamoura   Tel./Fax: (089) 321 268

Surgery: Casa de Saúde Santa Maria - Faro
Tel. (089) 802 106/7; 823 065

Emergency 24 hours   0936 - 415 299

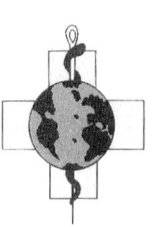

MEDICAL

LUZDOC
INTERNATIONAL MEDICAL SERVICE

A multilingual experienced team will give you medical attention and assistance for any problems you might have if you are ill away from home.

Rua 25 de Abril 12, Praia da Luz, 8600 Lagos
APPOINTMENTS & 24 Hr EMERGENCY COVER 082 789866
FAX 082 788216   MOBILE PHONE 0931 811988

Lloyd & Whyte
(Insurance Brokers)

A range of health care schemes for all your health care needs.

Head Office: Av. Dr. Mateus Teixeira de Azevedo, Lote 3 R/C
8800 TAVIRA. TEL: (081) 32 58 42 FAX: (081) 32 58 79
Brendon (Personal Insurance) Services

Multiclínica do Algarve

DENTAL SERVICES
- Cosmetic Dentistry
- Prosthetic Dentistry
- Orthodontics
- Dental Hygiene
- **Implants**

CHIROPRACTIC
- Back and Neck Pain
- Headache and Migraine
- Sports Injuries
- Sciatica

BENFARRAS, 8100 LOULÉ Tel: (089) 366 266 Fax: (089) 366268
on EN 125 between turnings to Vilamoura and Boliqueime. Benfarras near Boliqueime.

MEDLAGOS
24 Horas Diagnóstico + Tratamento
We care about **your** health

AMEIJEIRA DE CIMA, BELA VISTA, LOTE 2 R/C,
8600 LAGOS
TELEFONE (082) 760181   FAX (082) 760180

MOTORING

Importing vehicles

A relaxation of the regulations and cost involved in importing vehicles from other EU countries is said to be imminent, so the following may soon be obsolete but at the time of writing this is how things stand.

We are now moving into an era where Portugal has to fall into line with EU rules regarding the free movement of motor vehicles. Hitherto the Customs had been free to levy whatever taxes it thought fit on most articles of commerce. Until now buyers have been faced with the IA, *Imposto Automóvel*, a socialist archaism aimed at taxing the rich, which inflicts escalating taxes based on the cubic capacity of all private cars. At the time of writing a 2-litre car paid almost ten times the amount of tax levied on a car of less than 1-litre. However, there are rumours of tax revisions where tax on smaller capacity cars will be increased, and reduced on the larger engine sizes.

There is one exception. Fortuitously, some four-wheel drive makes are classed as working vehicles and escape the capacity tax; other four-wheel-drive vehicles based on passenger cars do not. This is why the Land Rover "Discovery" is marginally cheaper here than in the UK, while the Opel "Frontera" is nearly twice the UK price.

Regarding second hand vehicles, until very recently if a Portuguese or any other citizen imported a passenger car from another country, EU or otherwise, tax was levied in Portugal even if the car has had tax paid on it in its country of origin. Now, the situation appears to be easing, possibly as the result of an appeal by a Portuguese motor dealer to the European Court, and many appeals, some successful, in Portuguese courts. Consequently the authorities are showing signs of taking notice of EU regulations controlling the free passage of vehicles between EU countries.

The ACP has reported that from 1 January 1996, on paper at least, the authorities are required to accept a privately owned, imported car which has suitable homologation papers from its country of origin. Moreover, the formalities for acquiring the homologation documents from the agents are required to be completed within three weeks and not to cost more than 100ECUs. Despite this, a *despachante* has told us that the 1995 requirements are the strictest so far, involving a great deal more paperwork and,

MOTORING

so far as the Algarve is concerned, the absolute minimum time for the process is five months, but is usually more than a year.

The Car Tax

The aforementioned *Imposto Automóvel*, on new cars is as follows as from mid 1996.

To calculate the amount of tax due on a particular vehicle, establish the engine size in cubic centimetres, decide which **Capacity Band** it falls into, multiply this figure by the appropriate **Tax per c.c.** and from the resulting figure deduct the **Factor**.

The taxes shown do not include IVA, which is levied on the total value of the car plus tax.

Capacity band	Tax per cc	Factor	Example	To pay
Up to 1000	261	50300	983	206263
1001-1250	596	385863	1189	322781
1251-1500	1399	1383385	1435	624180
1501-1750	2013	2308911	1700	1113189
1751-2000	3395	4372715	1980	2349385
2001-2500	3273	4490007	2300	3037893
Over 2500	2050	1457259	5600	10022741

The taxes shown above are for the engine sizes shown in the column headed **Example**.

For used cars, a further deduction may be made according to the age of the car at the following rates:

1 - 2 yrs 10%; 2 - 3 yrs 15%; 3 - 4 yrs 20%; over 4 yrs 25%.

The IA (*Imposto Automóvel*) is applied to all vehicles imported by Portuguese residents. So far as the *Alfândega* is concerned, this means:

- Portuguese citizens.
- Foreigners with residential permit.

Import concessions

Many new members coming into the country from EU countries, especially Germany and Holland, will wish to take advantage of the import concession for EU citizens making a change of residence and bringing their cars with them. Precise details of the requirements for this process are laid out in Decree Law 264 of 30 July 1993. However, beware! Local customs offices may have their own interpretation of the law.

MOTORING

The conditions are:

- ❏ The car has to be matriculated in its owner's own country.
- ❏ The car registration documents must be the regular ones from the owner's country, not export documents.
- ❏ The car must have been in its owner's name for at least six months before coming to Portugal.
- ❏ The owner has to be from an EU country.
- ❏ The owner has to have a driving licence.
- ❏ The owner cannot have worked for profit in Portugal during the year preceding the one in which he cancelled residence in his own country. Persons cancelling residence in 1996 cannot have earned money in Portugal during 1995.
- ❏ The owner cannot have a Portuguese *residência* before moving to Portugal.
- ❏ The applicant must have lived in his own country for at least six months before moving to Portugal.

The documents required are:

- ❏ Vehicle registration document
- ❏ Passport
- ❏ Driving licence
- ❏ Número de Contribuinte
- ❏ Certificate issue by the *Junta de Freguesia* of your intended residence to confirm that you live there.
- ❏ Document from your own country proving change of residence to Portugal. In France this is called *Changement de Domicile*, in Germany an *Ameldung*, and for UK residents an equivalent document will be issued by the British Consulate on production of the certificate of residence from your *Junta de Freguesia*. Only documents in English, French or Portuguese are acceptable. Those from Germany, or any other country, must be translated into Portuguese by an approved agency. This document should state the date of departure from your own country.
- ❏ Certificate issue by the *Finanças* in the area where you intend to reside. This shows any income generated in Portugal in the three years preceding document 6. It is arranged by filling in a form at the *Finanças* office.

MOTORING

- ❏ Two diagonally opposite 3/4 view photographs of the car taken to show the front and one side, and the rear and the other side.
- ❏ The instruction book for the car.
- ❏ The size of the tyres.
- ❏ The engine number.

The last four items (8-11) are for the *Direcção-Geral de Viação* for a process called V5 which records all the technical data of the car after it has been inspected by a test centre. The matriculation process also calls for five declarations, two forms - DVL and 13 - and four small cards.

You can do all this yourself or you can employ a customs agent. A good *despachante* will do all the leg-work for you. Your only requirement would be to take your car to an inspection centre for a prearranged appointment, and to sign a paper to confirm that the car is waiting for the decision of the customs director. Meanwhile, you can drive the car with a *Guia de Circulação*, which can be renewed ad infinitum, until the customs director makes his decision. As soon as this is given, the agent starts the matriculation process and will deliver the Portuguese plates.

In the interim, the only persons who can drive the car are yourself and your immediate family, that is your father, spouse or children.

It is important that as soon as you have the Change of Residence certificate you immediately apply for a *residência*, because the Customs may want to see it.

Tourist vehicles

Early in 1993 new rules were introduced regarding tourist vehicles, that is to say private vehicles registered in countries other than Portugal, belonging to non-residents. So far as Portuguese customs are concerned, there are two categories of tourist car owner: long-term and short-term.

Long-term visitors

Long-term tourists are those staying for long periods with friends or in hotels. They are allowed to keep a foreign-registered car in this country for a maximum of 180 days from the date of the stamp in their *Guia de Circulação* (circulation permit). After that,

MOTORING

the car must be taken out of the country. Bringing it back in again that year is not permitted. Nor is it permitted to bring in another car in its place.

With abandonment of border controls, this law lends itself to malpractice. It does not cater for the car owner, who arrives with the intention of staying as a short-term visitor for 30 days and then decides to stay on. He can make his way to the *Alfândega* in leisurely way to obtain a *Guia* and extend his stay by a further 180 days.

The following procedure is expected of long-term tourists:

> ❏ Within four days of entering the country, visit a customs office and ask for a *Guia de Circulação*.
> ❏ On this form the clerk should enter details of yourself and your car. Have it stamped by the *Alfândega*.
> ❏ Take this form to the police, the GNR, within four days. The police will check the vehicle details, stamp the *Guia*, retain the duplicate and hand the original back to you. You must have it available in the car at all times.
> ❏ When taking your car out of the country, hand in the *Guia* to a customs office near the border.

Short-term visitors

For practical reasons short-term visitors - those intending to remain in the country for 30 days or less - do not require a *Guia de Circulação*. During the tourist season the customs would not be able to cope. However if you have bought your car under some kind of tax-free arrangement, such as that operating in Andorra; and it bears customs identification such as the French TT prefix plates or the German Z prefix plates, you should get yourself a *Guia*. The road police regularly check cars with these licence plates.

Residents and the six-month regulation

One other category of car owner faces problems. This is a person who has had a home here for a number of years, has a residential visa, but only brings his car in for six months every

MOTORING

year. He retains his national licence plates. Knowing that it is illegal for him to be driving a foreign-registered car, he shows his passport and foreign driving licence if stopped by the police. Eventually, he decides he wishes to keep his car here permanently.

This is regarded by the customs as the direct importation of a second-hand vehicle by a resident. The IA will be assessed on engine size as if it were a new car. The biggest deduction given is 10 % for a car more than two years old. For example, an owner wishing to bring in a well-loved, 12-year-old Mercedes-Benz 240 (engine between 2,001cc and 2,500cc) should expect to pay 3,050,000$ less 10 %, which works out at 2,745,000$ or rather more than the car costs new.

Permission to Drive

If you own a Portuguese registered car and you wish anyone other than yourself to drive it they should carry with them, in the car, the following declaration. It can now be typed on ordinary white paper taken by you, the owner to the notary's office to be notarised.

Incidentally if you go to your insurer and ask them about this they will tell you that the *Declaração* below is unnecessary. They wil be thinking only of insurance. AFPOP checked this out with the police and they were told quite firmly that the permission-to-drive document was a legal requirement and that failure to be able to produce it if stopped could result in an on-the-spot fine.

Fill in the details as follows:

A.	Car owner's full name
B	Nationality of above
C	Owner's Passport number
C2	Address of owner of car
D	Make and model of your car
E	Car registration
F	Full name of second driver
G	Nationality of second driver
H	Second driver's passport number
I	Car owner's pace of residence and the date
J	Owners full name again with signature above it.

MOTORING

> DECLARAÇÃO
>
> Eu,......A................., de nacionalidade ..B..., portador do passaporte No....C........, residente na ....C2..................., proprietário do automóvel......D......... matrícula.....E....., declaro para todos os fins convincentes e em especial, para fazer-se perante as autoridades Aduaneinas e de Trânsito, que autorizo ....F........., de nacionalidade...G...., portador de passaporte No.....H........ a utilizar o referido automóvel para viagens turísticas e pessoais dentro e fora do território Nacional de Portugal.
>
> Place of residence and date.......I..........(e.g. Alvor, 20 Maio, 1991)
>
> ....J......................

These are the rules regarding who can drive what as of January 1996.

> - Residents who have applied for and obtained a residential visa, *Autorização de Residência*, are required to convert to a Portuguese driving licence within one year.
> - A foreign resident who imports a vehicle which is registered abroad must matriculate it. (See the section on concessionary importation).
> - A foreign resident holding a Portuguese driving licence may drive any Portuguese registered car whoever the owner.
> - A non-resident may drive a foreign or Portuguese registered car but if stopped by the police must be able to show that he or she is not resident and is not working in Portugal.
> - Non-residents who drive cars which are not registered in their name must be able to produce a notarised 'permission to drive' declaration from the registered owner. **Spouses are not exempt**.

What the British driving licence lacks is a photograph of the holder. This is probably why the traffic police here prefer the international driving licence issued by the English motoring organisations. It does have a photograph, is good for a year, and can be bought over the counter at any AA or RAC office in the UK or, we are told by the RAC, obtained from an *Automóvel Clube de Portugal* office.

MOTORING

The EU ruling regarding driving licences, removing the obligation to change them when transferring residence, comes into effect in July 1996. It will be interesting to see whether the *Direcção-Geral de Viação* will recognise this.

Drink and drive

The tragically high road accident rate in Portugal brought about swingeing changes in the drink and drive laws with effect from October 1992. These changes are important because they bring the minimum alcohol level down to a point halfway between the extremely stringent Swedish limit and that in the UK.

Portuguese law states the limit in terms of grams per litre of blood, the maximum legal limit being 0.5grams per litre, rather than the almost universal and more convenient milligrams per centilitre. The police breathalysers are calibrated in grams per litre also, so for the purposes of this chapter the limits are stated in the same way. Comparing the laws in other countries, the Swedish maximum is 0.25 grams per litre while in the UK it is currently 0.80 gms/l. The new Portuguese parameters and the sentences quoted are as follows:

Alcohol level	Fine in contos
Between 0.5 and 0.79 gms/l	20 - 100
Between 0.8 and 1.1 gms/l	40 - 200
Over 1.2gms/l	Judgement in court

A recommended way to control one's drinking is to think in terms of units of alcohol. One unit taken on an empty stomach will raise the alcohol/blood level to 20mg/cl; your liver will break this down in one hour. Thus, two units will be absorbed in two hours, four units in four hours, and so on. Alcohol taken on a full stomach is absorbed more slowly, delaying build-up in the blood.

Be warned that lightweight ladies require less than this, heavyweight males can take more. Figures indicate that weight for weight the female sex needs less alcohol than the male to bring the alcohol/blood ratio up to a given level.

As a rough guide, listed here are the amounts of various drinks equivalent to one unit.

MOTORING

Drink	% Alc.	Ml.	Fl.oz UK	Fl.oz.USA
Spirits	40	25	0.9	1.1
Port	12	85	3	3.6
Vermouth/Sherry	16	63	2	3
Wine	9	111	4	5
Beer	5.5	180	6.5	7.8

The less academically inclined might like to take as the standard measure that well-tried utensil, the giveaway 300ml tumbler, distributed by Highland Clan and BP among others in Portugal.

Half an inch, 12mm, of whisky in the bottom of one of these is equivalent to one unit of alcohol.

A not-too-podgy "finger" would be two units. It's a sobering thought that a "finger" is the measure which will take you up to the legal limit. Three fingers, catching your system at the wrong moment, could land you in prison.

Incidentally, the same glass filled to the brim with Portuguese beer holds roughly half of an imperial pint and is equivalent to a little under two units. A large sherry glass holds 7.5cl or 3fluid oz.

Safe drinking

Take two units before dinner, one unit one hour later and one unit one further hour after that. The great danger is the brandy after dinner! Having had an aperitif before the meal, and two or three glasses of wine with it, the blood alcohol will build up slowly. After dinner, as the stomach empties, the final brandy will be absorbed quickly and push the already high alcohol/blood level way above the limit.

So the answer's a lemon: cut a generous slice out of it, divide that slice into two, squeeze the two halves into your gin and tonic, add two lumps of ice, enjoy your drink, and find a graduate of Alcoholics Anonymous to drive you home.

Getting a driving licence

The *Automóvel Clube de Portugal* stated some time ago that Article 46 of Decreto Regulamentar No 47/87 of 29 July 1987 sets down quite clearly that citizens of the European Union must

MOTORING

acquire a Portuguese driving licence within one year of their residential visa being granted. Citizens of other countries must obtain a licence immediately their *residência* is granted. Much has changed since then, but as of April 1996 the European Union driving licence is still not recognised in this country. If you have a residential visa, in Portuguese law you are a Portuguese citizen. Therefore you must hold a Portuguese driving licence.

To obtain a licence, the requirements are as listed on the next page. It is assumed you have passed a driving test in your own country. This is acceptable to the *Direcção Geral de Viação* who administer these things.

If you have not passed a test, you will have to take one here in Portugal. The alternative is to go back to your own country and do it there. For Britons this would mean obtaining a British provisional licence, taking lessons and then waiting months for a test, which you may or may not pass.

It may be more economical to do it through a Portuguese driving school. Sad to say in a great many cases, just how quickly and easily you pass the test really depends on the size of your wallet.

Assuming that you already have a driving licence issued in your own country, the documents you need to obtain a Portuguese permit to drive are as follows:

- ❏ Your residential visa
- ❏ A Portuguese identity card
- ❏ Your original driving licence
- ❏ Two passport-size photographs
- ❏ A medical certificate. If you are under 60 years of age a *Centro de Saúde* will provide one. Or you can go to your own doctor.
- ❏ One form No. 921
- ❏ One form No. 922 with a *fiscal* stamp of 600$

If you are less than 65 years old, the licence you acquire will be valid until you reach that age. When that day comes you must re-apply, submitting a further medical certificate. This licence will last until you reach the age of 70.

After reaching 70 years, subsequent licences are good for two

MOTORING

years only. Each renewal will require a certificate from the chief medical officer in your area.

Your licence can be obtained through a local driving school. For a fee they will deal with the paperwork, dispatch it to the *Direcção de Viação* of your region, and eventually you will get your licence. You will be given a receipt, which doubles as a permit to drive, while you are awaiting delivery.

If you have time on your hands, it is better to take a day off and go to the regional licensing centre yourself. Algarveans have found the officials at Faro most helpful and you will get your licence in less than half the time. Moreover, the receipt they hand to you is recognised by the police. Some of the papers doled out by driving schools have been turned down by the *Brigada de Trânsito* making roadside checks.

When you hand over the paperwork for your licence, you will be asked to surrender your national licence. This is correct in EU law and you are breaking the law to apply for a duplicate licence. The Portuguese licence is valid in all EU countries.

There used to be a requirement for a certificate of good character from your consulate. This is no longer a requirement for British subjects.

Driving in Portugal

Portugal is renowned for being one of the easiest countries in Europe in which to have a road accident. Contributory factors are the carriageway format on major highways, an overwhelming proportion of first generation drivers, the national temperament and corruption in the driving test system.

National temperament manifests itself in a passion for overtaking under any circumstances, especially if the driver is behind the wheel of one of the two top German makes, or the car in front is being driven by a woman.

The surfeit of first generation drivers on Portuguese roads is a socio-historic phenomenon. Prior to 25 April 1974, Portugal was virtually a two class society with only a restricted number of people able to afford anything better than a bicycle. As a result, only a small proportion of today's Portuguese drivers were brought up in car-owning families, thus the majority lacked parental guidance in the critical formative period.

MOTORING

The "panic lane"

There are no written rules covering these first two contingencies, but there are some for the road format. Even major roads, like the trans-Algarve EN125 and the main Lisbon road south, are virtually two-lane highways with traffic moving in opposite directions. The wide, hard shoulder flanking the two middle lanes is not for general use; it is not meant to be a slow lane. It is intended for specific types of traffic. The following vehicles may stay in it permanently:

- Emergency services
- Pedestrians
- Slow moving vehicles and mule carts.
- Its temporary uses are:
- For slower traffic to pull into to allow faster vehicles to pass.
- For broken-down vehicles until they are removed.

You will quickly find, hopefully before it's not too late, that the main function of this secondary lane is not written in any Highway Code. Many, many times in even a short journey you will be confronted with two or even three cars abreast, coming at you in the opposite direction. The only reaction, fortunately a natural one, is to pull over into this hard shoulder to avoid catastrophe. We have christened it the "panic lane".

Sometimes drivers are slow to react, or the "panic lane" is occupied by a "tricyc" or a rubbish bin. The consequences are usually devastating and bloody. Of course there is a spin-off. When the tragic air disaster happened at Faro airport, the speed with which the emergency services dealt with the casualties was put down to the expertise they had acquired on the EN125. It is labelled along with the *Marginal* as one of the most dangerous roads in Europe.

Hazards to watch out for:

- Obstructions in the "panic lane" on main roads. They can inhibit your ability to dodge overtakers coming in the opposite direction.
- Double overtaking.
- Non-observance of "Stop" signs.

MOTORING

- Motorcyclists from the opposite direction cutting across your bows into an acute junction on your right.
- Absence of rear lights on motorcycles away from the main highways.
- Trucks on minor roads immediately after the lunch break.
  Avoid high speed on minor roads, winding or otherwise.

The official view

The authorities admit that driving standards in Portugal are in need of improvement. It is hoped that real improvement will come from driver education and that standards and practices will be improved in driving schools. In addition, heavier fines for driving offences have been promulgated.

Documentation to carry at all times

Random roadside checks are a way of life on Portuguese roads. One day the police will be checking big trucks, the next day commercial vans and the following day cars. They used to have a passion for MiniMokes, especially those rented by tourists with pretty girls in them.

If stopped, get out of the car, preferably with the following documents in your hand. You will be fined if any one of the following is not with you in the car:

- Driving licence.
- Your green insurance card.
- The green and blue car *livretes*. Some police forces now accept notarised copies of these.
- Identity card or passport.
- Permission-to-drive document if necessary.

It is not necessary to hold original documents in the car. Photocopies of each document are acceptable providing they have been notarised. There is no need to have the insurance certificate notarised.

British tourists unaccustomed to continental motoring should note that in Portugal, as in most European countries, there is no such thing as having seven days to produce your driving licence.

MOTORING

It has to be with you in the car at all times.

International driving licences issued by the British AA or RAC are useful in Portugal. This is because the police prefer a document with a photograph in it.

Common offences

You will also be fined for the following:

- ❏ Not wearing a seatbelt at all times.
- ❏ Failure to have a red triangle in the car.
- ❏ The wrong type of red triangle. It must be model No. DGV A001.
- ❏ Less than 2mm of tread on your tyres.
- ❏ Tyres of a size different from the size shown on your car papers.
- ❏ Unserviceable wipers.
- ❏ Faulty headlamp, side lamp, indicator, stop light.

There are strict new laws on drinking and driving with the lower alcohol limit being set half way between Sweden's very low limit and the British one. This is all defined earlier in this chapter under a separate heading.

It is the Law that all vehicles display in a prominent position (eg on the dashboard) visible to an official of the GNR standing outside the car, a plate or tab giving the owner's name and address. The use of seat belts is obligatory at all times. Where seat belts are installed for rear seats they must by law be used.

It is forbidden to carry children below the age of 12 in the front seat of a car.

Payment of fines

In line with a law which came into effect on 12 December 1991, traffic fines incurred by owners of a Portuguese driving licence are NOT payable to an apprehending official of the GNR. Instead, the GNR official gives the offender a *"multa"* (offence form), completed on the spot, which the offender must take within 15 days to any *Posto da GNR* where a *Guia Mod* 1-A is issued. This must be taken on the same day to any *Finanças* where the fine is paid.

In the case of non-residents or holders of non-Portuguese driving licences (tourists, immigrants etc.), fines are always paid

MOTORING

on the spot and are likely to be more than if you were a resident. Despite the fact that every responsible body urges tourists not to carry too much cash with them, the Portuguese Tourist Board is urging that tourists carry enough money with them to pay on the spot fines. This can be as much as 40,000$.

Don't think that because you're a tourist you will get away with it. The rank and file of the GNR appear to have no interest at all in the promotion of tourism.

Reporting of accidents

In the event of a serious road accident:

- ❏ Wait until the police appear. If you are in a populated area the grapevine telegraph will have them on the scene very quickly. If you are out in the country, leave someone to guard the car, find a phone and dial 115. You should be answered by someone with a grasp of languages. Or persuade the other driver to do the phoning.
- ❏ Insist that the GNR take a statement from you as well as the other driver. The police tend to take a statement only from the driver speaking their native tongue and ignore the other driver if he is a foreigner. If the policeman refuses, ask his name and rank (Portuguese for this, please). Then go with someone who speaks Portuguese to the nearest police station and make a report there. Only a few GNR officers, as distinct from the *Brigada de Trânsito*, speak any language other than their own. Those who do are most likely to speak either English or French.
- ❏ Insist on an immediate breathalyser test for yourself and the other driver.
- ❏ Obtain the following information from the other driver:
    His name
    The name and address of his insurance company
    The number of his insurance document *(No. Apólice)*.

In the event of an accident involving a third party being injured, you are strongly advised to allow the insurance companies to resolve everything between themselves. Do not become personally involved in any way. Taking a sympathetic attitude and maybe visiting an injured party in hospital or at home places one on the firing line for all sorts of claims from families and friends of the injured party.

MOTORING

Buying and selling cars

One of the most frequent omissions when cars change ownership is that the buyer of your old car fails to register it in his name. It remains on the main computer in Lisbon as your car, and you remain legally responsible for it while your name is there. If it is involved in an accident or an infraction of the law, you can be called upon to pay for any fines or damages. If you refuse, you can be hauled up before court and made to pay the fines in addition to the court fees and your lawyer's costs.

Mind you, the buyer does not get off scot free if you persist in the matter. For failing to register the car in his own name within 30 days, he can be fined up to 100 *contos* and the vehicle can be impounded. What is more, there seems to be no legal reason, since the car is registered in your name, that you should not retake possession of it!

If you buy a used car from either a friend or a dealer, both the buyer and the vendor must follow the correct procedure, which is as follows:

> ❏ Both parties should fill in a *Contrato Verbal de Compra e Venda* (*Declaração para Registo de Propriedade*).
> ❏ When signed, the forms should be notarised with the purchaser's signature authenticated.
> ❏ Have the replacement car registered in your name at the *Conservatória* of your district within 30 days of the transaction for the reasons stated above.

Do not hand over the keys of your car until the purchaser has paid you for it and can show you a notarised copy of the *Guia de Substituição de Livrete*. Also, insist on evidence that he has applied for the new *Título de Propriedade* so that it is registered in his name. Obtaining a *Título de Propriedade* takes about three months. Refer to the banking chapter on how to deal with dud cheques if you're dealing with a stranger and are sufficiently naive not to demand cash.

It is a good idea to retain notarised copies of the small green and blue documents, usually referred to as the *livrete*, of your old car.

MOTORING

Buying a new car and trading in your old one

In the euphoria of becoming the owner of a new car and getting a good trade-in allowance for your old faithful, there is a tendency to assume that the concessionaires from whom you buy your new car will automatically attend to all the formalities, but there can be problems. The legal snag here is that you do not know who the buyer is. The normal procedure is that you will be asked to sign a *Contrato Verbal de Compra e Venda* with the buyer's name left blank. In return, you hand over to the concessionaire the two-document *livrete* of your old car and think nothing more about it. At this point you should also write out a receipt and get the buyer to sign it to aid proof of new ownership of the car. What usually happens to your old car is that the concessionaire will have a tame used-car dealer who takes your old car off his hands. This dealer will then fancy-up your trade-in and sell it on. You have to rely on him to make sure that the ultimate recipient of the old faithful has it registered in his or her own name.

The most you can do to prove you have sold the car is to ensure that the invoice for the new car shows full details of your old car and the price allowed for it. Having got it, keep it in the family archives indefinitely, or until you leave the country, lock, stock and barrel forever more.

Giving up motoring

Strictly speaking, the vendor of a car which he doesn't intend to replace should include the following information in the receipt:

- ❏ The make, model type, body number, registration plate of the car.
- ❏ Vendor's name, address, and identity card number.
- ❏ Full identification of the purchaser, or the intermediary, if there is one.
- ❏ Date of the transaction and the price paid.
- ❏ An undertaking that the purchaser/intermediary will provide a photocopy of the completed contract as well as a photocopy of the *Guia de Substituição* issued in the name of the new owner by the *Conservatória de Registo*.
- ❏ The notarised signature of the intermediary or purchaser on the receipt.

MOTORING

Highway Code

Until a couple of years ago Portugal did not have a Highway Code as such. The very first one became law on 1st October 1994. As one would expect, it ratifies much existing law, in some cases acting as a reminder of long abandoned customs (such as stopping at Stop signs), with the object of reducing Portugal's terrifying road accident rate. In one area the authorities appear to have been realistic in raising the speed limit on main roads and reducing it in built-up areas.

Speed limits

Road category	Cars	Light vans	Buses	Trucks
Built up areas	50	50	50	50
Side roads	90 (70)	70 (70)	80	70
Main highways	100 (80)	90 (80)	90	80
Motorways	120 (100)	110 (90)	110	90

* The figures in parentheses are for vehicles with a trailer attached

Fines for speeding or not speeding

Exceeding the speed limit by:	Fine in *contos*
Less than 30 km/h	10 - 50
30 - 50 km/h	20 - 100
More than 50 km/h	40 - 200
Up to 30 km/h on the motorway	10
Going so slowly as to obstruct traffic	5 - 25

Many regulations, such as the ones referring to alcohol abuse, remain unchanged in the Highway Code and are dealt with detail earlier in this chapter. The fines for transgression of these laws are revealed in the new code and are laid out in the section headed "Drink and Drive".

There have always been various degrees of traffic offences. They are now clearly defined in the new code as Light, Serious, and Very Serious. Only the last named will be dealt with in court; the rest will be dealt with by the police with fines.

Light offences:

- ❏ Treating officers of the law with disrespect
- ❏ Driving on the left hand side of the road

MOTORING

- Failure to give pedestrians right of way on crossings
- Exceeding the speed limit by up to 30 km/h
- Failure to observe STOP signs
- Repeatedly crossing the solid white line
- Driving under the influence of alcohol (0,5 to 0,75 grms/l) or drugs
- Stopping or parking on the hard shoulder of main roads
- Driving without lights when this is called for (e.g. in heavy rain).

Serious:

- Stopping or parking on the hard shoulder within 50 metres of an intersection
- Parking at night on the hard shoulder of motorways
- Exceeding the speed limit by up to 60 km/h
- Alcohol reading of more than 0,8 grms/l
- Driving under the influence of drugs
- Entering or leaving highways by other than the designated roads
- Driving without lights
- Failure to dip headlights for oncoming traffic
- Dangerous U-turns
- Dangerous overtaking

Very Serious:

- Alcohol level more than 1.2 grms/l.
- Driving without a licence
- Causing accidents

New regulations for light vans and pickups

New regulations call for a *Isenção de Horário de Trabalho*, issued by *Direcção Geral de Viação*. To get this you need the following:

- A fiscal stamp for 243$
- Photocopies of the car *Livrete* and *Registo de Propriedade*
- The pink *Cartão de Empresário* to prove that you are self-employed
- Copy of your 1993 IRS reference showing that you pay business tax
- Receipt from the *Segurança Social* to prove that you pay *Caixa*

MOTORING

If someone who shares your home with you, such as your wife, drives the car, further documentation is required:

> ❏ A fiscal stamp for 243$
> ❏ An *atestado* from your *Junta de Freguesia* stating that you live in the same house. This is for exemption from limitation of working hours
> ❏ Document to prove that your relative makes regular payments to the *Segurança Social*. Play safe and get a receipt for the year

If the vehicle is genuinely for commercial use it is exempt from IVA, in which case its working hours will be limited. If it has been bought as a commercial vehicle, without IVA, but is being used for pleasure only by an owner who cannot prove that he pays business tax to the IRS or *Caixa,* he could be faced with extra tax.

Customs (Alfândega) Offices:

- ❏ Alfândega de Lisboa, Sede, Rua Terreiro do Trigo, 1100 Lisboa. tel (01) 888 35 76; fax (01) 888 36 86
- ❏ Deleg. Aduan. Alcântara Norte, Avenida Brasília, 1300 Lisboa. tel (01) 397 85 61; fax (01) 395 57 70
- ❏ Deleg. Aduan. Cais dos Soldados, Avenida Infante D. Henrique N° 95, 1100 Lisboa. tel (01) 888 19 10; fax (01) 888 23 48
- ❏ Deleg. Aduan. Jardim do Tabaco, Avenida Infante D. Henrique, 1100 Lisboa. tel (01) 888 37 77; fax (01) 888 88 98
- ❏ Deleg. Aduan. Xabregas, Avenida Infante D. Henrique, 1100 Lisboa. tel (01) 858 60 41; fax (01) 858 64 10
- ❏ Deleg. Aduan. Alverca, EN10, 2615 Alverca. tel (01) 957 06 21
- ❏ Deleg. Aduan. Aveiro, Ed. Tirtife - Moinhos, 3800 Aveiro. tel (034) 23 350; fax (034) 38 10 6
- ❏ Deleg. Aduan. Braga, Parque Industrial Celeiros, 4700 Braga. tel (053) 67 25 73; fax (053) 67 34 59
- ❏ Deleg. Aduan. Bragança, Avenida Abade de Baçal, 41, R/C Dt., 5300 Bragança. tel (073) 27 478; fax (073) 27 480
- ❏ Deleg. Ag. Aduan. Caia, 7350 Elvas.tel (068) 64 11 50; fax (068) 64 11 51
- ❏ Deleg. Aduan. Covilhã, Parque Industrial, 6200 Covilhã. tel (075) 33 13 58; fax (075) 33 16 63
- ❏ Deleg. Aduan. Faro, Avenida de República N° 3B, 8000 Faro. tel (089) 82 23 25; fax (089) 82 41 23

MOTORING

- ❏ Deleg. Aduan. Figueira da Foz, Cais da Alfândega 31, 3080 Figueira da Foz. tel (033) 35 565; fax (033) 29 424
- ❏ Deleg. Aduan. Freixeiro, EN 107, 4470 Maia. tel (02) 996 18 27; fax (02) 996 07 25
- ❏ Deleg. Aduan. Lagos, Rua Vedoria N° 3, 8600 Lagos. tel (082) 76 28 17; fax (082) 76 73 49
- ❏ Deleg. Aduan. Leixões, Avenida Centenários, Leça da Palmeira, 4450 Matosinhos. tel (02) 995 19 76; fax (02) 995, 86 07
- ❏ Deleg. Aduan. Olhão, Avenida 16 de Junho, 8700 Olhâo. tel (089) 70 20 20; fax (089) 70 41 97
- ❏ Deleg. Aduan. Peniche, Prageira, 2520 Peniche. tel (062) 78 78 51; fax (062) 78 16 96
- ❏ Deleg. Aduan. Portimão, Rua Júdice Biker N° 5, 8500 Portimão. tel (082) 24 239; fax (082) 41 55 29
- ❏ Alfândega do Porto, Sede, Rua Nova da Alfândega, 4000 Porto. tel (02) 200 04 37; fax (02) 31 59 02
- ❏ Deleg. Aduan. Setúbal, Praça da República, 2900 Setúbal. tel (065) 52 21 65; fax (065) 34 156
- ❏ Deleg. Aduan. Sines, Quinta da Sta. Isabel, 7520 Sines. tel (069) 62 40 01; fax (069) 63 51 76
- ❏ Deleg. Aduan. Valença, EN 13, 4930 Valença do Minho. tel (051) 82 42 17
- ❏ Deleg. Aduan. Viana do Castelo, Largo João T. Costa, 4900 Viana do Castelo. tel (058) 82 33 46; fax (058) 82 11 16
- ❏ Subdeleg. Aduan. Vilamoura, Marinha de Vilamoura, 8125 Quarteira. tel (089) 53 14 31; fax (089) 51 14 06
- ❏ Deleg. Aduan. Vila Real de Sto. António, Avenida da República 82-1°, 8900 Vila Real de Sto. António. tel (081) 53 14 31; fax (081) 51 14 06
- ❏ Deleg. Aduan. Vilar Formosa, Edifício CTT, Praça General Humberto Delgado, 6350 Almeida. tel (071) 52 142; fax (071) 53 227

Automóvel Clube de Portugal Offices

The ACP issues international driving licences and renders services (car importation, car documents, driving licences) at the following offices:

- ❏ Head office ACP, Rua Rosa Araújo, 24, 1200 Lisboa. tel (01) 356 39 31; fax (01) 57 47 32

MOTORING

- Avenida Dr Lourenço Peixinho, 89D, 3800 Aveiro.
  tel (034) 22 571; fax (034) 25 220
- Avenida Conde D.Henrique,72, 4700 Braga.
  tel (053) 27 01; fax (053) 61 10 26
- Avendia Sá Carneiro, Edif. Montezinho, Lj. AK, 5300 Bragança.
  tel (073) 25 070; fax (073) 25 071
- Rua de Sofia, 175, 3000 Coimbra. tel (039) 268 13; fax (039) 35003
- Rua Alcárcova de Baixo, 79, 7000 Évora.
  tel (066) 275 33; fax (066) 296 96
- Rua Francisco Barreto, 26 A, 8000 Faro. tel (089) 80 57 53/4;
  fax (089) 80 21 32.
- Avenida Saraiva de Carvalho, 140, 3080 Figueira da Foz.
  tel (033) 241 08; fax (033) 293 18
- Rua do Município, Lote B/1, Lote C, 2400 Leiria. tel (044) 82 3632;
  fax (044) 81 22 22
- Shopping Center Amoreiras, Loja 1122, Lisboa. tel (01) 387 18 80;
  fax (01) 69 14 42
- Rua Gonçalo Cristóvão, 2 a 6, 4000 Porto. tel (02) 316 732;
  fax (02) 316 698
- Centro Comercial Fonte Nova, Loja 17, Rua João Eloy 152,
  2900 Setúbal. tel (065) 392 37
- Avenida 1° de Maio, 199 r/c, 5000 Vila Real. tel (059) 756 50
  Rua da Paz, 36, 3500 Viseu. tel (032) 42 24 70; fax (032) 42 24 37

Roadworthiness test

It is most important to examine the green section of your *livrete* in order to establish which test date category your vehicle falls into. You will find it on the right-hand side, fourth entry down under the heading *Tipo*. Older cars may have the word *Particular* instead of *Passageiro* under the *Tipo* heading. The two words have the same meaning.

Looking forward, there has to come a time when cars are tested according to the month and year. The final digit system cannot last for ever and in any case it is grossly unfair. You may think that the last digit or letter of your licence plate number has some magic significance, that maybe it signifies the month of registration. In fact it doesn't mean a thing. The last digit of our previous car was 1 and it was matriculated in May 1985. The last letter of our current Renault Twingo is N and it was registered in April.

MOTORING

It has been said that test stations are under-utilised. We feel that this is only a temporary situation. It should not be overlooked that every year a few tens of thousands of vehicles are added to the test list and, thanks to the healthy Portuguese second-hand car market, not nearly that number are being scrapped. The test centres may be a little short of business at the moment, but their day will come.

A recent visit to a car test centre convinced us that in this area of activity the *Direcção-Geral de Viação*, in conjunction with private enterprise, has quickly got to grips with the car testing problem. This particular test station was fitted out with the latest German equipment with a rolling road for brake testing and low frequency vibrators for checking car suspension for worn steering, suspension joint and shock absorbers. There was also American equipment for exhaust analysis. The vehicle being tested is driven over a series of pits rather than being hoisted on lifts.

A feature of the system is that there are no repair facilities in the test station. Any afterwork would need to be done by a garage recommended by the testers or of your own choosing. However, the preferred procedure seems to be to have your car prepared for the test beforehand by one of a number of firms who specialise in this kind of work. Most main agents will do it for you for their specific make.

In the period during which a network of test stations was being established, cars were being given a "next test date" two years ahead. Enquiry of the ACP produced the information that this was a product of the previous law, when test stations were fewer that they are now. From now on, once your car has been tested you will be given a green slip bearing the date of your next test, which should be a year ahead.

MOTORING

- SPECIALISTS IN LEGALISING ALL TYPES OF VEHICLES
- GENERAL IMPORT EXPORT TRADING
- DRIVING LICENCES
- AGENCIES AND REPRESENTATIVES

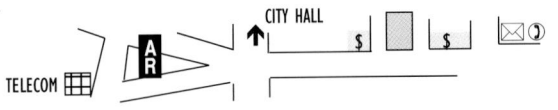

Largo Heliodoro Salgado, Edif. Vista Rio - 1º Andar - Sala 2A,
Apt. 547, 8500 Portimão
Tel (082) 414676/413531/417235/417236   Fax (082) 411471

MOTORING

Motoring dictionary

Accelerator	*Acelerador*
Align lights	*Alinhamento de faróis*
Adjust brakes	*Afinar travões*
Battery	*Bateria*
Braking system	*Travões*
Parking brake	*Travão de estacionamento*
Bodywork	*Carroçaria*
Bumper	*Pára-choques*
Chassis	*Quadro*
Chassis number	*Número de quadro*
Clutch	*Embraiagem*
Dashboard	*Tablier*
Exhaust pipe	*Tubo de escape*
Fan belt	*Correia da ventoinha*
Filter(oil)	*Filtro(óleo)*
Headlights main beam	*Faróis máximos*
Headlights dipped	*Faróis médios*
Sidelights	*Faróis mínimos*
Horn	*Buzina*
Indicator lights	*Pisca-pisca*
Lead-free	*Sem chumbo*
Number plate	*Chapa de matrícula*
Oil change	*Mudança de óleo*
Contact breaker points	*Platinados*
Puncture	*Furo*
Radiator	*Radiador*
Service	*Revisão*
Shock absorber	*Amortecedor*
Silencer	*Silencioso*
Sparking plugs	*Velas*
Steering wheel	*Volante*
Switch	*Interruptor*
Tow bar	*Dispositivo de engate para reboque*
Tyre (tubeless)	*Pneu (sem câmara)*
Wheel	*Roda*
Wheel balancing	*Calibragem de rodas*
Windscreen wipers	*Limpa párabrisas*
Windscreen washer	*Lava-vidros*
Workshop	*Oficina*

OFFSHORE COMPANIES

The pros and cons

There are arguments for and against these legal/financial devices, which are usually set up in one country to avoid the various property taxes in another country where property is located. So far as Portugal is concerned, the advantages of an offshore company can be applied to business or home ownership. The basic principle is that an individual who is buying property in one country sets up a company in another country (usually one in which tax legislation is benevolent) to purchase , let us say, a home. This company will then purchase the home, which becomes its property, and will pay all the necessary taxes associated with the purchase and day-to-day running of it. From then on, any changes of ownership can be made quite simply by transactions in the shares of the company rather then by going through the tax paying and legal hassle of selling it in the country where it is located. On paper the advantages are significant.

Should you wish to sell the property, you avoid by a transaction of shares in the company:

- Payment of SISA, property transfer tax
- Agents' fees, which can be up to 10% of the sale value of the property
- Capital gains tax
- Portuguese legal fees.

Should you die, you avoid:

- Inheritance tax by willing your shares in the company to your heirs.
- Having to make a Portuguese will, the expense and complication of declaring your assets, making a Deed of Qualification of heirs and subsequent registrations at the land registry and/or commercial registry.

Other possible advantages are:

- Anonymity of ownership
- Sequestration of assets in which the beneficial owner is resident.

OFFSHORE COMPANIES

If you decide to form an offshore company the following documents will be required in Portugal:

> - Certificate of Incorporation issued by the agency which incorporated the company.
> - Power of attorney to buy property overseas or powers to do whatever the client wishes to use the company for.
> - *Cartão de pessoa colectiva* obtained from the company registry in Lisbon (RNPC)

The foregoing is the bright side of the deal. Against this you have to set the cost of forming and maintaining the offshore company. Annual general meetings have to be held in the usual way and audited accounts and annual returns have to be filed yearly by the appointed or nominee directors, not the beneficial owner. The annual cost can be from a few hundred pounds sterling upwards. Failure to perform these formalities can result in the company being struck off the companies register with serious implications for the ownership of the property.

It should be borne in mind that there is a possibility of the EU introducing legislation against a device which deprives member countries of large amounts of tax. France and Spain have already legislated by imposing what is, in effect, fiscal penalties on any company based in a country not having a double tax treaty with them and owning immovable assets in their countries. The assumption is that countries not having double tax agreements are where tax-evading companies are located.

Already one of the minor penalties in Portugal is that you cannot claim remission of *Contribuição Autárquica* for the first 10 years of ownership as a normal owner can. Also, inheritance tax which you are so sedulously trying to avoid is not necessarily as drastic as the purveyors of offshore companies would have you believe. It is based on the *Valor Tributável*, the minimum taxable value of the house, not its market value, and is a small percentage of that figure if you are willing the house to wives or blood relatives such as sons or daughters. (See table on next page). The 76% so frequently quoted does not apply at all. The highest is 50% when you are willing the property to a person who has no blood or marital relationship.

OFFSHORE COMPANIES

Valor Tributável in *Contos*	Up to 500	500 to 2,000	2,000 to 5,000	5,000 to 10,000	10,000 to 25,000	25,000 to 50,000	Over 50,000
Children	0	4	7	10	14	18	23
Spouse and direct descendants	0	6	9	12	16	20	25
Previous generation & brothers	7	10	13	16	21	26	32
Third generation	13	17	21	25	31	38	45
Anyone else	16	20	25	36	39	43	50

The general opinion appears to be that forming an offshore company is especially valuable for people buying very expensive property, or by someone who intends to sell it fairly quickly with a large gain.

OFFSHORE COMPANIES

"OFFSHORE" COMPANIES

INTERNATIONAL COMPANY
SERVICES (PORTUGAL) LIMITADA

WE ARE PART OF THE ICSL GROUP - ONE OF THE WORLD'S LARGEST PROVIDERS OF OFFSHORE COMPANIES AND TRUSTS.

OUR PROFESSIONALLY QUALIFIED STAFF CAN ASSIST YOU TO INCORPORATE IN ALL MAJOR OFFSHORE JURISDICTIONS AND PROVIDE A COMPLETE ADMINISTRATIVE SERVICE INCLUDING ASSISTANCE WITH OPENING BANK ACCOUNTS IN AUSTRIA, SWITZERLAND, ISLE OF MAN, JERSEY, ETC.

FOR FAST AND HIGHLY CONFIDENTIAL SERVICE PLEASE CONTACT:
PAULO RÉFEGA   NIGEL ANTENEY-HOARE

TEL: +351 (82) 342601, FAX: +351 (82) 342259.
Internet: http//www.icsl.com E-mail: icsl@telepac.pt
PARQUE EMPRESARIAL ALGARVE, E.N. 125, APARTADO 246, 8400 LAGOA, PORTUGAL.

Abacus (Gibraltar) Limited

Property Holding, Trustee and Corporate Services

Trusts and holding companies can play a major role in tax planning and asset protection. In Gibraltar we have the expertise and ability to provide a fully professional, comprehensive trustee and corporate service to our clients worldwide.

For more information please contact:

Anne Darlington - Algarve Representative

Abacus Services (Gibraltar) Limited
Quinta Córrego da Zorra
Estrada de Vale do Lobo
Apt. 6, 8135 Almancil
Tel: 089-394780 Fax: 089-394125

Solutions
for Business

PASTIMES

Once you have settled down in your Portuguese home and got your affairs in order there will come the urge to find some kind of relaxation or pastime. Most pastimes are available if you go out and look for them. Just what you find will depend on where in Portugal you are and whether you are looking for a passive activity, like watching football or listening to good music, or an active one. In the latter category there is access to the whole gamut of leisure interests ranging from archaeology to wind-surfing or whatever. The difficulty you might come up against is that your chosen activity is practised by a small group at one end of Portugal and you are unfortunate enough to live at the other end. However, we have picked out a few examples of what goes on.

Sports

Association football, as in the rest of Europe, is something of a fetish and every town and village has a team to cheer and a football pitch of some kind to play on. If you are in a small community, taking an interest in the local club is a good way to make friends with the local inhabitants.

Rugby football is nothing like as popular as soccer, but for those who want to take part or watch from the sidelines there are clubs in Lisbon, Oporto and Loulé.

Cricket has a surprisingly long history in Portugal. It originated in Oporto but there are now clubs in Lisbon and at Barringtons, Vale do Lobo, in the Algarve as well.

Tennis is a sport which can be indulged in just about everywhere in Portugal. There are some excellent foreign-run tennis centres offering coaching and holding regular tournaments. Squash is also popular though facilities are much more limited.

Since Henry Cotton established the Penina golf course on the paddy fields west of Portimão, 16 more golf courses have been built, most of them in combination with high class urbanisations. A problem with golf in southern Portugal is the cost of the green fees. Residents have to take second place to tourists who sometimes buy combination hotel/golf package holidays. Golf in the Algarve is more expensive than in neighbouring Spain. It is not unknown, since the opening of the Via do Infante motorway, for keen resident golfers to drive over the border where they can get a couple of rounds for the price of one round in the Almancil area.

PASTIMES

The western Algarve has more affordable golf, with the exception of the Penina which is mainly reserved for hotel guests. However, we hear that this course is being enlarged and is likely to become more affordable and accessible.

For some years, bowls has been a developing pastime in the southern region. It is played by old and young alike. Its advantages are that it is usually played less aggressively than golf, and it does not demand such large areas of grass as the water-thirsty golf courses.

Boules or petanque is worthy of consideration as a garden game. It is very suitable for a dry, arid environment and makes an ideal after-dinner diversion. No sport could place less demands on the groundsman. On the other hand, croquet, which is having a revival, does call for a reasonably smooth lawn.

There is good sailing all around the coast of Portugal be it with wind-surfers, dinghies or cruisers. Lisbon's huge natural harbour is ideal for sailing with any kind of boat, as are the harbours at Setúbal, Oporto and Portimão The south coast, being more sheltered than the west coast, lends itself to small boat sailing and there are regattas right through the season under the auspices of the Portuguese National Sailing Federation. Major championships for Snipes and Dragons have been held at Vilamoura. Snipes and another very popular class, Lazers, are to be found at various clubs dotted along the coast. These clubs are friendly places with grand titles. You don't need to have a test to become a member, but if you intend to sail a dinghy or drive around in a motor boat, you will have to pass an examination, in Portuguese, to prove your proficiency. If you are interested in watching sailing, keep an eye on the local papers. Regattas go on right through the winter. There is even one at Faro on Christmas day.

Cultural pursuits

Music lovers are especially fortunate. In Lisbon and Oporto there are many concerts and recitals throughout the year. The Algarve has concerts from time to time, particularly in Lagos, Almancil and Faro, as well as an annual summer music festival with recitals in halls and churches the whole length of the region. The best advice is to watch the papers and public notices. The

PASTIMES

Bolshoi Ballet once visited Portimão and played to an audience which was miserably small simply because the event was not properly advertised and very few people knew about it.

There are societies and clubs for all sorts of cultural pursuits. One very active organisation is the Algarve Archaeological Association, which is constituted as a charitable organisation and organises visits to archaeological and historical sites all over Portugal. It supports Portuguese archaeology in every way it can. A companion association is the Historical Society in Lisbon.

For thespians there are plenty of amateur dramatic societies in Lisbon and Oporto, in some of the main provincial towns and in the Algarve. These societies are not all confined to expatriates. Some present a good opportunity to make Portuguese friends.

The spectacular quality of the light in southern Portugal offers wonderful opportunities for artists and photographers. Exhibitions of paintings and sculpture by local artists abound. It is surprising that there has never been a group of photographers in this country akin to the Californian school, which produced artists of the calibre of Ansel Adams. They revelled in the light and textures of the Californian desert and produced timeless photography. There are equal opportunities here in Portugal, especially, one feels, for those who are prepared to abandon colour for monochrome.

Special interest clubs

Car buffs are reasonably well catered for. Apart from the Portuguese Grand Prix at Estoril, national and international rallies take advantage of the ample rugged terrain. An international motor show is now held and is growing in importance in line with the burgeoning Portuguese car population. To keep in touch with events and developments, membership of the Automóvel Clube de Portugal is well worth the subscription. Not only does the Portuguese-language Clube journal tell you what has happened and what is about to happen, it also keeps you informed about the regular flow of new motoring laws.

There are a great many organisations where one can meet similarly minded people and at the same time raise funds for good causes or for specific charities, such as children's homes.

PASTIMES

It is a fundamental truth that the more you put into life, the more you get out of it. Nothing can be more rewarding than working for a voluntary organisation which provides a service to one's fellow human beings.

AFPOP, the Associação de Proprietários Estrangeiros em Portugal, is an example of a self-help association. From small beginnings it has been built up into a national association which now has almost 3,000 members. This has been achieved by a small nucleus of enthusiastic people who have devoted their time and expertise, as well as the use of their homes and equipment free of charge, and got a kick out of it. There are many other voluntary organisations which could, and do, benefit from this kind of enthusiasm.

Rotary and Lions Clubs are very active here, but they are Portuguese institutions and conduct all their business in that language. There is also an active 41 Club for ex-Round Tablers in the Algarve. Masonic lodges can now come out into the full light of day in this Catholic country. A number of them have been founded in various centres.

It is not uncommon for expatriate wives who may, or may not previously have been executives, to set up small businesses as a means of keeping their minds alive. In this context it is not out of place to mention Network, a very active association in the Algarve for women who run small or large businesses. This is a well-run organisation which draws members together for regular lunchtime meetings.

PETS & VETS

Pets, correctly termed companion animals although some of them are not animals at all, come in every shape and form from cockroaches by way of tarantulas and snakes via our common domestic pets to man-eating tigers. Fortunately, the run of the mill in this country are cats, dogs, cage birds such as canaries and birds of the parrot family, tortoises and terrapins, the occasional monkey, rabbits and the odd *burro*. It is impossible to deal with most of these in the space available. However, a few words about dogs seem not to be out of place since this is the one pet which is regulated by the law.

Dogs

There are now no restrictions on the import of dogs (or cats) from EU countries, but some paperwork is still required. For example, all dogs intended for permanent residence must have documentation showing that they have been inoculated against rabies. Government veterinarians also recommend that cats be given an anti-rabies vaccination although, in their case, it is not compulsory.

Owners importing pet dogs or cats from the UK must have one of the following for each animal:

- An export health certificate, form EC2902 issued not more than 48 hours prior to export and valid for ten days, signed by an approved veterinary surgeon, stating that the animal is free from signs of infectious or contagious disease including rabies and distemper.
- An official certificate stating that the dog has been injected with an approved anti-rabies vaccine. (The British Ministry of Agriculture states quite categorically that this is unnecessary. The rest of Europe thinks otherwise. You will find that the Portuguese authorities, and the authorities in any country through which the animal might pass en route to Portugal, will insist on it. Play safe and have one administered by an approved vet in the UK, (or your own country). And don't forget to take along the certificate saying that it has been done.)
- If you are travelling from the UK by ground transport there is a separate export/health certificate for France, EC2905, and another, EC2904, to get the animal through Spain. They are most unlikely to be needed, but it pays to have them.

PETS & VETS

Special import certificates are required for animals meant for commercial breeding purposes. They are obtainable on application to:

Ministério de Agricultura,
Largo da Academia Nacional das Belas Artes 2,
1200 Lisboa.

In the UK the Min of Ag will usually apply to the Portuguese authorities for you. It takes about three months to obtain the permit.

Import permits are not required for touring dogs belonging to holiday makers or visitors, but they should be accompanied by at least a rabies injection certificate. Now that European borders are wide open, documents are not usually demanded at customs posts, but it is essential to have them available, just in case. Remember too that Sweden has strict anti-rabies laws.

Local vaccination

All Portuguese resident dogs must be vaccinated annually against rabies. This can be done by your own vet, or by Government vets who travel from village to village, vaccinating licensed and sometimes unlicenced dogs which are presented to them by owners. A small charge is made, which is less than one would pay at a veterinary clinic.

In days gone by, any dogs which did not have owners were periodically rounded up as strays and put down.

Transportation by air

Some airlines allow small dogs to accompany their owners in the cabin; one would have to negotiate this with the individual carrier. Normally, dogs imported into Portugal by air cargo must be transported in a travel box constructed to a strict airline specification. It is conveyed in a special, pressurised and heated compartment situated below the flight deck. The necessary export documentation is attached to the box and processed by Portuguese customs on arrival. The British form, for dogs, cats and rabies susceptible mammals, is EXA 1 obtainable from:

The Ministry of Agriculture, Fisheries and Food,
Hook Rise South,
Tolworth, Surbiton KT6 7NF.

PETS & VETS

On arrival the animal will be given a perfunctory examination by the resident veterinary at the airport, while the owner, or his agent, deals with the customs formalities. Residents from EU countries should not have to pay IVA on their animals, but owners from non-EU countries should expect to pay IVA on the cost of the flight, any handling charges at the other end and the value of the dog.

However much you cherish your dog it does not pay to value it too highly. Otherwise you could face a big bill, which has to be paid in cash.

Licences

The law decrees that all dogs intended to be permanently resident in Portugal must be licenced on arrival and the licence must be renewed annually.

To obtain or renew a dog licence requires you go to your local *Junta de Freguesia* and your local *Câmara*. You will need the following documentation:

❏ Your dog's current anti-rabies injection certificate signed by an approved vet. It has been known for clerks in the *Câmara* to demand a notarised signature from the vet.

PETS & VETS

> ❏ A licence application form (modelo 446) obtained from your *Junta de Freguesia*.

Complete the form and take it back to the *Junta de Freguesia* who will verify on it that you are a resident.

Take this residential certificate and your dog's current rabies certificate to your local *Câmara*. After paying the licence fee (charges: 1.126$ for a dog or spayed bitch, 1.260$ for an unspayed bitch, 880$ for a renewal). You should then be issued with a dog licence, plus a numbered tag to affix to your dog's collar.

Licences are valid from May 31 to the same date the following year. They must be renewed during June or July at your local *Câmara*. Take with you the licence renewal form and a current anti-rabies certificate signed by an approved veterinary.

Perhaps the best tailpiece to wag is that the UK is at last showing signs of relaxing its strict anti-rabies regulations. Subject to a whole raft of form-filling, dogs for breeding purposes from closed breeding kennels are to be allowed into the UK without having to go through quarantine. Hopefully the relaxation will eventually be applied to pets. Before that can happen one imagines that there are vested interests to be overcome.

The foregoing is the exotic side of dog ownership in Portugal. Many less dewey-eyed, more practical dog lovers take a locally born dog into their care. The reasoning is that they are more likely to be resistant to the sand-fly and the heartworm. Another reason is that you like a dog as a companion rather than something to show off to your friends. Many of the local Twentieth Century Fox breed are extremely agreeable animals, nice people. It's a good idea to take a puppy of known parentage and bring it up from the beginning rather than taking a fancy one of the half wild dogs which roam the hillside and are very set in their ways.

Vets

None of our companion animals would be able to enjoy life and keep us company for any length of time without the services of the long-suffering veterinary. The poor vet has to face up to all sorts of ailments in various types of animal and by the nature of his profession none can tell him what is wrong with them when they feel off colour.

PETS & VETS

Canine complaints

Aside from the usual diseases endemic to dogs, such as distemper, there are two diseases especially endemic to Portugal, namely Leishmaniasis and Heart Worm. Either of them is extremely serious and can be fatal.

Leishmaniasis, often referred to as sand-fly disease, as its name suggests is spread by the sand-fly, an extremely small, night flying, blood-sucking insect. It is small enough to find its way through fly screens. More usually it stays outside dwellings and one way to protect your pet is to bring it indoors at night. The symptoms of Leishmaniasis are many and varied. Common signs are skin lesions, hair loss, weight loss, anemia, lethargy and diarrhoea. If it can be diagnosed and treated promptly, before there is any internal damage, the recovery rate is generally good. One problem with Leishmaniasis is that it can infect humans. Adults are less susceptible than children.

Heart worm larvae are transmitted by the bite of an infective mosquito. Adult worms can be as much as 25 cm (10 in.) long and inhabit the right ventricle of a dog's heart. When present in large numbers they cause the symptoms of heart disease, namely coughing, difficulty in breathing and reluctance to exercise. If untreated the disease is potentially fatal. Heartworm is also prevalent in the eastern states of the USA with the result that effective drugs have been developed and are now available here. Heart worm is difficult and dangerous to treat once it has started, therefore it's a good idea to have your dog's blood tested at an early age, say six months, and then give it a preventive pill, 'Heartgard', once a month to kill the worms before they reach the heart.

A less serious problem is that of ticks which can be a test of patience if you exercise your dog regularly in scrubland, especially if herds of goats have recently been grazing the ground. In the spring and early summer the problem is especially acute and your pet can come back home with half a dozen of these pests clinging to the coat. You can brush off most of these reddish, crablike creatures, but one or two may have got into the coat before they're spotted. Feeling through the coat later you find these bloated with blood. If you pull them off immediately you leave the

PETS & VETS

head of the tick embedded in the skin where it can cause irritation. It is best to put neat alcohol on the tick, or give it a quick spray of lighter gas or insecticide, and let it fall off by itself. Vets recommend a product called 'Frontline' as the best guarantee of freedom from ticks and fleas.

Clínica de Veterinária Canham

Dr. Ian McLaren
BSc. BVM & S, MRCVS.

TEL: 089 413449 FAX: 089 413447
EMERGENCY SERVICE: 0931 812273

SÍTIO DO TORREJÃO, AREEIRO - 8100 LOULÉ

CONSULTING HOURS:
MON-FRI: 9-10.30 AM
5-7 PM
SAT: 9-10.30 AM

Quality Accessories and Foods

ALVOR VETERINARY CLINIC
Dr. DAVID G. HOGGER * Dr. JAMES H. CAGNEY
Ladeira da Nora, Alvor, 8500 Portimão
(3kms from Alvor exit on Portimão bypass)
Tel: (082) 458340

Dr. Jeff Allen. BVM&S MRCVS DVM
Veterinary Surgeon
Consulting Hours

Mon to Fri: 9.00-10.30 am, 5.00-6.30 pm   **Sat:** 9.00-10.30 am
Qt dos Ciprestes · Sítio do Ferrel · EN 125 · Luz · Between 4 Estradas and Espiche
Tel. (082) 761827   Fax. (082) 782842   After hours: 0931 812152

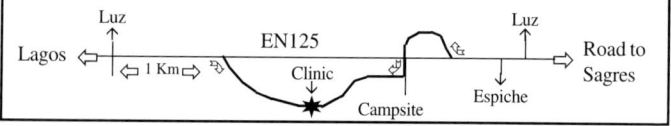

POLICE

Five forces

There are altogether four major uniformed police forces and one in plain-clothes in Portugal. The most obvious one is the khaki-clad *Guarda Nacional Republicana*, the GNR. They have been described as a paramilitary force, which they were in the first place. During the Salazar period when Portugal was virtually a police state, they were a force to be reckoned with. They are still the most influential and all pervading of Portugal's law-keepers and at times the most picturesque when, immaculately turned out, they mount their horses and go on patrol in pairs. Normally their mode of transport is an olive-green UMM 4x4 with a simple GNR emblem stencilled on the door.

The GNR can be very helpful. Away from the main towns you would report lost property to them, or complain about infringements of your civil rights. They are the people to contact if you have a road accident and they usually come quickly to the scene of break-ins and burglaries. When you dial 115 and ask for the police, it is the GNR who will arrive on your doorstep. Old habits die hard; they tend to know far more about you and your activities than you imagine.

A special section of the GNR, the *Brigada de Trânsito,* traffic police, patrols the main roads. Their duties, not in order of importance, are:

> ❏ To keep an eye on driver behaviour.
> ❏ Check observance of speed limits and overtaking zones.
> ❏ To conduct random roadside breathalyser tests.
> ❏ To ensure that the multitudinous construction and use regulations pertaining to commercial vehicles are being obeyed.

They have a passion for the last activity when they might be better occupied controlling the wanton overtaking habits of the motoring population away from the no-overtaking zones. They can be distinguished by their green and white saloons , with blue, red and white transverse lights on the roof. You will know they're around by the warning flashes from fellow-travellers' headlamps.

Another special section within the GNR is the *Brigada Fiscal.* Their main duties are to back up the *Alfândega*, the office-bound

POLICE

section of Customs, and most important, to endeavour to stem the trafficking of drugs in Portugal. You will also find them:

- At border customs posts.
- Doing roadside checks on foreign-registered cars to ensure that tax has been paid.
- Patrolling coastal roads.
- At sea checking for contraband.

In the cities there is a role for the blue-uniformed PSP, the *Policia de Segurança Pública*. Just a few of their duties are to:

- Guard the doors of *Câmaras*.
- Look after lost property.
- Control traffic.
- Control crowds.

A uniformed force which does not come into the eye of the general public is the maritime police, the *Polícia Marítima,* They have a mix of jobs. For instance they will:

- Issue licences for boat owners, for which there is a written and practical test, and three grades.
- Keep an eye open for misbehaviour on the beaches; illegally parked caravans for example, or water skiers operating too close inshore.
- Ensure that the fishing boats obey the regulations and have all the right licences. Did you know that you have to have one for a depth sounder?
- Do drug searches.
- Co-operate with the *Capitão do Porto* in controlling shipping.
- Endeavour to apply a whole raft of ancient laws with inadequate resources.

Finally we have the plain-clothes *Polícia Judiciária,* the criminal investigation police. Apart from robberies which you can report directly to them, they have to investigate a wide range of serious crimes from corruption - a growing abuse in public administration since the inflow of large EU subsidies - to murder, drug-running and fraud. They are based in the cities and major towns.

POOLS

Before you splash out....

Mention living in Portugal to a northern European and he will conjure up a vision of a white-painted villa with palm trees and swimming pools. It will most likely not occur to him that there is a lot of Portugal outside the southern region where people do not have pools but still manage to live a normal existence.

In fact, in Portugal pools are in many ways an Algarve phenomenon. One imagines there are more pools in the southern region than there are in the whole of the rest of the country. Their construction is highly developed in the Algarve using expertise culled from California, South Africa, Australia and wherever else there is a fund of experience in this activity.

One's own private pool is a great personal pleasure, especially to expatriates whose previous experience has been with public swimming baths. But as with so many things in life, the greater the pleasure the greater the pain. The P/P ratio can be much improved if you plan ahead, decide what you are going to use the pool for, and then go to a pool specialist to build it for you.

The man who is building your house will eagerly offer to build you a pool. There is a chance he might do a good job. Some builders are quite good at building pools; many are not. Alternatively, the builder will hire a specialist; then the question of cost comes into the equation. You might find it cheaper to choose your own specialist with a known track record. The point is that by employing a specialist you can demand a guarantee. If there are problems, you have a come-back which a specialist can't dodge as easily as a builder will do, if he can. Moreover, insurance companies look more kindly on professionally-built pools.

What so often happens with builders' pools is that the deep end will become less deep because of a large rock, or another expensive-to-shift boulder will call for an alteration to the shape. We know of a builder's pool that is sliding down a hillside.

A pool is a relatively fragile shell. The more structurally sound this shell is - with ample steel reinforcement and gunned concrete - the less likely it is to crack, especially when we have one of those earth tremors, that are by no means unknown on the fault line which passes through the southern, pool region.

The main types of pool are brick, concrete, liner and GRP

POOLS

(fibreglass). Brick pools are usually built by house builders and are constructed around brick walls on a concrete floor. The walls are then heavily rendered with concrete to which a tile lining is attached. Concrete pools start with the same brick shape and a concrete floor, but are then given a thick, reinforced concrete lining which is afterwards rendered and faced with tiles.

Liner pools are constructed by first digging the appropriate size and shape of hole and constructing a pre-fabricated, galvanised steel shell inside it. The ground is then infilled up to the exterior of the shell. Finally, a plastic liner, exactly tailored to the shape of the shell is dropped in. GRP pools are relatively small to enable them to be transported by road to the site, where they are dropped into a prepared excavation. There is usually no tiling, the surface of the material being adequate without this.

Location and design

If you have the space, some thought should be given to the location of the pool. It is a fact of life that children, and some grown-ups, scream or shout when they are in or around pools. If you are fond of peace and quiet and have enough ground area, it may pay to locate your pool well away from the house, maybe with dense shrubs in between. There is safety to be considered here: with the pool unsighted from the house you would always need a grown-up on duty to monitor children. A pool-side bar might be the answer.

Getting into and out of the pool has also to be considered at the design stage. For example, the less agile among us would opt for steps into the pool rather than having to swarm up and down a fancy chromium ladder.

Your pool does not have to be rectangular. It can be any shape you like. Round and kidney shapes are popular options. We know of one that is the shape of a jet airliner. If you are an all-the-year-round swimmer you will probably go for a rectangular pool because the shape lends itself to a roll-up cover.

There is also the possibility of having some colour other than the usual shades of blue. Why not emerald green, or midnight blue, or even black? Dark colours help to heat the water by absorbing infra-red radiation from the sun. We feel that brown should be avoided.

POOLS

A very popular feature in our own pool is the "panic ledge," a 25cm wide shelf around the deep end, about 120cm below water level, on which less competent swimmers can stand when they have made it to the "other end". Another good idea is to have the sides of the pool radiused into the bottom, rather than making a sharp corner. It makes it easier to use one of those expensive, but effective creepy-crawly suction cleaners. It is also essential to make provision for underwater lighting at the design stage.

It is essential, too, to make provision for a pool-side shower and a suitable notice to encourage guests to use it. Perspiration carried into the pool encourages algae, and suntan oil makes a greasy rim round the waterline. Moreover, when coming out of the pool it is good to be able wash off the chemicals.

Building in brick and concrete

Nowadays, by far the greatest number of Algarve pools are made this way. The designer has complete freedom to make exactly the shape the client asks for, and the detail of the interior of the pool can be more easily controlled.

Bearing in mind the aforementioned earth tremors, which you ignore at your peril, we favour the reinforced concrete type. Having built this reinforcement, the concrete lining should be applied with a pressure gun. It is quite possible to build shuttering inside the reinforcing and pour the concrete. This way you can have a thicker shell. But the usual way is to use the Gunite process by which liquid concrete is literally hosed at the sides of the pool using a powerful pump, a special hose and nozzle, and a strong man.

The advantage of Gunite is that the concrete is free of airholes and is of greater mechanical integrity. Ideally, the concrete mix should be made with salt-free sand (rarely used but available) and applied within three hours of mixing. Since this is not much longer than an Algarve lunch hour, and there is a tendency to start gunning just before the dinner bell goes, it pays for your building surveyor, or yourself, to be around at the time. This is the critical stage. If you are a perfectionist, you will write this requirement into the original specification and have someone trustworthy to keep an eye on the proceedings. Obviously it is impossible to gun the whole of the interior at one go, but one can ensure that the batch

POOLS

of concrete is used up as soon as it is mixed.

The choice of colour can often be left until the last moment. Portugal is the land of tiles, *azulejos*, and there is infinite choice. If you opt for radiused bottom edges in your pool, you will have to choose from samples of the tiny mosaic tiles which are needed to accommodate the radius between the bottom and the sides. They come in a large range of colours. A bonus with this type of tile is that it is non-slippery, thanks to the large amount of grouting.

Building a liner pool

The main advantage of these pools is that they are tremor-proof. Although they are popular in more moderate climes, the prolonged exposure to ultra-violet light in the Algarve causes them to deteriorate relatively quickly. Ten years is a good life span. The plastic liners are substantial and come in attractive surface designs, but after a period of years they become susceptible to over enthusiastic Portuguese pool cleaners and acquire rents and tears which call for emptying the pool to make repairs. The cost of replacing the water is expensive. The cost of replacing the liner is very much more so. Repairs to the steel lining may be necessary too, due to rust.

Once your pool is built it will have to be surrounded with a paved terrace. The generally accepted medium for this is the rough surfaced *ladrilhos*. Avoid glazed tiles anywhere near the pool area; they are lethally slippery to wet feet.

Incidentally, if you propose to let your house, it is essential to mark the deep end with approved signs on the edges of the pool, and to have a " no diving " sign at the shallow end.

Maintenance and cleaning

Your pool will need a pump and alongside it a filter system. In a normal pool house you will find an electric pump with a time-switch, a large filter filled with special sand, and an array of pipes and valves. If you intend to look after the pool yourself, you will learn which are the vacuum, skimmer and lower outlet valves and the sequence in which they should be operated.

You will also learn how to maintain the contents of the pool at the correct pH value and with an adequate chlorine content. The

POOLS

chemicals used for the maintenance of " freshwater " pools - chlorine powder and hydrochloric acid - are quite dangerous if handled carelessly, but not beyond the capabilities of a responsible adult or teenager. Professional pool cleaners are currently charging upwards of 10,000$ a month. Pool maintenance takes about an hour a week in the summer, and is minimal once the water temperature drops below 19ºC.

An alternative to using chemicals is to have a salt-water pool using electrolysis to keep the chemical content of the water at the correct level. The extra expense of the equipment appears to be justified. We have yet to discover how the expense of replacing the solid copper anodes compares with the cost of chlorine. The latter is ridiculously expensive bearing in mind how common a chemical it is.

Pool law

- ❏ Do shower before and after using the pool.
- ❏ Do not run or chase round the pool.
- ❏ Do not push another person into the water.
- ❏ Do not use glasses or bottles around the pool.
- ❏ Do place a "no diving" sign at the shallow end.
- ❏ Do not leave children unattended for even a few minutes.
- ❏ Do make sure that non-swimming children wear armbands.

POST

Making the best of the mail

In common with every other service in Portugal the postal service is improving quite rapidly. Generally it is now no better or worse than that in other EU countries. If there are delays, put them down to geography.

On one score, in the Algarve at least, the service is lax. This is delivery to private addresses in new urbanisations. In one well established urbanisation the mail is still delivered into a bucket hanging under the rafters of a shelter in a *quinta*.

In such cases the answer is to rent a box number, an *apartado*, in the nearest post office offering this facility. It costs a little over 1,000$ per year to rent one of these lock-up boxes. You will be issued with your own key; the person who sorts the mail inserts it into the back of the box. Incidentally, when posting letters don't be put off by the notice "*Cartas*" on the box. This means letters as well as postcards.

A frustrating aspect of the *Correio* is the requirement to collect registered mail or parcels from a main post office. You will receive an *Aviso de Recepção* giving you so many days to collect your post. If you happen to be out of the country and turn up too late, you stand a good chance of losing it. It is meant to be returned to sender, but parcels don't get that far. Here an *apartado* number can help, especially if you patronise a sub-office in a village. The post-mistress will most likely be your friend, know you and put your package on one side.

The normal post can now be rapid; we sometimes receive a letter only three or four days after it was posted in northen Europe. Or one can wait weeks (very often the delay is not in Portugal).

The best advice is to reckon on ten days to get a letter from other European countries, and be prepared to wait a couple of weeks for one from the USA.

Four choices

As part of the process of improvement, the CTT has instituted two new types of mail, *Correio Azul* and *Correspondências Internacionais SAL*. So there are now four choices:

POST

EMS is a national service within continental Portugal and is intended mainly for parcels. The lowest charge weight is 250 grams (about 9oz).
CORREIO AZUL is the priority service which is meant to ensure delivery in Portugal the next day. Often it does, but in so doing it is said to slow down all other mail. It is excellent, but expensive.
NORMAL is what we've always been used to. It goes by surface to most parts of Portugal and by air to international destinations.
ECONÓMICO means SAL. It is a purely international service which is claimed to be cheaper than air mail, but faster than surface mail. It is a mix of surface mail within Portugal and air mail outside, in common with normal mail. However, being the cheapest option one can reckon on it being the slowest.

Envelope sizes

To enable their sorting machinery to operate as efficiently as possible the CTT has set minimum and maximum limits on the sizes of envelopes.

If you go inside or outside these limits the mail has to be sorted by hand; expect to pay a lot extra for the privilege of posting your king-size cards this Christmas.

They also ask you to use light coloured envelopes and write in dark coloured ink. They could, just possibly, turn down that trendy, dark red envelope bought in your home country. Stationers know better than to sell them in Portugal. Here are the sizes for standard letters and postcards:

	ENVELOPES	
	Minimum	Maximum
Length	140mm	235mm
Width	90mm	120mm
Thickness	5mm	
	POSTCARDS	
	Minimum	Maximum
Length	140mm	148mm
Width	90mm	110mm
Thickness	150grms / sq metre	

POST

CHARGES

From the beginning of March 1996 there was a general increase in postal rates. The main increases were for mail within Portugal, and in the lower weight categories of European and Intercontinental mail.

There was one temporary saving to be made. When buying stamps (*selos*) from vending machines, the 70$ stamps, for 20gr standard letters remained valid for a time.

National Mail

Portugal, Madeira and Azores

Weight	Azul	Normal
Up to 20gr Std	80$	47$
Up to 20gr from machines	75	45
Up to 20gr Non-std		80
20-100gr	120	80
100-250gr	280	155
250-500gr	510	280
500-2.000gr	800	510
Postcards		47

Europa

Special rate to EU countries, including Spain, for Standard letter under 20gr - 78$, from machines 75$.

All european countries

Weight	Azul	Normal
Under 20gr Std	350$	98$
Under 20gr Non-std		180
20-100gr	500	205
100-250gr	750	410
250-500gr	1.000	750
500-1.000gr	1.500	1.300
1.000-2.000gr	2.300	2.000
Postcards		98

POST

Intercontinental

Weight	Azul	Normal
Under 20gr Std	350$	140$
Under 20gr Non-std	225	230
20-100gr	500	330
100-250gr	950	760
250-500gr	1.500	1.450
500-1.000gr	2.700	2.550
1.000-2.000gr	4.500	4.400
Postcards		140

	National	International
Registo	200$	315$
Aviso Recepção	100$	315$

PROPERTY

Buying land or property

First steps

Having established that you have permission to build a house on a piece of land, or are buying an existing house, the time has come to draw up a **promissory contract**. This legally binding document should contain the following:

> - Full identification of the vendor and you, the purchaser.
> - A description of the land.
> - Its registration number if it has one.
> - Its article number at the tax office.
> - Its boundaries.
> - Its superficial area.

It is also imperative that the registries are searched for any hidden debts attached to the property. This information is available at the *Conservatória de Registo Predial* and your *advogado* should be extremely diligent at this stage in the proceedings. He or she should be made aware that you know that *advogados* are responsible for the results of any negligence in this respect. Sloppiness at this stage could eventually result in your losing the property years after it has become your home.

There is a separate chapter in this handbook on choosing an *advogado*.

In this respect there are four situations to avoid when purchasing property:

> - Don't try to get by without a lawyer.
> - Don't allow one and the same *advogado* to act for you and the vendor.
> - Don't use other than an independent lawyer recommended by an independent body such as a consulate, embassy, association (such as AFPOP), or friends.
> - Beware of any offer to undertake the whole transaction, or place purchase money in the agent's account.

To act for you if you are not on the spot to sign personally, an

PROPERTY

advogado will need a power of attorney. Thanks to the Hague Convention, this may be drawn up by a public notary in your own country, or by a Portuguese consulate or embassy, and notarised there.

You might also consider joining AFPOP, the Association of Foreign Property Owners in Portugal. Their aim is to offer a helping hand, they know a great deal about the legal fraternity in the Algarve and have available a fund of know-how about the machinations of the property business and its operators.

Having firmly decided that you want to spend all or part of your life in this sunny clime, write yourself a little notice saying: "BUYER BEWARE". Put it in a place where you will see it every time you go out in the morning.

The promissory contract is the first important document you will sign, or have signed for you. Until you come to execute this document, do not part with any money whatsoever to a vendor, his agent, or any other person except the lawyer.

The temptation to put money up front is inherent in many northerners. Resist it. Giving in has enabled many property dealers and builders to live in a style to which they are not properly accustomed.

The deposit you pay will normally be 10 to 20% of the purchase price. There are safeguards and penalties once the promissory contract is signed. If you drop out, you lose your deposit. If the seller reneges, he has to pay back twice the amount of the deposit. An alternative is for the non-guilty party to ask for a specific judgement in court (Article 830 civil code) in which the judge condemns the guilty party to sign the deeds.

PROPERTY

Final purchase

Before you become owner of the land you must pay **SISA**, the property transfer tax. This is achieved by you, or one of your *advogado's* staff, taking the promissory contract and *Contribuinte* numbers of the vendor and purchaser to the local *Finanças* and paying the money. For this purpose the purchaser, if a foreigner, is issued with a temporary *Número de Contribuinte.*

If you are buying a newly built flat, it is well worth reminding your lawyer that under a decree law published in 1991, a proportion of the original SISA for the land will be deducted from the payment the purchaser is to make.

Note: this is only enforced at the request of the interested party and only for the first purchase apartment.

For apartments, the SISA paid on the land is deducted in proportion to the relationship of the value of the apartment to that of the whole property.

The last step is signing the *escritura*, the title deeds to the land. This will be drawn up by the public notary. He will want to see the following documents:

- If you are buying a house and it has been built after 1951, a *Certidão de Habitação* (certificate of habitation).
- Proof of registration of the land, its description and number, in the *Conservatória de Registo Predial* records. If it does not have a number, evidence of a search made in the last three months.
- The *Caderneta Predial* (rates document) with the previous owner's name on it, and the *valor tributável* (rateable value) to bear out that the land, or house and land, has been registered for tax purposes.
- The *Finanças* reference number or proof that it has been applied for.
- It is up to the *advogado* to check that the description of the property in the *Finanças* files matches up with the description in the land registry.
- The lawyer's power of attorney if he is signing for you.
- The receipt from the *Finanças* confirming that SISA has been paid, or confirmation that it is exempt.
- A draft complementary document if you are buying into a development with its own usage rules.

PROPERTY

Eventually, you will go by appointment to the notary's office where the *escritura* has been prepared. It will be read out to you prior to your signing it. It is really best for the buyer to be present, with an interpreter if he doesn't speak the language, since the document, naturally, will be written in Portuguese.

After signing, immediately order notarised copies of the *escritura* from the office staff. Pay for these and for the preparation of the *escritura*. The fee depends on the number of pages and the stamp duty. Allow for about 1.5 % of the value of the land; or 11% if it is a deed of gift.

Precautions

During the Algarve property boom it was not unknown for a vendor to rush off, sell land or property to another buyer and hurriedly register it at another notary public before the first buyer has had time to do his registration.

A more likely problem now, one which has caused much anguish in the past and will continue to do so until the civil law is changed, is the procedure for creditors to put a charge on property. This calls for a creditor to put a charge on by registering it in an entry book on the counter of the *Conservatória de Registo Predial* office and then for it to be transferred to the main registry (the "Big Book") at a later date, when the workload permits. The problem is that while the entry in the book on the counter is legally binding, it does not appear on the the land registry until it is entered in the "Big Book". If the intervening period were a matter of days this would be fine and dandy. Sadly, the period can be anything from as little as a few days to a month or two, or 14 months in one case.

Thus there is a danger period, even before your acquisition of the certificate from the land registry and the notarisation of your deed of conveyance (*escritura*). The land registry certificate is valid for six months. You have to add to that the delay between entries in the book on the counter and their transfer to the "Big Book". Let's assume that it is four months. Thus when the day comes to notarise the *escritura*, the notary will accept the land registry certificate, if it is valid within the six month period. At any time in the 10 months preceding the date on the deed, a creditor of the vendors may have put a charge on your future property

PROPERTY

without it appearing on the land registry certificate. Consequently, you register the property in your name and the charge is yours without your being aware of it.

Meanwhile, the creditor keeps warning the vendor, threatening him with court action. The vendor happily ignores this. The creditor takes the case to court and wins it. Your property will have to be sold off to pay the creditor. The first thing you will know about it is when a man in uniform knocks on your door, checks your identity, and asks you to sign for a document notifying you that your property is to be auctioned.

It has happened that the charge may have appeared on the certificate and the buyer or his representative have failed to notice it, the notary has assumed the buyer knew about it and accepted it, and therefore did not mention it.

The way to avoid this is for you and/or your *advogado* to go to the *Conservatória de Registo Predial* on the day of the sale, before signing the *escritura*, and check all entries. A lax *advogado* will not do this for you automatically.

The reason for all this is important. In Portuguese law, title is only enforceable against third parties AFTER registration at the land registry, not by paying SISA or signing *escrituras*.

In the fullness of time you will receive documentation showing that ownership of the land has been transferred to your name. The document will show where the entry has been made in the files, the book and the page number.

The pertinent information will automatically be transferred to the tax office and you will be given a permanent fiscal number, *Número de Contribuinte*, showing your new address. What you should do is check the address, and if necessary change it to one where you want the rates demands to go to.

Proud owner

You should eventually have in your possession notarised copies of the following documents:

- ❏ The *Certidão de Teor* of the *Conservatória de Registo Predial,* the all-important land registry certificate.
- ❏ The *Caderneta Predial* for the property with your name on it.
- ❏ The *escritura*.

PROPERTY

- A *Contribuinte* card with your name and number on it. The address on this should be the same as the property if you intend to live there. You will be asked for this number when you come to pay for anything from taxes to a new typewriter ribbon.
- If it is an existing house which has been built after 1951, a *Certidão de Habitação*.

You can now sleep soundly in your bed at night.

Money

It is worth knowing that the Portuguese banks are keen to lend money for mortgages, although the lending rate is higher here than in countries further north.

Moreover, Decree-law 255/93 states that if you buy property with a loan from a bank you no longer need formal deeds at the notary and the costs that go with them. Alternatively you can use a simple certification of signatures on a form to be supplied by the bank lending the money. However, the bank's charges for this seem to be little different from the notarial charges. Either way, provisional registrations of acquisition and mortgage (the bank's guarantee) are to be paid for by the bank.

Exemption from ContribuiçãoAutárquica

Residents in Portugal, including expatriates holding a valid residential visa, should be aware that subject to the conditions below they may be exempt from rates on their property. Some people do not know of their entitlement, pay rates for several years, and then apply for exemption in the mistaken belief that the years already paid will be refunded.

The law on this subject is as follows:

According to the *Contribuição Autárquica* Code, (article 12b), urban property for residential purposes - with habitation licence - built as a permanent residence for an individual (not for a company wherever based), is exempt from rates for a period of 10 years as long as the property's rateable value is not superior to Esc. 10,000,000 (ten million escudos), and that it is occupied for the above purpose within six months of the deed of purchase or completion of building. The exemption starts from the date of the deed or completion of the building.

PROPERTY

An application (*requerimento*) needs to be submitted to the head of the local tax office enclosing the property's documents to substantiate what is being requested within 90 days from one of the two above dates. Forms are available in every *Finanças* department.

If the individual only uses the property for his permanent residence after the above mentioned 90 days, or if the exemption request is submitted beyond that period, the exemption will start on the following year but will not go on for 10 years. Rates will have to be paid on the year in which they would have been due if the request for exemption had been submitted in time; i.e. if a property is bought for permanent residence on 1st October 1991, one would have to file for an exemption before the end of 1991. Should one apply for it, say, in January 1993, the exemption would start as from January 1994 until January 2001. One would therefore get the benefit of eight years exemption.

If the property has not already been registered at the tax office, it will have to be first valued for tax purposes, and only then will the owner know whether or not the exemption has been granted.

A point to remember is that rates demands will always be sent to the address given on your original application for a *contribuinte* number until a change of address form is submitted. For convenience, lawyers will often fill in the forms using their office address - for instance when the client is buying a country building plot, or there is no postal service to the property being purchased. Unfortunately the tax office refuses to accept *apartado* numbers, so rates demands can, and sometimes do, "get lost in the post".

If you are worried that you have not received the expected rates demands in September and April, go to your local tax office and ask to look for your name in the computer listing of all property owners, to see if any payment is outstanding.

The tax official can issue a form which allows you to pay rates without the usual green bill. While you are at the tax office, ask for a form to change your fiscal address to a more suitable one where mail is sure to reach you. Remember to take your original *contribuinte* card, or a copy, with you so that the details can be verified.

Note: If you are a few days late with your application in the first year, you pay for that year and then have exemption for the

PROPERTY

remaining nine years. If the property changes owners during the 10-year period and no application for relief has been made, the second owner can also apply for relief. If he is prompt, that is 90 days from purchase, he gets 10 years relief. Subsequent owners have the same concession. Thus, if the property continually changes hands in less than 10 year periods it can be forever exempt! The loss of tax, of course, is made up for by the numerous payments of SISA.

Some tax offices will give you exemption from *Contribuição Autárquica* even if your property's rateable value is more than 10 million escudos, but it will be for less than 10 years.

Land Expropriation

With the improvement of road communications goes the possibility that part of your land may be appropriated for road building. The following procedure proved to be effective in local developments in the Lagos area where the EN125 to Sagres is being re-aligned and improved.

The first move is to submit to your local *Câmara* a request, in Portuguese, for a certificate of the area expropriated. In due course you will be asked to collect this certificate.

With this certificate and your *caderneta predial* in your hand, make off to the *Finanças* and present them to the *Chefe da Repartição de Finanças* of your *Câmara*. In due course you will receive the revised *caderneta* and an offer of a sum of money as compensation. Then register the alteration at the Land Registry, with the expropriation document and the *caderneta*.

In the case in point, officials from the Lagos *Câmara* made a personal visit to finalise the paperwork. Moreover, a cheque was handed over the day the owner of the land and his wife signed their acceptance of the offer.

Checklist:

> ❏ Letter in Portuguese requesting a certificate of the area to be expropriated. This will acquire for you the next item.
> ❏ Certificate of land area.
> ❏ *Caderneta predial* of the property affected.
>   AFPOP has available a pro forma letter in Portuguese covering the application for a certificate.

PROPERTY

Let us take care of your problems
★ Property Management ★ Sales & Rentals ★ Insurance ★
★ Construction & Maintenance ★ Motor Importation, etc. ★

We are a long established company with years of experience in all facets of hands-on management, concentrating on the areas from Quinta do Lago to Vilamoura and offer a thoroughly professional service.

| Apartado 43
Almancil 8135 | **brian
stephens
lda.** | Tel. 089 395320
395729
Fax. 089 395355 |

RESIDENCY

Residents' responsibilities

The government department which handles matters relating to residence permits, *Serviço de Estrangeiros e Fronteiras*, has a 10-point list headed "The main responsibilities of foreigners residing in Portugal". Here it is:

- **Respect for the law** - Foreigners residing in Portugal shall abide by the laws of Portugal and, as foreigners, those Portuguese laws which govern foreign nationals (Art. 67, Decree-Law Nº 59/93 of 3rd March and Para 1, Art. 15, Constitution of the Portuguese Republic).
- **Duty to notify** - Foreigners residing in Portugal shall notify the *Serviço de Estrangeiros e Fronteiras* (Foreigners and Frontier Services) of any change in their address, profession, marital status and/or nationality within a period of 8 days starting as from the date the change occurs (Art. 61, Decree Law Nº 59/93 of 3rd March).
- **Prolonged absence** - Foreigners residing in Portugal shall notify the *Serviço de Estrangeiros e Fronteiras* of their intention to absent themselves from Portugal for more than 90 days, such notification to be made prior to departure (Art. 61, Decree-Law Nº 59/93 of 3rd March).
- **Renewal of residence permit** - Whenever residence permit holders wish to have their permits renewed, the *Serviço de Estrangeiros e Fronteiras* shall be notified of this intention within 45 days prior to the date on which the residence permit expires (Art. 58, Decree-Law Nº 59/93 of 3rd March).
- **Withdrawal of residence permits** - Residence permits may be withdrawn if they are held by foreigners who live in Portugal for a period of less than 6 months in each year (consecutive or intermittent), by foreigners who do not fulfil the pre-requisites to live in Portugal as a resident foreigner of who have feopardised public law and order, national safety and/or international relations with other EU member states (Art. 62, Decree-Law Nº 59/93 of 3rd March).
- **Failure to notify** - Foreigner residents failing to notify the authorities as stipulated in Para 2 and 3 above shall be liable for payment of a sum currently ranging from 6 to 24 thousand escudos (Art. 106, Decree-Law Nº 59/93 of 3rd March).

RESIDENCY

- **Staying on after expiry of authorised period** - Foreigners who stay on in Portugal after the validity of their residence permit has expired shall be liable for payment of a sum currently ranging form 12 to 96 thousand escudos (Art. 99, Decree-Law Nº 59/93 of 3rd March).
- **Delay in renewing residence permits** - Foreigner residents allowing their residence permits to expire and/or delaying renewal thereof shall be liable for payment of a sum currently of 24 thousand escudos (Art. 59, Decree-Law Nº 59/93 of 3rd March).
- **Declaration on entry** - On re-entering Portugal by a frontier without border control, coming from another EU member state, foreigner residents who are not EU nationals are required to notify the authorities of their return within a period of 3 working days as from the date of re-entry. Notification may be made to the *Serviço de Estrangeiros*, to the *Policia de Segurança Pública* (Police) or to the *Guarda Nacional Republicana* (National Republican Guard) (Art. 11, Decree-Law Nº 59/93 of 3rd March). Failure to comply with this requirements shall entail payment of a sum currently ranging from 20 to 100 thousand escudos (Art. 100 of the same law).
- **Special regime** - EU citizens come under the special regime laid down in Decree-Law Nº 60/93 of 3rd March.

Residence permits

The rules governing permission to reside in Portugal have recently been drastically revised for two reasons. The first of these changes came as a result of Decree Law 60/93, promulgated on 16 February 1993, activated early March, which brought into effect various EU directives relating to the free movement of citizens of EU countries within the Community.

The second was a panic move to hold in check a massive influx of non-Portuguese speaking immigrants from the country's erstwhile colonies in Africa. The latter legislation, unintentionally one feels, also encompassed many retired people from countries outside the EU who had taken up residence in Portugal as perpetual tourists and did not have residential visas. Overnight they became illegal immigrants.

In the event, the massive invasion from the colonies did not

RESIDENCY

materialise on the scale anticipated and the situation regarding elderly, retired, non-EU citizens remained where it always had been, subject to the general law.

EU citizens

The text of the all-important Decree Law 60/93 is long-winded and convoluted. Should you wish to read the small print, an English translation of it is available to members of AFPOP for a small fee. What follows is a précis of the law as it affects the majority of non-Portuguese EU citizens.

An important change in the law, very much to the benefit of EU citizens, is that it is now possible to apply for a residential visa at your local office of the *Serviços de Estrangeiros e Fronteiras* instead of having the tiresome business of going to a Portuguese consulate outside the country to do it. Maybe there's something to be said for the Common Market after all.

People who have an automatic entitlement to a residential visa allowing them to reside in Portugal (includes Madeira and the Azores) are:

- ❏ Employees of Portuguese companies who are citizens of an EU country.
- ❏ Citizens of an EU country with their own properly constituted business in Portugal.
- ❏ Citizens of an EU country who have worked in a Community country either as employees or self-employed. This covers retired people living in Portugal on a pension, disability or otherwise, so long as they have sufficient means not to become a burden on the State in an emergency. (See later for insurance and financial requirements).*
- ❏ Students who are citizens of EU countries and have their own resources.
- ❏ Members of the families of the above, be they parents, spouses, or children, who have been neither employed nor self-employed. (See later).
- ❏ The spouse, and dependents under the age of 21, of people from EU countries who have come to work here.

    * The retired people (ex-workers) referred to in item 3 are required to have:

RESIDENCY

> ● An adequate retirement pension, or disability pension as the result of a work accident.
> ● State health insurance in their own country (*Credencial Pensionária*).

As a matter of interest, Decree Law 60/93 defines "sufficient resources" as the amount that Portugal provides to its citizens on social support programs. In practice, the *Estrangeiros* office likes to see a bank statement showing reserves of about 500,000$, or a letter from your bank manager stating that you regularly import significant amounts of cash. Foreign students are required to prove to the appropriate authority that:

> ❏ They have enough resources not to require social support.
> ❏ They are enrolled in a recognised establishment for the furtherance of their professional development.
> ❏ All their family are covered by an all-risk health insurance.

Types of residence permits

Three different types of *residência* will be issued to EU citizens:

> ❏ Residence card (or visa) for a citizen of a European Union country.
> ❏ Temporary residence card.
> ❏ Permanent residence card.
>
> The first category of card will be issued to:
>
> Workers from within the EU who are employed in Portugal for a period of one year or longer. (If their contract is for less than a year but renewal would take their employment over a year, they still qualify).
>
> Self-employed people with businesses.
>
> The retired EU citizens with adequate pensions and all-risks health insurance mentioned earlier.
>
> Members of the families of the above.

Validity

Workers will be issued with a five-year visa which will be

RESIDENCY

renewed for periods of 10 years.

Retired people will be given a two-year visa renewable for periods of five years. The *Estrangeiros* office will require the following documentation:

> - Four passport-size photographs.
> - Form Mod. 700 (supplied by the office).
> - Form Mod. 320 (supplied by the office).
> - A bank statement showing you have a substantial deposit, or a letter from your bank stating you regularly import money for use here.
> - Proof of retirement.
> - A *Credencial Pensionária*.

The last named document is taken as proof that you have health insurance in your own country. The basis for the *Credencial* is the aforementioned proof of retirement. One of your own government's pension payment slips translated into Portuguese by an approved translator is accepted. To get a *Credencial,* take the slip and the translation with your passport to an office of the *Segurança Social*. You get it the same day if you go to the regional head office, otherwise be prepared to wait a week or so.

Student visas will be valid for one year. If the course is for longer than that, it will be renewed annually.

Interrrupted residence for periods not exceeding six months, or military service, will not affect the validity of the visa.

Temporary residence cards

This type of visa is for temporary workers and their families from EU countries who come here to work for a Portuguese employer, or for a service company, for a period of more than three months but less than a year.

A seasonal worker from an EU country can remain in Portugal without a visa provided he holds a work permit registered with the *Inspecção Geral de Trabalho,* or its equivalent in Madeira or the Azores.

Permanent residence cards

These appear to be for younger people who wish to settle permanently in Portugal. The rules are stricter in that a request for

RESIDENCY

a residence card must be made on the form provided within three months of arriving in Portugal. Applicants with work contracts must apply for renewals within 15 days of renewal of the contract.

The *Serviço de Estrangeiros e Fronteiras* are responsible for obtaining all the information required properly to establish the "situation" of the applicant.

Information about an applicant's criminal record may be requested if justified.

Non-EU citizens

Non-working, non-EU citizens include Norwegian and Swiss people from Europe as well as the more obvious North Americans, Japanese, Hong Kongese and whatever.

General Portuguese law applies to any citizen from a country outside the EU. To obtain an *Autorização de Residência,* a residential visa, is an exhaustive process.

Not so long ago it was necessary to obtain a *Visto para Residência,* a tourist visa, in your own country before coming here as a tourist. The *Visto* allowed you to stay for 60 days and it could be extended twice. If you then decided that you would like to live in Portugal you had to return home and apply for an *Autorização de Residência* at a Portuguese consulate there.

Nowadays the *Visto para Residência* is half of the form you fill in on the 'plane coming to Portugal. This should be retained and if you stay more than 60 days you should go to an office of the *Serviço de Estrangeiros e Fronteiras* and renew it. If you're late with this formality you will be fined.

If you decide that you would like to live here you will have to go out of Portugal to a consulate in Spain, for example, and apply for an *Autorização de Residência* there. The following documentation is called for:

- ❏ Three photocopies of every page of the applicants passport (including blank pages). Two of the copies to be notarised.
- ❏ If married and supported by the husband, three notarised copies of the marriage certificate translated into Portuguese by an approved translator.
- ❏ Three copies of a certificate of medical insurance translated into Portuguese by an approved translator. Two copies to be notarised.

RESIDENCY

- For a single, person copies of their bank statements over the last three months. If married, three copies of a letter from the husband, translated into Portuguese, to certify that he is supporting his wife. This should quote the husband's name and passport number and the applicant's name and passport number. Two copies to be notarised.
- If married, three copies of the husband's passport. Two copies to be notarised.
- Three copies of the *escritura* of the applicant's home. Two copies to be notarised. (If the couple, or the single applicant do not own a home a certificate from their *freguesia* testifying that they reside in the area).
- Three copies of the applicant's criminal record translated into Portuguese. Two copies to be notarised.
- An authorisation from the appropriate consulate in Lisbon certifying details of the applicant's birth certificate. Two copies to be notarised.
- Three passport size colour photographs of the applicant.

Serviço de Estrangeiros e Fronteiras offices:

LISBON (Head office) - Rua Conselheiro José Silvestre Ribeiro,4, 1600 Lisboa. Tel (01) 7141027 / 7141179; Fax (01) 7140332.

LISBON - Av. António Augusto de Aguiar, 20, 1000 Lisboa. Tel (01) 523324; Fax (01) 524053.

COIMBRA - Rua Pedro Monteiro, 70, 3000 Coimbra. Tel (039) 716776; Fax (039) 724470.

FARO - Rua Dr José de Matos, 14, 8000 Faro. Tel (089) 805822; Fax (089) 801566.

FUNCHAL - Rua Nova da Rochinha, 1-B, 9000 Funchal. Tel (091) 32177; Fax (091) 31918.

PONTA DELGADA - Rua Marquês da Praia e Montforte, Apt. 256, 9500 Ponta Delgada. Tel (096) 26791; Fax (096) 24422.

PORTO - Rua D. João IV, 536, Apt. 4819, 4013 Porto Codex. Tel (02) 319982; Fax (02) 311211.

RESTAURANTS & FOOD

Portuguese cuisine

Writing in 1893, Fialho de Almeida enthused: "...without a doubt the Portuguese is the most refined, the most succulent cuisine in the world." He went on to give credit to the voyages of discovery which gave Portugal the first choice of new ingredients and skills inherited from the Arabs who passed on the casserole and the art of frying.

A hundred years on we might feel that Fialho was rather overstating the case. Arriving in Porto from France in the fifties and patronising the best restaurants there, the main impression we gained was of the size of the portions rather than the finesse of their preparation. Forty years on the situation has improved. Students of gastronomy will find exotic Portuguese dishes in the better Lisbon and Porto restaurants, and Portuguese friends will take them to small restaurants specialising in classic Portuguese cookery.

But, for us, the charm of Portuguese cuisine is away from the two main cities. Wherever you are in Portugal, it pays handsomely to seek out regional specialities, if only to try them once. The regions and the small towns away from the coast have so much to offer. There you will find cooking in which the quality of the ingredients is beyond reproach, and helpings that are generous. Northern Europeans may have difficulty in coming to terms with some of the watery soups. But in the north-eastern regions of Portugal the stews made with pork, sausages and beans are sturdy and nourishing, reflecting the cold nights and the hard, working conditions of country people. On both the west and south coasts you will find wonderful fish dishes.

Working down Portugal from the north to the south, from the snows of Trás-os-Montes to the sand, sun and heat of the Algarve, there are a few typical dishes one should look out for, either because they are special to Portugal, a delight to the palate, or just plain nourishing.

Soups are a feature of Portuguese peasant life because they can be cooked in a cauldron on an open fire. *Sopa de castanhas piladas*, dried chestnuts and butter beans made into a thick, typically nourishing soup. In common with *caldo verde* it originated in the Trás-os-Montes region. The real version includes garlic sausage, and the *galega* cabbage is shredded to the consistency of green grass.

RESTAURANTS & FOOD

In the northern provinces there are a few peasant dishes made from left-over bread which are worth a try. Most of us who live in Portugal relish those huge, craggy loaves made with that white flour which seems to have all the nourishing qualities of wholemeal. Even in rustic homes there are left-overs of bread, stale bread, and the people of the north use these to make *açordas* and *migas*. There are *açordas de marisco, açorda de bacalhau* and *açorda alentejana*, the last a soup made with fresh coriander. In the three Beira provinces one finds *migas* which tend to be made with *broa de milho*, maize bread, and follow the same pattern but with meat instead of fish. *Ensopados* and *sopas secas* also incorporate bread. We can't wait to try *sopa de cavalo cansado*, tired horse soup, with pieces of bread soaked in red wine and sprinkled with sugar.

Stews, for the foregoing practical reasons, feature on the menu in all the northern provinces. Beef, goat and pork are the principal ingredients with the addition of fresh fish in the *Litoral*, and *bacalhau* everywhere. There are also the *sarrabulhos*, blood stews, incorporating the gore of the animal being cooked. Don't be put off by the description. They are both tasty and nourishing. Incidentally, an Oriental touch in the cooking process is the classic Portuguese *refogado*. This is the custom of frying the onion and herbs together before adding the ingredients of, say, a stew. It certainly draws the flavour out of the herbs and is one of the characteristics of Indian curry cooking. Presumably these ideas were brought back by the Portuguese navigators and explorers, and have become traditions.

Beans, rice, and garlic sausage figure prominently in stews, shades of the French *cassoulet*. Garlic sausage (*chouriço*) is to be found in infinite variety and would merit a chapter of its own. Beans, rich in protein, are a feature of Portuguese cuisine as evidenced by the huge sacks of dried beans on market stalls. One would dearly love to know what they are all used for. Portuguese rice is every bit as good as the imported variety, at half the price.

Some may regard the humble *porco* with disdain, but it is undoubtedly a main feature of country life. Families or small groups of village folk will nurture their precious pig, slaughtering it with due ceremony on a kind of rough, wooden altar. There are delicious recipes for every little bit of it, inside and out, including the ears and the tail. And, of course, in certain

RESTAURANTS & FOOD

cases it is denied maturity in order to provide that great delicacy, roast suckling pig, once a speciality of the Beira provinces but now appreciated throughout the land.

The southern region, once one of the most poverty stricken provinces in the whole of Portugal, now prospers as a result of a large expatriate population and tourism. To satisfy the latter activity, sardines are major offerings at waterside grills. They were once a major industry in Portimão. They are still one of the best and cheapest foods available and much appreciated by the local populace. The humble motorcycle, replacing the *burro*, has made a difference here. Purveyors of *sardinhas*, with a box of fish on the pillion of their motorcycles, range far inland madly blowing their horns to announce their presence.

Other Algarvean specialities are the *cataplanas*, stuffed *lulas*, sea bass and seam bream, and the all-pervading *frango piri-piri*. If you order the last mentioned expect to wait for half an hour or more while it is cooked on a wood-fired grill. If the "piri-piri" is not chilli-hot enough don't hesitate to ask for the *molho piri-piri* to liven it up. The area of Foia, uphill of Monchique, is renowned as the area for this delicacy and certainly there are restaurants there which excel in it. But there is no need to be a mountaineer. Some of the best chicken piri-piri we have tasted has been sampled well away from the Serra de Monchique.

There are occasional moans about the local custom of chopping up chicken with a blunt weapon, leaving it full of bone debris, rather than dissecting it. This seems to have its roots in Chinese cooking. The Chinese are said to do it to bring out the flavour of the marrow in the bones, but they use a sharp weapon and wash the chicken under running water to remove any sharp splinters of bone.

Breaking away from tradition

Just a few words about salted cod *"fiel amigo"* one of the most widely sold foods. This commodity is popular right through the Mediterranean latitudes, but in Portugal it is almost revered. It is on sale everywhere, its quality defined by a decree law of 1976. There are five grades, ranging from *miúdo* (the offcuts) to *especialidade*, which is self explanatory. The shopkeeper will cut you off a length utilising a wicked looking guillotine, or you can buy it in the big supermarkets chopped and wrapped. Different countries have their own way of de-salting it. Here in Portugal, 12

RESTAURANTS & FOOD

hours soaking in clean water appears to be enough, longer for the thicker, middle section of the fish, changing the water two or three times. If *bacalhau* appears to be expensive, remember that it doubles in size when soaked. The best way to decide whether you like it or not is to order one of the traditional *bacalhau* dishes in a restaurant. The writer's favourite is *bacalhau à Brás*.

Another spin-off from Portuguese colonialism is turkey (*perú*). *Bifes de perú,* turkey steaks, are readily available all year round. Apart from all the Portuguese ways of cooking them, they are a good substitute for veal and make splendid *escalopes à milanesa* or any other kind of escalope or schnitzel you fancy.

Quick supermarket chicken glossary

Frango	Chicken
C/Miúdos	Bits and pieces, giblets.
S/Miúdos	Whole chicken without the giblets
Churrasco	Whole chicken split for the barbecue
Fricassé	Chopped up remains of what is left after the legs and breast have been removed. Very cheap and mainly bone.
Perna	Legs and thigh
Peito	Breast

Shopping for food

In the last six years the whole aspect of shopping for food has changed. The supermarkets have become bigger, hypermarkets have sprung up and many of those little goodies that we were homesick for, like Bird's Custard and Marmite, are now available but at a price rather more than one would pay at home.

There is still room for the local shops which increasingly style themselves *mini mercados*. Away from the tourist areas and the tourist season you find their prices are usually a little more than those in the big supermarkets. Against this, one should take into account the extra cost of petrol to drive to the supermarket, as well as the goodwill and friendships created by shopping locally. Their produce will usually be better, either bought from the nearest district vegetable market or obtained from local growers.

The traditional vegetable and fish markets located in all towns must not be ignored. There you will find fresh vegetables from

RESTAURANTS & FOOD

local growers, always in season, and not available out of season. Don't buy all your requirements from the first stall that hits your eye. Time spent on reconnaissance is seldom wasted. Walk right around the market and then pick and choose. One special kind of market local to us, and which can be found elsewhere, is the Saturday morning market in Lagos where stall-holders, Portuguese and expatriates, take over the bus station and display their wares. Here you will find at bargain prices superb, naturally-grown vegetables and every kind of country produce straight out of the garden. One Britisher will provide parsnips by request. This vegetable appears to be virtually unknown in Portugal.

What does stand out from supermarket to supermarket and from one *mini mercado* to another is the difference in retail prices. There appears to be no control or agreement. Especially in the holiday areas, the mark-up is obviously intended for the tourists. Residents are wise to shop elsewhere. This applies especially to imported specialities like Kellogg's cornflakes or Nescafé. Portuguese cornflakes are quite as palatable as the imported variety. There is nothing wrong with Portuguese coffee from Brazil, although we're not quite sure about the indigenous brand of freeze-dried coffee. Pasta (*massa* in Portuguese) is cheaper than the Italian brands and equally as good. However, there's no Portuguese equivalent of *tagliatelli*.

If you are a compulsive shopper and live close to the Spanish border, a shopping trip to the nearest large Spanish town or city is worthwhile. If you look around, you will find things you can't buy in Portugal, some will be cheaper than they are here, some will be more expensive, some will be better. We bring back olive oil, sherry (almost unobtainable in Portugal), tins of stuffed olives, tins of *tomate frito*, hot green peppers and Gordon's gin.

Breaking away

It is remarkable how similar basic Portuguese foodstuffs are to those in Southern Italy, even to items like *bacalhau* which is *baccala* in Italy. And then there is the preponderance of *massa*. If you can lay hands on an old copy of Elisabeth David's *Italian Cooking,* or one of the many Italian cook books, you can have a ball with local ingredients which are not available fresh in Northern Europe.

RESTAURANTS & FOOD

SALFINO
MEXICAN RESTAURANT

Portimão
R. Cândido dos Reis 14
Tel. 082/22938

PIZZA service
HOME DELIVERY
PIZZA **SPECIALISTS**
Open from:
12 pm -3 pm and 6 pm - 11 pm
☎ 416 834

Borges & Guerreiro
TRAVESSA MANUEL DIAS BARÃO, N° 7 - PORTIMÃO

INTERNATIONAL AND PORTUGUESE CUISINE

LOTA
RESTAURANTE
PASTELARIA

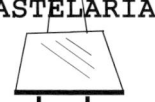

We serve snacks, meals and pastries

BREAKFAST ♦ TAKE AWAY
WE SPEAK ENGLISH
OPEN ALL YEAR

8 am to midnight / summer until 2 am
De: *José Cabrita Lourenço*
RUA DA PRAIA - EDIFÍCIO VISTA MAR
8365 ARMAÇÃO DE PERA - Tel. 082-313503

CAPACHO

8500
Alvor

RESTAURANTE

Portuguese Cuisine
different dish everyday

GRILL

-- CERVEJARIA --

SNACK BAR

☎ 458 126

Rua Poeta António Aleixo - Edifício Valmar

RESTAURANTS & FOOD

No Patio
Restaurante e Bar

...in the old area of Lagos
...with excellent cuisine
...with scandinavian charm
...for a delightful dinner
...looking forward to seeing you

Open All Year except
Nov. - Jan. - Feb.

Closed on Mondays

Rua Lançarote de
Freitas, 46
8600 Lagos

Tel. (082) 763777

RESTAURANTE TÍPICO   **COZINHA PORTUGUESA**

OPEN ALL
YEAR

CLOSED ON
THURSDAYS

ROASTS

STEWS

CHARCOAL
GRILL

MESA POSTA
R E S T A U R A N T E

ROTUNDA DO VAU, 8500 PORTIMÃO   TEL. 082 - 414 582

---

setere   Distributor

YOUR BRITISH STORE

Your favourite British brands.
TESCO foods ◆ ARGOS catalogue.
Household & Electrical goods ◆ Linens, etc.
Make a visit, you will immediately feel at home.
Apartado 919 - 8125 Vilamoura
Tel: (089) 328370 / 380865   Fax: 328375

Loulé
EN 125
Vilamoura   Quarteira

TYPICAL HOUSE
International Cuisine

We've a great choice:

STEAK ON THE STONE, FISH OR MEAT FONDUE, STEAK ON THE WOODEN BOARD, EXCELLENT CATAPLANA AND TUNAFISH OR SWORFISH ON THE CASSEROLE. PORTUGUESE SPECIAL DISHES. LOVELY, TYPICAL ATMOSPHERE. A MUST FOR LUNCH OR DINNER.

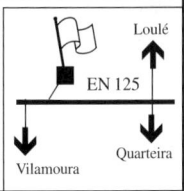

O Barafundas
RESTAURANTE

We accept Partys and Birthdays!
Open from 12.00 pm - 3.00 pm and 6.00 pm - 2.00 am

Av. Sá Carneiro, Montechoro (junto à Farmácia) • 8200 Albufeira • Tel. (089) 54 29 51

SECURITY

If you were setting up a company to operate the crime of burglary it would just have to be called "Ladrão Lda" and be situated in the Algarve. There are rich pickings in the southern region of Portugal where there are hundreds of homes full of the nice things in life, jewellery, cash and all kinds of home entertainment equipment All this coupled with a relaxed frame of mind among the owners of property. An added bonus is that many properties are left empty for much of the year.

Sad to say, burglary is a booming business. It is the number one crime in terms of turnover and has the highest percentage of unsolved cases. Its proliferation is due mainly to the large numbers of young people needing money to buy drugs.

There are three main types of burglar:

Professional - Male or female, fit, non-aggressive, agile, opportunist. They are likely to run rather than pick a fight.

Youngsters - Operating singly or in groups, after money to pay for drugs. Sometimes managed by an adult with the same object.

Aggressive - A variety of the genus football thug, he will beat down your front-door and make life miserable for you. He's soon caught and effectively dealt with by the GNR.

The loot

Unless they are specialists, burglars are looking for money, jewellery, radios, TVs, VCR's, Walkmans, cameras. Anything readily convertible into cash. Specialists may go for antiques, pictures, valuable rugs and the like.

The vulnerable

Thieves are looking for an easy, soft target. Their ideal is a house with easy entry, no occupants, a minimum amount of lights, no dogs and a good escape route.

Fortifications

The only way any burglar can get into your house is through a door or a window, unless you have an extremely large chimney. Make life difficult for him with the following precautions:

- ❏ Fit double locks to all the doors.
- ❏ Fit old-fashioned sliding bolts on the outside doors engaging with striking plates sunk into the wall.

SECURITY

- Install grilles on all windows, and don't forget the small ones. The thickness of the bars has to be big enough to defy one of those large reinforcing rod cutters. One or two bedroom window grilles should be hinged for emergency exit.
- Outside doors should have solid panels. They should have heavy-duty hinges through-bolted to the door and connected to the wall by rawl-bolts. Aluminium doors should have double, reinforced panels. If the door has an inset window, fit a grille attached with through-bolts.
- If the perimeter is a small one, build a wire mesh fence with a razor-wire topping round the property.
- Sliding windows need special locks and precautions should be taken to prevent them being lifted out.
- Double glazing is some protection. Wire mesh interleaving is no barrier to a sledgehammer.

Psychological precautions

- Signs on equipment indicating that it is registered with the GNR.
- Tape recordings of a savage dog barking triggered off by a proximity light switch.
- Dummy cameras mounted high on the wall near the proximity lights.
- If you go out during the day, leave the outside gate open. Thieves don't like being caught by a sudden arrival. A friend found a tin box about 28 x 20 x 15cm, painted it red and had a sign-painter write the family name of one of his German friends on it. It was fixed high on the outside wall of his home in a position readily visible from the road.

Lighting

- Outside illumination on all sides with proximity switches.
- Intermittent lighting inside the house. Control table lamps with inexpensive plug-in timers.

Protective habits

- Never open the door automatically if you are alone. A safety chain is a desirable addition whether you're female or antique male.
- Don't leave the key under the doormat or in the nearest plant pot.
- Close all the grilles when you leave the house.
- Switch on the precaution lights regularly at night.

SECURITY

Maids

- ❏ Portuguese maids are almost without exception as honest as the day is long, and loyal with it. But they do talk to their husbands and their husbands talk to friends in the bar. A maid will boast about her mistress's jewellery and it's common knowledge within days.
- ❏ Don't let them see your jewellery or where you keep it.
- ❏ If you have a floor safe, locate it in a room which is not accessed by your employees.
- ❏ If you do have a taped dog bark, never ever play it when your employees are around.

Dogs

These are very personal things and a great deterrent. They should be left inside the house where they can't be the recipients of poisoned titbits. Choose one with a loyal temperament, a good, deep bark and sharp teeth.

Even if you don't have a dog, get yourself a warning notice and mount it in a prominent position. They are available from *drogarias* with a picture of a dog and a warning message in Portuguese. The picture is very important.

SECURITY

Electronic devices

Consult your security equipment retailer about these. He knows far more than we do what is available. In many cases, too much publicity about his wares and methods is not a good thing. Here's a start:

- ❏ Alarms to scare off intruders and warn your neighbours. Make sure they're well protected from being set-off accidentally. Neighbours and police get very annoyed about false alarms and quickly come to ignore them.
- ❏ An electronic beam system all round the perimeter of your property is good but expensive. The alarms should be installed to ring either inside or outside the house at will.
- ❏ A whole variety of indoor alarms setting off outside hooters is available. They work off exotic proximity switches and can be very effective. But do make sure that they cannot be set off by a dog or cat.

Neighbourhood watch

This is effective if carried out conscientiously. Unfortunately, on many urbanisations in the Algarve there are few neighbours to do the watching during the winter months.

Protecting your valuables

There are various types of safe available from the security specialists. The size and maybe the type will be determined by what you intend to put in it. It is doubtful whether any of them will defy the attentions of a professional safe-breaker. However, even a steel box or gun cabinet made of heavy gauge steel secured with mortise locks and fastened to the wall and the floor could protect radios and pocket cameras from youthful snatch-thieves.

Certainly if you are second home for long periods, leave as few valuables as possible in the house. Valuable carpets, televisions and VCRs can be put into store. Jewellery and cameras can go with you to your other home. If you insure valuables, read the small print carefully. You will most probably find that cameras, tape recorders and the like are only insured when they are safely locked away in a steel box. If you leave them lying aroud and a snatch-thief scoops them up, you are unlikely to be compensated. If they belong to guests, they may be claimed for on the owner's travel insurance.

TAXES

Tax no longer lax

Some of us feel pretty smart about taxation on our income. We reckon that by living not quite in our own country and not quite in Portugal, we can avoid taxation in both. But as the Portuguese administration becomes more and more computerised this grey zone becomes less and less grey.

Time was when many expatriates regarded Portugal as a tax haven, maybe paying a nominal amount of tax in their own country and considering that sufficient. So far as the British are concerned this is no longer so. There is now a considerable exchange of information between the British Inland Revenue and the Portuguese tax authorities. A number of residents have had polite invitations to visit the IRS office and have then been put through an inquisition concerning their worldwide income. The inquisitor makes little effort to hide the fact that he was fully informed by HM Inland Revenue about their UK income from untaxed interest or investment.

The Portuguese IRS have full access to all bank accounts and the foregoing situation is usually triggered off by regular movements of large amounts of cash into and out of your Portuguese account.

Should the foregoing happen to you it is best to take a tax advisor with you or you may indavertently answer questions which you need not have responded to.

Imposto único

Decreto-Lei 106/88 heralded a new income-tax system, *imposto único*. It was, in effect, a reform of direct taxation to replace the old schedular tax system which was self-defeating in its complexity. It was felt that the new tax system would be easier for everyone to understand and be easier to administer. Maybe there were hopes that the habit of tax-paying might catch on.

The tax is sub-divided into two main headings and is levied on worldwide income:

- ❏ IRS, *Impostos sobre o Rendimento das Pessoas Singulares*, Personal Income Tax.
- ❏ IRC, *Imposto sobre o Rendimento das Pessoas Colectivas*, groups of people; in other words Corporation Tax.

TAXES

So far as the tax authorities are concerned, all residents must file a return of their world wide income even if they are paying tax in their own country under a double tax agreement. One does not have to have a *residência*, a residential visa, to be deemed a resident by the *Finanças*. If you spend more than 183 days a year in Portugal, either at one time or cumulatively, you are reckoned to be resident. Needless to say you automatically become a resident if you have a permanent home here.

IRS

As the law says, this is a tax on the global income of individuals. The foreign population is divided into two groups:

> a. Non resident, paying tax on Portuguese income
> b. Resident, paying tax on worldwide income
>   Income is sub-divided into the following official categories:
> - Wages and salaries
> - Self employed
> - Commercial or industrial
> - Agricultural
> - Investment
> - Rented property
> - Capital gains
> - Pensions
> - Gambling, including lotteries

There is a tax form to be filled in, Modelo IRS1. You will have to go to the tax office to collect, and pay for it. This is the law of the land. Not all foreign taxpayers realise that it is up to them to go to the tax office and obtain a form. It doesn't come through the post unrequited like it does back home. Moreover, if you overlook this either involuntarily or on purpose, you cannot claim ignorance of the law and you may be liable to fines or even prison for the offence.

If you are a member of AFPOP, they have a dummy form with a translation of all the headings. However, the requirements are not easily understood and it is really in one's best interest to employ an accountant, much preferably Portuguese who speaks your own language, to do the job for you. This could save you at

TAXES

least the accountant's fees because he will be able to claim all kinds of allowances and any medical expenses for you. In this context it pays to save all bills and take them along with you.

IRC

This is a business tax and applies to companies and commercial bodies as below:

- Companies with their head office in Portugese territory whose activities are mainly commercial, agricultural or industrial.
- Groups with their head offices and management on Portuguese territory, who do not pay IRS or IRC by way of the individuals or companies from which they are constituted.
- Global income of groups of individuals who do not have a head office or management structure in Portugal and who would normally pay IRS. Typically these would be groups of professional people. Family companies, the equivalent of a UK trust, are included in this category.
- There are other variations on the theme which your accountant will explain.

IRS tax on pensions

Tax on pensions is of very special interest to foreign residents, many of whom are retired. Here's how it works for them if pensions are their sole source of income. The computation is very simple. It is calculated like this:

- The first 400,000$ of your pension is excluded from tax.
- Half the amount in excess of the above, up to 1,000,000$ is free of tax.
- Medical insurance, doctors fees and medicines are deductible.
- Foreign taxes can be claimed as an expense.
- If your country of origin has a double taxation agreement with Portugal and tax is deducted from your pension at source, you are not liable to pay Portuguese tax. (Fill in your name and address on a tax form, pin a notarised copy of your annual tax return to it - in the case of UK citizens your P60 - and take it to the *Finanças*. They will take note of the details).

TAXES

Tax rates on personal income *(other than pensions)*

To arrive at an approximation of how much tax you are likely to have to pay before allowances, the following table may help. Simply calculate the percentage of your taxable income, which varies according to your income bracket, and deduct from it the figure in the third column.

Taxable income Esc millions	Percentage	Deduct
0 -0.45	16	nil
0.45-0.85	20	18,000$
0.85-1.25	27.5	81,750$
1.25-3.00	35	175,500$
over 3.00	40	325,000$

Contribuição autárquica *(Property tax)*

This is a general tax on land or buildings levied by the local authority, the *Câmara Municipal*, to finance their public services, building programs and the like. The tax is paid by property owners, not tenants, for their own benefit.

Tax is due on each parcel of land and whatever building have permanently existed on it for more than a year. The property is valued in three classifications: *Prédio Rústico*, *Prédio Urbano* or *Prédio Misto*. These classifications are defined in the fiscal register, the *Matriz Predial* and are as follows:

Prédio Rústico

- Non-building land outside an urban site.
- Agricultural land providing an agricultural income.
- Non-agricultural land of low value, which may or may not have secondary buildings on it unsuitable for habitation.
- Land on urban sites which provides either an agricultural income or, by law, provides no income at all.
- Houses and buildings strictly devoted to agriculture located on agricultural land, or financially independent of the land they are on.

Prédio Urbano

- Buildings for residential, commercial or professional use, with the necessary licences to practice if for the latter.

TAXES

- Building land, either inside or outside urban sites, that has been licensed for building on the title deeds or has subsequently been given a building licence.
- Other land, outside urbanisations, which has not been licensed for building but is not categorised as *Prédio Rústico*.
- Buildings or homes which have a different licence or a different purpose from the aformentioned categories in the *Urbano* category.

The Finances office uses the land's fiscal value as the basis for its calculation for *Prédio Rústico* or *Prédio Urbano*. The flat rate for the former is 0.8% while the latter is calulated on the a variable, between 1.1% and 1.3%, depending on the value of the property.

Around March or April each year, property owners receive a notification printed in green on buff paper from the *Direcção das Contribuições e Impostos* of the *Ministério das Finanças* in Lisbon stating the amount of tax to be paid. If the value is above a certain amount, you may be allowed to pay it in two instalments, the first in April and the second one in September.

Bear in mind that if you pay SISA on the property, you are relieved of the necessity to pay *Contribuição Autárquica* for a period, depending on the rateable value, *Valor Tributável*. When that period is over, you start to pay the year after. The figures are altered every year, but the table below gives a good guide to the length of time you can expect to be exempt from *Contribuição Autárquica*.

Rateable value contos	Years owner occupied	Years if rented
Up to 7,000	10	20
7,000 to 10,500	10	8
10,500 to 14,000	10	6
17,500 to 21,000	4	2
21,000 to 25,200	4	n/a

The places to pay it are:

- At the *Finanças* of your local *Câmara*.
- At a main post office.
- At the *Banco Português do Atlântico* by cheque if you are a customer, otherwise with cash. (This bank will allow you to draw cash with your credit card and then hand the cash with your bill to the same teller. He will receipt it and retain half the form).

TAXES

Inheritance tax

Inheritance tax is paid by the heirs of a resident or non-resident who held property (moveable or fixed) in Portugal. The rate of tax is dependant not only on the value of assets, but also on the relationship between the deceased and the beneficiary. Under English law, for instance, inheritance tax does not apply between spouses. This is not the case in Portugal. Furthermore, here it is extremely expensive to leave a large portion of one's estate to a non-relative.

Briefly, the rate of the tax is calculated as follows:

Following the "de cujus" death, the beneficiaries' appointed executor or solicitor has 30 days to present to the tax office in Portugal a certified copy of the death certificate. Within 60 days of the death, a list of all assets must be given to the tax office. Assets are divided into two parts: active and passive (debts). Within the first section are included bank accounts, property, moveables, shares and share certificates, cars, right down to personal items. In the second section, one must declare debts, namely mortgages in Portugal, personal borrowings and unpaid bills, including those for funeral expenses.

The tax office will then sum up all the assets and calculate the tax in accordance with the following table. It is relatively simple to quantify the moveable assets; the beneficiary does just that when submitting the list. For property, however, the tax is calculated on the basis of the table and the rateable value of the property, shown in your *Caderneta Predial*, if it has been updated as it should be every six months.

There are discounts on the tax to pay if its liquidation is immediate. On the other hand, the tax office may allow you to pay in instalments, with interest.

The above is not applicable to:

    a) Assets outside Portugal;

    b) Assets owned by offshore companies of which the deceased is the beneficiary owner.

TAXES

IMPOSTO SOBRE SUCESSÕES E DOAÇÕES

Contos	up to 700	700 2,750	2,750 7,000	7,000 13,750	13,750 34,500	34,500 68,500	over 68,500
Your children	0	4	7	10	14	18	23
Between husband & wife	0	6	9	12	16	20	25
Relatives or sisters and brothers	7	10	13	16	21	26	32
3rd Generation	13	17	21	25	31	38	45
Outside the family	16	20	25	30	36	43	50

Married couples are calculated using the following sequence:

>If one partner receives more than 95% or more of the joint income, it is divided by 1.85 to arrive at the taxable income.
>If the above does not apply, the income is divided by two.
>The relevant rate is applied to one of the above.
>The resultant is multiplied by two.

Capital gains tax

Classified as type G income, capital gains tax is levied on the sale of the following types of property. The variable rate peaks at 20%.

>Freehold Property
>Lease and rental rights
>Shares in quoted companies
>Stock held for less than two years
>"Intellectual property" (presumably this means copyright of books and works of art)
>Exempt from capital gains tax are:
>Bonds and unit trusts
>Assets purchased by individuals before 1 January 1989.

Rental income tax

When assessing income from rents, the taxman first of all makes a 35% reduction to arrive at the net taxable income.

TAXES

Individual owners pay 16 to 40 % depending on the amount. Offshore companies pay a flat rate of 25%.

SISA

SISA is levied when a property is transferred from one owner to another. The rates are as follows.

Rustic property is charged at 8% of the amount declared in the deed that conveys the property. For example, if a piece of land is sold for three million escudos, the tax payable will be 240,000$.

Land for construction, in other words building land, is charged at 10% of the declared value.

Where urban property is designated for habitation, no SISA is levied if the declared price is less than 10 million escudos. Above this price, tax is levied on a sliding scale levelling out at 27,800,000$. Higher than that a flat rate of 10% is charged. Some of the intermediate rates are shown below as a rough guide. There are intermediate steps between the values shown.

Esc. Value	Tax	Esc. Value	Tax
10,400,000	20,000	27,000,000	2,548,995
15,200,000	343,998	25,200,000	2,080.995
20,000.000	976,996	Above 27,800,000	10 %

SISA must be paid a few days before the signing of the deed. If SISA is due on the transaction, the receipt proving payment is one of the documents you must present to the notary before he will agree to draw up the final deed for signature. The receipt remains in the notary's files so if you wish to retain a copy mention this to your lawyer before the document is sent to the notary. Otherwise, you will have to ask for a copy from the notary's office and that is more expensive.

In transactions between non-Portuguese nationals, the contract price is sometimes stated in another currency. If this happens, a letter from a local bank has to be produced within three days of the request for SISA payment showing the prevailing rate of exchange for the SISA calculation. Bear in mind that if out of the total cost, a specific amount is being paid for furniture and fittings, this may be noted in the *escritura*. It will not affect the amount of SISA levied since this is based on the total amount, but it does establish a value for the property in any future transaction.

TAXES

From December 1995 the *Valor Tributável*, which has been unchanged for a number of years, will be changed according to the following table.

Date of registration	Multiple
Prior to 31 Dec. 1988	1.3
1991	1.15
1992	1.1
1993	1.05

Tax avoidance

In UK law, and one imagines in the law of other countries, it is every citizens' birthright to minimise their tax burden by legal means. There are experts of your own nationality practicing in Portugal who are eager to help you to do this. As ever, if you do use the services of these specialist accountants be sure to have a written estimate of what their charges will be before you instruct them in any way.

Tax evasion

Deceit or lying to deprive the taxman of his just dues is illegal, in any country. With many people of all nationalities it is something of a hobby. The computer and closer co-operation between national tax authorities are stacking the odds against this particular pastime.

In many European countries, Portugal included, there are taxmen adept at the assessment of income by the outward signs of it, namely lifestyle, fancy cars and large houses. They relate this to the movement of money in the victim's bank account and draw their conclusions accordingly. Additionally, in Portugal there is a reward for information from the public at large.

TELEPHONES

Clearing the lines

Only a few years ago the section of the CTT responsible for the telephone system changed its name to Telecom Portugal. Almost at once the Portuguese telephone system took a turn for the better. New buildings with digital exchanges sprung up and people in those areas who had been waiting for years for a phone suddenly got one. Not only did they get one, but it worked with astonishing clarity and alacrity.

Foreign numbers, which previously took a dozen or so tries before you got through, now responded immediately. Moreover, fax machines became practical. It is fair to say that in 1991 Portuguese tele-communications moved into the 20th century.

Some of the old exchanges are still operational. You can tell where they are because the numbers in that area all have five digits. Digital numbers have six digits.

Where the system is still lacking is the itemisation of telephone bills, which are presented monthly with an annual promise of change which never materialises. At the moment the sum total of information you are given is the call charge and the number of periods you have used. By all means go to your local Telecom Portugal office where you will be allowed to see an itemised list of calls lasting more than 25 periods and not including *Interurbana*. You must make a note of the numbers there and then. Because of an obscure decree law on the privacy of communication, *Artº 34 Inviolabilidade do Domicílio e da Correspondência,* you are not allowed to have a record. Before you are allowed to take a copy of the bill away with you, the last four digits of the numbers will be indelibly deleted by the assistant. It is difficult not to see this as a delightful, typically Portuguese, avoiding manoeuvre.

The method of charging for phone calls in the second most expensive telephone system in Europe is worthy of an explanation. First let us explain that, in common with many other European countries, Telecom Portugal charges are based on the "period" system. Elsewhere it is termed a pulse, a method which lends itself to computerisation, but is difficult for the layman to understand. A telephone pulse or "period" is a variable length of time, expressed in seconds, at a fixed price. In Portugal the "period" can be as long as 540 seconds (9 minutes) for a cheap rate local call,

TELEPHONES

and as short as 4.3 seconds, or less, for an intercontinental call. The fixed charge for each of these variable pulse/periods is 12$50 including IVA.

If you need an example, take two extremes. When calling any European country outside Portugal in Zone 1 during the day you will be charged 12$50 for every 4.7 seconds talking time. If you are calling your neighbour after 22.00hr you can chat for as long as nine minutes for the same 12$50.

Inside Portugal there are five different call types as follows:

Local calls to numbers beginning with the same three digits as your own.

Regional calls made within your own area without dialling an area code.

Interurbana calls made to numbers outside your telephone area. Charges are reduced if the distance is less than 50km.

Comunicações Automáticas Zona 1 calls made to EU countries outside Portugal (see list).

Comunicações Automáticas Zona 2 calls to the rest of Europe. See the following page.

Within the above types of call there are time bands in which the charges vary according to the time of day. For the table below we have calculated the very approximate **cost per minute** based on a five minute call. In parentheses is the number of seconds per pulse/period. Readers with a mathematical turn of mind will appreciate that it is impossible to give an exact figure.

Time bands	*1000-1300* *1400-1800*	*0800-1000* *1300-1400* *1800-2200*	*2200-0800* *Holidays* *Sat & Sunday*
Local	12$50(3min)	12$50(6min)	12$50(9min)
Regional	125$00(30s)	24$00(32s)	20(42s)
Interurbana	*0800-2000*	*2000-2200*	*2200-0800*
Less than 50km	35$60(21s)	25$00(30s)	17$80(42s)
More than 50km	71$20(10.5s)	50$00(15s)	35$60(21s)

TELEPHONES

One can dial calls outside Portugal to the two *Zonas de Comunicações Automática* shown below:

Zona 1 - All of the European Union plus the Faroe Islands, Gibraltar, Iceland, Morocco, Norway, Switzerland and the Vatican City.

Zona 2 - Albania, Algeria, Armenia, Azerbeijan, Bielo-Russia, Bosnia-Herzgovina, Bulgaria, Cyprus, Croatia, Yugoslavia, Estonia, Georgia, Greenland, Hungary, Lithuania, Macedonia, Malta, Moldavia, Poland, Czech Republic, Republic of Slovakia, Rumania, Russian Federation, Tajicistan, Tunisia, Turkey, Turkestan, Ukraine.

Call charges are:

Zone/Time	0700-0900 1300-1400 2100-2400	0900-1300 1400-2100 2100-2400	0000-0700 Weekends & Holidays
Com Aut Z1	115$38(6.5s)	131$60(5.7s)	93$00(8.0s)
Com Aut Z2	144$23(5.2s)	174$42(4.3s)	121$50(6.0s)

Zona 3 - Countries not included in Zones 1 and 2.

It does not pay to underestimate the cost of interurban calls over 50km radius. We assume this is measured between exchanges. A call from Alvor to Faro can cost as much as a call from Alvor to Lisbon. During working hours a five minute *Interurbana* call costs 425$ between either of these exchanges.

Intercontinental calls vary over a wide spectrum. If you are concerned about the cost, dial 098 for information.

For information on other areas dial:

    090 For the interurban area within Portugal

    099 For European and Mediterranean countries.

The one concession seems likely to find few takers. Pensioners and retired people receiving less than the minimum national income qualify for a 60% reduction of the *assinatura* plus 25 free pulses per month.

A useful service number is 118. This will give you the name and address to match a phone number. Or treat it as directory enquiry for phone numbers. A charge of 22$60 is made for this service.

TELEPHONES

DIT

Anyone who regularly makes international calls from Portugal will be painfully aware of the swinging charges inflicted by Telecom Portugal, the second most expensive in Europe.

Dial International Telecom, a new UK based service using US technology is now offering a call-back service for which substantial savings are claimed. The principle is that one is allocated a UK number to call from your home, mobile or whatever. Within 20 seconds you will be given a UK line into which you dial your DIT PIN number followed by the number you require. You will then be connected to that number and charged from then on, not from the time you start the procedure.

There is a once-and-for-all charge of £50 to join the service and you are expected to pay a minimum of £25 per month. The cost of your calls will be deducted from this. Any of the charge not used up will be carried over to the following month. DIT tell us that it is possible to suspend payments until it is used up.

Charges are calculated in US dollars and converted to Sterling at the going rate. At the present time, a one minute full rate call from Portugal to the UK is charged at 131$. The DIT charge for the same call would be 115$

An extra cost is the requirement for a telephone with tone entry. The Telecom Portugal system currently works on the pulse system and the handsets do not, so far, have a tone button or switch. Remember too that DIT does not replace your Portuguese line, or the monthly bill, although that would naturally be less.

DIY callback

We feel that for those of us who have talkative families in the UK, it still pays to buy them a Mercury subscription, or that of one of the other Telecom independents in the UK who submit itemised bills, and arrange your own call-back system. Your relatives or friends then send you the bill which usually turns out to be about half of what it would be if the call originated in the Telecom Portugal network.

TELEPHONES

Mobile telephones

Cellular telephone networks have come late in the day to Portugal. That is no hardship because, as a result, the technology is state of the art and is reckoned to be the best in Europe. Operating on the digital GSM system, which is rapidly becoming the standard, it is administered by Telecel Lda, a joint venture between Telecom Portugal, Marconi and TMN. One of the snags is that the handsets are expensive compared with the UK for example, where they are usually offered as an incentive to subscribe to a call-expensive system. However, the cost of calls in Portugal appears to be within reason although they are by no means cheap. There are three price bands which cater for different levels of usage and all calls are charged at the inter-regional rate. There is no such thing as a local call. The machines, portable telephones, yuppy dummies, call them what you will, vary from 42,000$ to 120,000$.

Telecel charges are based on a once-only joining fee followed by a monthly charge and then the call charges themselves. Costs are as follows, the prices are per minute:

Monthly charge	Mobile to Telecom 0900-1300 1400-2200	Mobile to Telecom 1300-1400 2200-0900	Mobile to mobile 0900-1300 1400-2200	Mobile to mobile 1300-1400 2200-0900
4,200$ *Especial* 10 min. free	135$00	30$00	95$00	32$50
8,500$ *Valor* 60 min. free	95$00	32$50	35$00	25$00
9,250$ *Mais*	53$00 (1) * 51$50 (2) 59$50 (3)	35$00	35$00	25$00

* (1) First 500 min. (2) Following 1,000 min (3) From 1,500 on

A comparison of these charges with those for regular Telecom Portugal calls can be an interesting pastime. An *especial* subscriber calling his home or office a couple of kilometers away during prime time will be paying the same rate as if he were calling Stockholm on Telecom Portugal. The minimum charge, 25$ off

TELEPHONES

peak, is the same as a prime time Telecom Portugal regional call.

Telephone adapters

Whatever the rights or wrongs of the practice, many Brits are tempted to install British Telecom telephones or faxes in their homes, mainly because there is a wider choice of instruments. To achieve this they usually call in a Portuguese telephone engineer to change the plug to fit the Telecom Portugal socket. Because British market phone connectors are different from those of other EU countries they will find that although they can make outgoing calls quite satisfactorily, the phone will not ring for incoming calls.

Should this happen a small "black" box (it's actually white) is available to make the connection. This has optional connectors for the modern Telecom Portugal sockets or the older screw-in or three pin sockets. It works equally well with phones, faxes or answerphones.

Colin Burgess

Telephone Adaptors: UK / Portuguese ♦ Just plug in
No need to visit, we can send your orders cash on delivery
Computers: Bespoke programming
            Hardware / Software supplied & repaired

Tel: 082 - 761953 or Fax: 082 - 761952

TELEVISION

General

This entertainment medium is unusual in that no television licence is called for in Portugal. Originally there were two national channels, now there are two extra ones, both enlivened by the injection of private enterprise money.

A large section of the expatriate population is quite happy with Portuguese national television, which can be excellent if you are able to endure its unbelievable and quite unforgivable inability to mount any program on time, except live football.

Most of the films shown are somewhat erstwhile. Others are classics from dusty Californian archives, dear to the hearts of devotees of the film. They are usually in the original language with dubbed sub-titles and are a help when learning Portuguese. The national channels' arts and documentary coverage is excellent with sometimes superb camera work. The motor racing coverage is better than average too.

Satellite TV equipment

Portugal is on the edge of the Astra coverage area. Viewers can receive a restricted selection of Sky transmissions without a decoder card and the full selection with one. They can also receive Eurosport and CNN in addition to RTL and a number of German stations. As a result, fixed satellite dishes are sprouting everywhere, adding their multitude to an older, smaller population of large, motorised dishes. The fixed dishes are very practical and in the last few years prices have come down sufficiently to make them affordable. It is now possible to buy a cheapy system from a cash and carry for as little as 32,000$. However, the reception of this equipment is somewhat limited and the southern tip of Portugal and the Barlavento requires something more techinically advanced. Prices have tumbled since the last edition of this book and one can now have a single system which will receive the Sky channels, Eurosport and many of the German transmissions for around 50,000$. All of the foregoing excludes fitting which can vary between 10,000$ and 15,000$ if done professionally. A dual system with offset dish, which will recieve the excellent BBC World News transmissions, plus the Euro Business and News channels and many more European channels, will set you back

TELEVISION

about 120,000$ including fitting. Motorised dishes are really for the enthusiasts, the positioner unit can be affected by mains voltage variations, and they can be generally more temperamental.

If you enjoy sound radio, the BBC radio channels, including the World Radio, can be received loud and clear on the audio channels of Astra.

Satellite cards

The legality of the use of UK-issued cards to receive the Sky transmissions is something of a grey area. Sky are only licensed to sell them in the UK. It would be an offence for them knowingly to sell them to viewers anywhere else. However, they can have little control over part-time expatriates who take their cards on holiday with them, or residents to have a friend "spark" one in their home country. They tell us that they have never taken action against individuals on this score. There are indications that ere long Sky might move into Europe, which would rationalise the situation, but it's taking time.

The alternative to these cards was, for a while, smartcards which, for about 12,000$00, allowed viewers to receive all the Sky pay-channels and represented quite a saving apart from appearing to be permanent. Of course, such devices are highly illegal on their home ground and the right to use them here is extremely doubtful. For a long time there has been a running battle between the smarties and Sky who changed the code frequently, causing the owners of these cards to have them recoded at frequent, 1.000$ per time, intervals. Recently Sky dealt a major blow when they went to the expense of issuing a new high-tech card which seems to have out-smarted the smarties for the time being.

Receiving BBC television

Brits who have become accustomed to the undoubted excellence of BBC television can receive BBC World Service programmes beamed from Intelsat VI. Compared with Sky, an expensive outfit is required with a large dish (180cm minimum for Portugal) and a D2 Mac receiver with a Eurocrypt M decoder. The dish has to be mounted separately, with a different orientation

TELEVISION

from an Astra dish. And, of course, you have to pay for a card. To receive BBC World Service TV transmissions you require a second fixed dish, total cost is about 250,000$.

Should British readers have a complete satellite set-up in the UK, there would be no objection to bringing the whole caboodle - System I television set, dish, receiver and LNB - to Portugal and using it as a dedicated, satellite-only receiver. You might need a bigger dish and more potent LNB to receive the weak Sky signals we get here. You would then have to purchase a second, System B/G television set to receive Portuguese programs. It seems hardly worth the trouble.

ALGARVE SATELLITE CENTRE

- Dishes from 95cm to 1.4m (prices 49,000$00 to 89,000$00)
- All suitable for Astra 1D or Eutelsat 13º
  BBC World, MCM, TV5, RAI UNO + RAI DUE etc.
- Dish sharing systems available
- Systems available with Astra 1E - Digital Wide Band LNB
- Efficient Electronic repairs carried out in our fully equipped workshop

Edifício Panorama, Rua Vasco de Gama (behind the Bus Station), 8600 Lagos
Tel 082 764121   Fax 082 764905

MARC ELECTRÓNICA PORTUGAL
de Marc Arthur Wentink
Sítio do Poço Seco, Armazém 5/6
Cardosas - 8500 Portimão
ELECTRÓNICA   Tel.: 082-492470 Fax: 082-411742

♦ all you need for satellite-tv
♦ own technical department
♦ quick response -
   3 service cars on the road

TIMESHARE

Take your time

Some people get a lot of satisfaction out of timeshare. A great many more endure anguish and worry. At least that's how it appears to the interested onlooker. Maybe one hears more about the bad cases than the good ones. Certainly in the Algarve the image of timeshare is smirched by the activity of timeshare touts, and the touts act that way only because the companies they work for encourage them to do so.

The principle of timeshare is that you purchase for cash through a timeshare club or syndicate the right to use accommodation, or a type of accommodation, in the shape of a house or apartment for a fixed period of time, usually measured in weeks. On top of the original investment there will be charges for maintenance and management.

At first sight it is an attractive prospect to invest a few thousand pounds to ensure that you can go to a familiar " holiday home " every year, or exchange with other timeshare owners. Some of the established and more responsible clubs have timeshare members as far away as America.

It is all very well if you manage to invest in one through a reliable company. Even then you would be excessively naive to expect to get any return on your investment or even get your original stake back if you wished to. You have to bear in mind that service charges can escalate astronomically; it is not unknown for them to double the year after you sign up. And take into account the cost of airfares when comparing timeshare with the cost of booking a holiday through a travel agency.

The real problems can crop up if you are inveigled by one of the touts who infest the popular tourist areas in Portugal into visiting a timeshare complex employing high-pressure sales tactics.

The laws

This problem was so bad that as long ago as 1981 the Portuguese Government promulgated special laws to protect purchasers: *Decreto-lei* 355/81 followed by *Decreto-lei* 368/83. Since that time there has been further legislation to ensure that timeshare owners get not only a fair deal in relation to the

TIMESHARE

property they are timesharing, but also the services and facilities linked to it.

The law concerned was *Decreto-Lei* 130/89. This has now been superseded by *Decreto-Lei* 275/93 of 5 August 1993. Its objects are twofold: to improve the quality and working of timeshare resorts and to give better protection to purchasers.

Apart from decreeing that not more than 60 % of any new development can be used for timeshare, this new decree law enhances the protection given by 130/89 and weighs the odds even more heavily in favour of the purchaser. It indicates that the Portuguese Government is well aware of the pitfalls awaiting purchasers when they come up against a certain very prevalent breed of timeshare developer. Purchasers should take comfort in the fact that the law is on their side and bear the following points firmly in mind if they are hell-bent on buying timeshare. They have the following protection:

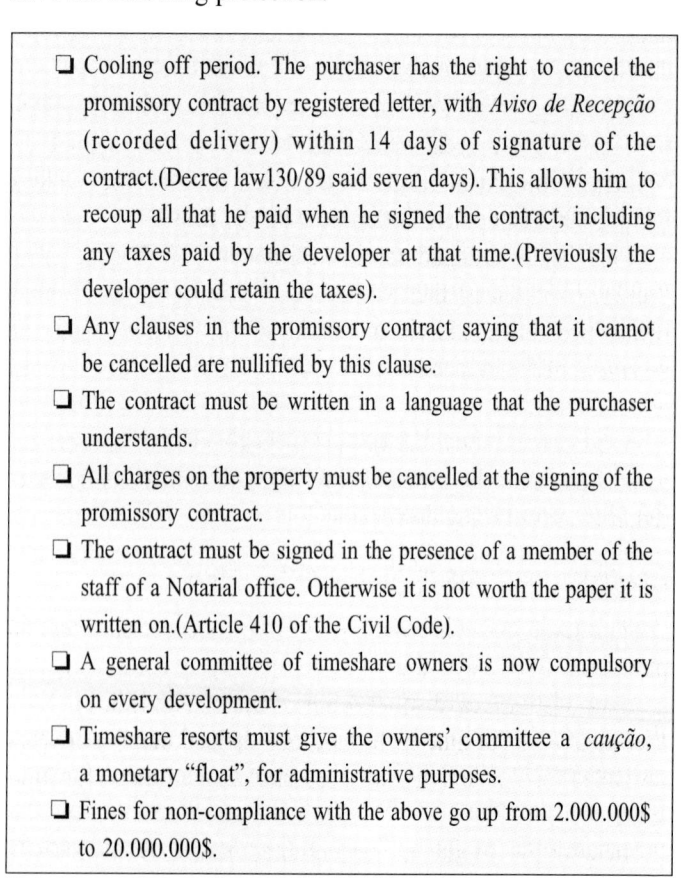

- ❏ Cooling off period. The purchaser has the right to cancel the promissory contract by registered letter, with *Aviso de Recepção* (recorded delivery) within 14 days of signature of the contract.(Decree law130/89 said seven days). This allows him to recoup all that he paid when he signed the contract, including any taxes paid by the developer at that time.(Previously the developer could retain the taxes).
- ❏ Any clauses in the promissory contract saying that it cannot be cancelled are nullified by this clause.
- ❏ The contract must be written in a language that the purchaser understands.
- ❏ All charges on the property must be cancelled at the signing of the promissory contract.
- ❏ The contract must be signed in the presence of a member of the staff of a Notarial office. Otherwise it is not worth the paper it is written on.(Article 410 of the Civil Code).
- ❏ A general committee of timeshare owners is now compulsory on every development.
- ❏ Timeshare resorts must give the owners' committee a *caução*, a monetary "float", for administrative purposes.
- ❏ Fines for non-compliance with the above go up from 2.000.000$ to 20.000.000$.

TIMESHARE

The main points of the new laws are that two aspects of timeshare are now recognised. The law sees them as the *Direito Real a Habitação Periódica*, REAL TIMESHARE RIGHTS TO OWNERSHIP and the *Direito Obrigatório de Habitação Turística*, CONTRACTUAL TIME SHARE RIGHTS.

Real timeshare rights to ownership

This section refers to a property sold for part-time ownership of a specific property for so many weeks, one week minimum, over a period which can be in perpetuity or for a minimum period of 30 years. Whether it be in perpetuity or for a restricted number of years, this REAL RIGHT OF OWNERSHIP will henceforth be the subject of a Land Registry like any other property.

In August 1993, new regulations were brought in which decree that the developer must prepare an *escritura* which describes the development as a "Timeshare" with many more documents to go with it. One of these has to be full approval from the *Direcção Geral de Turismo*.

According to the 1989 decree law, a full notarised *escritura* was required for each week sold. It had to describe all the elements of the unit AND gives a complete list of all the services, facilities and equipment which go with the title.

This is all changed in the decree law of August 1993. Presumably because the law feels that developers are now so firmly tied down, individual purchasers no longer require an *escritura*. All they need is to certify signatures in front of any notarial clerk.

We fail to see how the individual buyer is as well protected as he was under the previous law, since the notary is not even required to check any documents!

Contractual rights of tourist occupation

This covers what is basically Club type occupation where the purchaser only buys the right to occupy a certain type of accommodation (as distinct from a specific building), for a specified period of time each year, for a defined number of years.

Rules for this activity are even stricter than those for time-share.

In addition to the aforementioned REAL TIMESHARE

TIMESHARE

RIGHTS TO OWNERSHIP, they are:

> ❏ The Contract shall specify the number of contracts that the promoters propose to issue as well as their value. The Tourist Board will then issue an authorisation which must be quoted in every Contract.
> ❏ The vendors must also deposit with the authorities a guarantee equal to one third of the total sale value.

Having seen what has happened in Spain, where tourists have been relieved of a great deal of money by the shadier side of the timeshare industry, the Portuguese Government is trying to clean up a murky area of the tourist market. The Civil Governor of the Algarve is also clamping down hard on touts, and has made many of their activities illegal. But they still operate.

If you are attracted to the idea of timeshare there are certain golden rules:

> ❏ Don't do anything, or sign anything whatsoever, until you get back home and have talked to friends, or one of the established timeshare owners' associations.
> ❏ Under no circumstances fall for a sales pitch that offers inducements or tells you that the offer is for a limited period, like that day. So very often the large enticements being offered if you sign on the spot are an indication that the end product is not a good buy. And very often the generous free gifts don't turn out to be what they're made out to be.

TRAVEL

By air

This is the favourite mode of transport with both holidaymakers and regular travellers between Portugal and northern Europe and farther afield. You have only to look at the map and the cost of flights to see why. It is relatively cheap and quick, less than three hours from most northern European airports even to Portugal's most southerly airport.

In the past it has not been so economical getting out of Portugal due to the mistaken efforts of the central government to make their national airline cost effective by controlling charter prices. Now this policy is changing.

Fares

At last the airlines operating in and out of Portugal are being de-regulated. The bureaucracy in Lisbon has finally given up the hopeless attempt to make TAP profitable by price-fixing. Now things are looking up. During the past year, controls have progressively been removed and we are at last able to buy economy flights to the UK and elsewhere. In this context, British operators appear to have been dragging their feet. German and Dutch operators have been offering reduced price fares for more than a year. It is very encouraging to find one operator even offering single ticket flights to the UK at reasonable prices. This is good news because, for some quite illogical reason, the scheduled airlines charge more for a single ticket than they do for an "Apex" return.

If economy is the order of the day, it is important to choose the date you intend flying. The most expensive time to fly scheduled airline or charter is Easter, high Summer (mid-July to mid-September) and Christmas. School half-term breaks also attract high fares. Other EU countries have roughly the same premium-price periods.

Expect to buy your flights for less in the periods between these dates. There will not be the same startling reductions if you are starting from Portugal as there would be if you bought your ticket in the UK. But there will be reductions.

If you aim to fly from either end at minimum cost it pays to shop around, preferably by telephone. Don't give up if an agent

TRAVEL

tells you there are no seats left on a flight. In all countries, airlines allocate blocks of seats to agents. When they have sold them they have a strong tendency to tell the customer that the flight is full, rather than directing him or her to another travel agent who might have seats available.

If you must fly on a certain day and cannot get a booking, go to the airport with your bag packed and with all your documents in order. Go to the desk of the airline you wish to travel with, ask for the station manager of that particular carrier and explain your problem. Very often there are spare seats because of the aforementioned situation. Or if the flight is genuinely full, someone may not show up and you may be offered a seat at the last moment. We have been told that if flights are underbooked, with a lot of spare seats, you can go to the airport and do a face-to-face deal with the station manager for a seat. Naturally the airlines are not keen to publicise this.

Excess baggage

Excess baggage is a worry to a great many travellers. Most golfers know by now that their clubs and golf-bags are not counted in the baggage weight. We have also found that charter airlines have got around to the fact that holidaymakers tend to return home with rather more weight than they arrived with, and are reasonably tolerant about extra baggage weight on flights out of the holiday centres.

Domestic and long-haul flights

Portugal is a beautiful country and there are good value internal flights and packages which will take you for short breaks to Lisbon, Oporto, Madeira and the Azores.

Lisbon airport is not everyone's favourite because of the difficulty of finding one's way around it. The resulting lost connections have cost it friends. One popular alternative for dwellers in the southern region when making long-haul flights is to fly direct from Faro to London and take a break in the British capital. Travellers to the USA have been known to take a ticket to the UK and then to book on from there with a British travel agent, taking advantage of the very keen prices available between the UK and the North American continent. Otherwise, the only transatlantic flights from Portugal originate in Lisbon.

TRAVEL

Spanish option

Now that the Via do Infante is in place from Guia/Ferreiras in the Algarve to the Spanish border, dwellers in the south of Portugal have the option of taking European flights from Seville.

Seville is little further from Portimão than Gatwick is from the British Midlands. It is certainly nearer to the Algarve than Lisbon and the airport facilities are good. However, there are no transatlantic flights and the fares to northern Europe tend to be more than they are from Faro.

By road

Compared with flying, this is expensive but pleasant if you take your time and make a holiday of it. Otherwise it's an expensive chore if you start from the UK, mainly because of the cost of ferries. Continental motorists are more fortunate in this respect.

We learnt early in life that Portugal was a long way from northern Europe. By road it is 2,123km from Brussels to Lisbon, 2,319 from Amsterdam, 2,229 from London taking the shortest sea crossing. Even Santander in northern Spain is virtually a two-day journey from the Algarve.

Via France

Everyone has their favourite route. The diehards do it by autoroute, others make diversions. Approaching Portugal by road, one is compelled to cross France and Spain. In both countries the autoroutes can be boring and expensive. If there is time to spare, it is worthwhile taking a look at the historic ground one is traversing.

Rural France has a charm of its own. A Michelin map and a good navigator can take you from north to south on excellent "yellow" roads without a single sighting of a *garde mobile* or a *motard* police motorcyclist. These gentlemen can impose a maximum fine of 900F on the spot, and they don't hesitate to do so. If you are in a hurry and taking the western route, bear in mind that although the autoroute from Tours to Bordeaux is expensive, the excellent dual carriageway through the Landes, from Bordeaux to the Spanish border, is free.

TRAVEL

Via Spain

Spanish roads, once so bad, are now excellent and it really is advisable keeping on them and away from Portuguese roads for as long as possible. In northern Spain the main road from Burgos to Valladolid is now to motorway-standard and it is free. The same goes for the N1 from Burgos to Madrid. There are Algarveans who take the motorway from Madrid via Córdoba and Seville to reach their homes, but it is an awfully long way round to stay on good roads. The Spaniards are developing a good through route from Pamplona, via Soria, Segovia, Avila and Caceres which is worth a try if you intend to cross into Portugal at Badajoz. This crossing is handy for both Lisbon and the most southerly region.

Channel crossings

The island race has the problem of getting on to the European continent via a sea crossing. We used to have the simplistic philosophy that a motor car, on even slow roads, travels more quickly than the fastest ship. Therefore, if you are in a hurry it has got to be quicker to take the shortest Channel crossing, find the nearest autoroute and get your foot down. This philosophy does not take into account the desire to stop for food, petrol, and sheer fatigue. Also, maybe, to pay the odd speeding fine.

Nowadays we take the longest possible sea-crossing, like the P&O or Brittany Ferries routes to northern Spain, taking advantage of the reduced prices to AFPOP members. Even then it is a sobering thought that having got to Santander or Bilbao, the road journey into southern Portugal is the thick end of 1,000km.

Within Portugal

Once inside Portugal the pace has to slacken because there is very little motorway to get you from A to B quickly. In the north there is a vital north-south motorway between Lisbon and Oporto, but we will have to wait for an equally vital north-south autoroute between Lisbon and the increasingly important Algarve. The Via do Infante in the south gets you from A to the middle of nowhere in the Algarve very quickly; thereafter the highway's progress to the west is bogged down in bureaucracy and, perhaps, that particular national trait which was aptly summed up by Rosemary Macaulay when she wrote that Portuguese officialdom always has a better use for public funds than what they were intended for.

Coach travel

Of course not everyone has a car. If you wish, you can travel by coach. It was cheaper than flying before the airline industry was liberalised. This is not necessarily the case anymore. However, there are a number of people who are allergic to aviation and for them there is a regular bus service from Lisbon to Paris, with feeder services from the Algarve to Lisbon and from the French capital to points north. Starting from Portimão in the early morning, one can be in Paris at 6.0pm the following day. Travellers to the UK have to cross Paris from south to north on a service bus, then a coach will carry them cross-channel arriving in London about midday, two days after leaving Portugal.

By rail

There is a feeling of comfortable Victorian adventure about the whole idea of travelling to Portugal by rail. As ever, one has to traverse France to Paris, where a connection can be made to anywhere in Europe. There has to be a change of trains at the Portuguese border because the Portuguese rail gauge is not the same as that in the rest of Europe. Otherwise it is quite straightforward. An attraction is that rail fares within Portugal are so frugal that one can afford to travel first class. Another is that trains are comfortable with good rolling stock. Moreover, rail travel gives you another view of this fascinating country.

Assistência e Serviço
Aeroportuário Lda.

* **Aviation Charter Seat Sales** * **Low prices** * **Special offers** *
Rua Casa do Povo 1, Almancil 8135, Algarve, Portugal
Tel. (089) 399973 / (089) 399869 Fax. (089) 399926

WATER

Domestic supply

The domestic water supply in Portugal comes under three main headings:

- ❏ Piped mains water originating from boreholes or reservoirs and controlled by local authorities.
- ❏ Natural springs.
- ❏ Private boreholes.

Mains water

Town water supply is one of the services which seems to have escaped nationalisation. Main towns have had their piped supply for very many years. Only in the last few years have pipe networks been expanded to take in the larger urbanisations which have sprung up, mainly in the Algarve, during the last 20 years.

Mains water is metered and priced in three bands according to the amount you use. If you live in a modest apartment without a swimming pool and take showers rather than baths, you will use only a few cubic metres in the course of the two-month charge period. However, should you aspire to lawns and pools, you will use many cubic metres of water and, because you've used a lot, will be charged about ten times the price per cubic metre as your more frugal neighbour.

It pays to keep a two-monthly record of your water usage. The "meter reader" does not in fact read your meter. Usage is estimated by the *Câmara* accounts department. If you use more than you are being debited for, when the meter is eventually read properly you may find yourself faced with a monstrous bill because all the excess will be charged at the most expensive rate. You will have to pay it and argue later.

Paying your water bill.

A *factura* will come through your door or into your letterbox every two months, except during the summer when the May-June period is extended by a month to make it May-July. This enables the meter reader to have an August holiday and deliver

WATER

your next bill two months later, in September. After that there's a one month period between bills to make up.

When it comes to paying the *factura* you have a choice between ancient and modern:

> ❏ Pay by direct debit.
> ❏ Pay the meter reader, who also delivers the bill to your door. He will receipt the bill giving his Christian name. Make a note of this name. Our's is Ângelo.
> ❏ If you are out when the meter reader calls, you will have to wait until the end of the month when, on the last two working days, a special office is opened at the *Câmara*. Inside is a long table with a line of gentlemen sitting behind it. These are the meter readers. Above each one is a little notice hanging from a wire, bearing his name. We easily spot the smiling face of Ângelo, give him the *factura* and a cheque, indulge in a friendly handshake and go away with a nice, comfy feeling that we are at last sharing the life and traditions of the Portuguese people.
> ❏ If you miss this charming ceremony, you will have to go to the accounts department in the *Câmara*, not the *Finanças*, and pay the bill to one of the clerks there. He may be a bit grumpy at being disturbed and will add a *multa*, a fine, for late paying. So don't go with a cheque already written out for the amount on the *factura*.
> ❏ Finally, you can pay the bill any time during the month at your local *Junta de Freguesia*. At least the two charming ladies in our's do it for us. They will take the *factura* and your cheque, put them in an envelope and give you their own receipt.

Natural spring water

Portuguese people tend to be connoisseurs of water. They will debate the qualities of the water from various springs and enthuse over their qualities just like a wine buff rhapsodising over a good vintage. Spring water comes from various sources.

> ❏ You may be one of the lucky ones and have your own private spring in your garden.
> ❏ If you live in a hilly district, go off with your car boot crammed with containers to your favourite spring to collect a week's supply.

WATER

> ❏ At the local *mini-mercado*, buy a few five-litre containers of one of the nationally distributed bottled waters such as *Luso*, *Alardo*, *Monchique*, or whatever.

Old habits die hard. Even in towns where the tap-water is eminently suitable for drinking, a large proportion of the immigrant population sticks to its favourite bottled "brew".

Boreholes

Before the advent of piped water in the urbanisations built by *estrangeiros*, many boreholes were sunk to draw water from the underground water table. The vast majority of these, sunk for domestic use, require a licence from the *Câmara*. Quite rightly the *Câmara* consider the water below their territory to be a communal asset. If you don't have a licence, they are quite likely to plug your borehole by pouring concrete down it. They in their turn extract water for their pipe network by drilling boreholes.

A grand survey of the water resources of the Algarve is continually under way. The authorities would dearly like to know the whereabouts of every borehole and well more than 15 metres deep. Being aware that there were hundreds if not thousands of unregistered boreholes and wells, especially in the southern region, they were pragmatic and in 1994 declared an amnesty against fines for everyone who registered their well or borehole before the end of August. It was then extended until the end of September and there have been further extensions.

The people who would like to know about your well or borehole are the *Delegação Regional do Ambiente e Recursos*, Rua Gambia, 33, in Faro. Should you decide to come clean, you will require:

> ❏ Your passport or identity card.
> ❏ An attestation from your local *Freguesia* confirming that you are a householder.
> ❏ A photocopy of the 1:250,000 scale map of your area showing the location of the well or borehole.
> ❏ The horse-power rating of your pump.

WATER

Coping with calcium

Hard water is endemic to the Algarve. Most of the domestic supply is extracted from underground tables by means of boreholes or wells, often hundreds of metres deep. The water has got there by permeating layers of rock and limestone, dissolving calcium and other elements on the way.

Although calcium is essential to the well-being of most of us, an excess of it can drastically reduce the performance of apparatus such as electric kettles, washing machines, dishwashers and gas water heaters by depositing a layer of calcium which acts as an excellent heat insulator. A coating as little as 0.5mm thick can increase heating costs by as much as 40%. Gas water heaters are particularly vulnerable and should be descaled annually.

The degree of hardness can vary and there are companies in Portugal who specialise in measuring this. It is usually stated in milligrams/litre or parts per million. If your water is rated at 150 ppm or more, it is worth treating. What has to be borne in mind is that calcium is one of the most important elements in our bodies and that a good supply of it is especially important for pregnant women, growing children and the elderly. Hard water is considered by dieticians to be an essential part of the normal diet.

The foregoing should be borne in mind when considering water softeners. Ion exchange water softeners, using salt, have been around for many years. They operate by removing the calcium carbonate from the water and replacing it with sodium salts. This is fine, but the treated water now contains sodium salts which render it unsuitable for children and the elderly. Therefore, if this kind of water softener is chosen, it should be installed downstream of the drinking water supply, not in the main. Modern ion-exchange water softeners are more compact than they used to be, but they are still bulky and need to be installed where they can be easily recharged with salt. On cheaper models, re-generation is controlled by a timer. More exotic ones are controlled by flow meters which re-generate only when necessary. Whichever you choose, ensure that it complies with EU standards which ensure that it doesn't contaminate the mains supply or breed bacteria.

Magnetic descalers are an alternative to water softeners and their manufacturers claim they stop limescale forming. Some of

WATER

them have a strong permanent magnet; others utilise a battery or mains electricity to produce a magnetic field. Their action is to destabilise the calcium carbonate and prevent it depositing as limescale. A snag in the past has been that they do not prevent scum in hand basins or evaporation staining in sinks.

A new type of electronic conditioner has recently appeared on the market which, it is claimed, gets over the shortcomings of the old magnetic softeners by feeding a series of varying low frequency radio waves into the water supply. It keeps the calcium carbonate so thoroughly in suspension that the water supply has all the characteristics of soft water. It dissolves limescale in shower heads, kettles and water heaters while at the same time eliminating scum in hand basins. A personal test showed that after ony a few days the improvement in the quality of the water was significant . Moreover it can be easily installed in less than an hour without disturbing any plumbing.

Corrosion

A problem afflicting owners of villas built before the easy availability of copper plumbing pipe in Portugal, is that the galvanised iron or steel plumbing pipe embedded in the floors and walls of houses is corroding and leaking. It calls for major building work on exterior and interior surfaces to get at the sources of the leaks. In some cases the only solution has been to completely re-plumb the affected house.

Water conservation

Most of the Portuguese population in the country areas of Portugal do not use a lot of water. The majority of the older, small Portuguese houses in the countryside have no running water. Most of the new ones in town areas, built since the Revolution, do. In the southern region it is the foreign residents with their lawns and golf courses, the tourists and the large farmers who are the main users. We have excepted pools because once they are filled the only water they consume is that lost by evaporation in mid-summer, and in the country they double up as static water tanks for fighting fires. So it is up to us to play our part in conserving water when and wherever we can. It is a serious matter because the underground water table in the Algarve is being so seriously depleted and replaced by sea water that

WATER

boreholes as much as four kilometres inland are producing water which is brackish.

Incidentally, it's no good borehole owners complacently sticking their noses in the air and claiming that the water shortage does not affect them. The underground lakes and water tables from which they derive their H_2O are as much a part of the public water supply as the reservoirs. They do not have a bottomless, personal lake located beneath their property from which it is their God-given right to draw as much water as they think fit.

We need water to drink, to cook with, to wash with, to water our food gardens with and, finally, to water our flower gardens. That is roughly the order of priorities. Here are just a few ways, major and minor, of saving it.

- Replace your lawn with a patterned *calçada* area.
- Use a cover on your pool to inhibit evaporation.
- Choose a light coloured car. It will need washing less often.
- Irrigate your garden once a week, giving it a good soak, rather than watering a little every day.
- Take a shower instead of a bath.
- Using a bowl inside the sink for the washing-up. (Don't use washing up water on the garden, but it makes a good weedkiller on paths and *calçadas*.)
- Don't leave the tap running when cleaning your teeth.
- In the summer, take a cold shower instead of a hot one to avoid the wasteful warming-up period.
- A British-size house brick placed upright in the loo cistern will reduce the amount of water flushed to waste. (Remember that it is only the portion of brick which stands above the low water mark in the cistern which does any good.)

Ingenious members of the community will have their own private ways of conserving water. In the house the main object of the exercise is to catch the water before it goes down the drain to waste.

WATER

THE GOLDEN RULE
IS TO ENGAGE BRAIN
BEFORE OPERATING
TAP.

Seeing is believing!

- No installation
- No plumbing
- No wiring
- Light weight
- Runs off domestic power supply
- Truly portable
- Low running costs
- Set up indoors or outside

Softub®
"The Spa of Infinite Possibilities"

JORO Lda. Rua 5 de Outubro 200 - 8135 Almancil Tel 089 393202 Fax 393201

JORO Lda.   Member of   Water Quality Association

KINETICO   GENESIS

ion exchange water softeners.
Non electric, automatic,
5-year guarantee.
Reverse osmosis and distillation units

The world's most advanced
countertop water distiller

Rua 5 de Outubro 200, 8135 Almancil - Tel. 089 393202 - Fax. 089 393201

WILLS

Making one is easy

Most people do not like making Wills. Quite why is not immediately obvious, because it is basically so simple. One explanation might be that it is tempting fate to make a will; the reality is that it is tempting fate not to make one.

A Will is quite simply a document stating what you want to happen to your belongings when you die. If you don't leave instructions (which is known as dying intestate) the law of one's own country has rules on how the property should be divided up amongst your surviving relatives. These rules may mean that the property is distributed in a way in which you would not have approved. That is one reason why writing a Will can save your family a considerable amount of trouble.

In Portugal it is not essential to use a lawyer for drawing up a Will, but it is strongly advisable to do so. Although you may have a very clear idea of how you wish your belongings to be divided, a lawyer will be able to draft the Will in terms that are completely unambiguous. The validity of a Will needs to be proved after a person's death. It is important then that there should be absolutely no misunderstandings about what was actually intended.

It is, of course, possible for your Portuguese assets to be incorporated in an English Will. However, it will be a lengthy process to have that Will proved in Portugal. Moreover, English Wills normally include trusts, which are an unknown concept in Portuguese law. They make it unbelievably complicated to register the property.

If you have gone to the trouble to produce an English Will, it is no great problem to prepare a Portuguese Will for what will normally be fairly restricted assets.

Writing a Portuguese Will need not take more than a few hours. Dying without having made one could cause your family months, or years, of problems. You probably had trouble grappling with the Portuguese legal system when buying your property. Imagine the trouble your family would have trying to sort out the estate after your death, probably under circumstances which might make it very difficult for them to come to Portugal in person.

WILLS

In Portugal there is the choice of making two types of Will, a Private Will and a Public Will.

PublicWill

A Public Will is written into the notarial books (in the same way as an *escritura*). It goes as follows:

- The testator, and the testator alone, will be provided with legalised photocopies for his own records.
- A few notarial offices will allow a third party to check that a Will has been made, and the date. No one is allowed to see its contents or a copy of them.
- It must be written in Portuguese and signed in front of the notary in the presence of two witnesses.
- A translator will have to be present if the testator or the two witnesses cannot speak Portuguese. That is unless the notary can translate the document for you into your language.

PrivateWill

This is a handwritten document, also signed before a notary and two witnesses. A Private Will has the following attributes:

- It is not written into the notarial books but will be handed back to the testator after the notary has approved it.
- It will be validated by a *minuta de aprovação* which testifies to the validity of the document.
- It must be handwritten as clearly as possible.
- It can be written in any language and may be in any national form. (This means that a lawyer in your own country should be able to prepare a draft for you. In practice, only one notary in the Algarve will accept an English draft).
  When notarised, place your Private Will in a safe place, such as a bank.

You should ensure that an English draft incorporates a clause on the law of "quick succession ". This is a common clause in English Wills and covers the case where both spouses, for example, are involved in a traffic accident. This ensures that if

WILLS

one spouse dies within, say, 30 days of the other's death, the inheritance is set aside and all the possessions are passed on to the next in line to inherit. This then avoids inheritance tax having to be paid twice on the same assets.

If there is a Will in your own country, it is sensible to ensure that the wording in both Wills is such that they don't conflict.

The snag with a Private Will is that no copy of it is kept in the notarial records. If you lose your notarised copy it is just as if you had made no Portuguese Will at all. The Public Will, in fact, is extremely private and quite safe.

Executors

In your own country it would not be at all unusual for a member of the family to be appointed as executor, that is the person responsible for ensuring that the deceased's wishes are carried out. With Portuguese assets and a Portuguese Will this could be an unfair burden. A qualified executor should be appointed, although this is not required by Portuguese law. A Portuguese lawyer would be a good choice. It is important here to appoint him before the testator's death and to name him in the Will, at the same time agreeing with him the fees that he will charge. If a bank or a non-Portuguese speaking lawyer is named as executor they will almost certainly have to instruct a Portuguese lawyer after the death. His fees would then be an open-ended expense which might be almost impossible to control.

Safety measures

- ❏ If you have a lawyer in your native country, make sure he is *au fait* with the contents of your Portuguese Will. Conversely, ensure that your Portuguese lawyer speaks your language and fully understands your wishes.
- ❏ Go back to your lawyer in your home country and instruct him to add a codicil to your Will saying just when and at what notarial office a Will on your Portuguese property was done. This is important because the expression in your main Will, "worldwide assets" or "assets wherever situated", includes Portugal.
- ❏ Keep an up-to-date account of all your assets in Portugal - property, bank accounts, insurance policies etc. Leave note with your

WILLS

> Portuguese lawyer indicating where they are deposited.
> ❏ If you have a spouse, make sure your bank accounts and car are in joint names. This ensures that the survivor has cash and transport available while the estate is being settled. Otherwise it can take time.

Inheritance tax

If the deceased was resident in Portugal, the inheritance tax declarations and the payment of taxes have to be made within 30 days, and there is another 60 days to produce a list of assets. If the deceased was resident outside Portugal, there are six months in which to complete the formalities.

The heirs should be made aware that inheritance and any other outstanding taxes must be paid before any change in the title can take place. They can make a private sales contract, but transfer of title can only take place after the inheritance has been accepted officially and the inheritance tax paid.

Heirs should be told exactly who the executor is so that they can make contact with him in the event of death to help them in administering and distributing the inheritance. Keep a close eye on the likely level of inheritance tax that is due to be paid, and discuss with the heirs just how this money is to be raised if they don't want to sell the property they are inheriting.

Bear in mind that inheritance tax is geared to the relationship of the person you leave it to. Leaving property to your wife or next of kin attracts low taxes. Leaving it to someone who is not a blood relation can attract up to 50% inheritance tax on the nominal value of your property.

All in all, making a Portuguese Will is a sensible precaution to save the heirs problems. It is essential financial planning which should be undertaken without any delay if one has assets in Portugal. It is equally sensible to prepare a Will in your own country. Wills should always be kept up-to-date and reviewed regularly to take account of changing financial and domestic circumstances.

WINE

Portuguese table wines

Wine writers have a jargon of their own verging on poetry. We read some time ago of a wine with delectable scents of jasmine, lime oil acidity and pine oil swirling together with the fruit of raspberries and plums. The imagination boggles. This was a wine selling for less than a fiver in British supermarkets, and for about half that price here.

We prefer the pragmatic approach: it has been said of beers that none of them are bad, it's just that some are better than others. The same goes for Portuguese wine. Ordinary Portuguese wines can be excellent. Put 500$ in our hand and we can promise to buy a better bottle of wine in Portugal than we would ever buy for the equivalent price in France. Moreover, what you get will be Portuguese wine. There is no need for the Portuguese wine growers to bulk up their wine with the produce of Algeria and Argentina.

Wine making in Portugal is undergoing enormous changes. At the turn of the century Portuguese wine-making was not the most advanced in the world. Under various regimes, moribund methods were enshrined in law. Co-ops were built with huge concrete vats devoid of temperature control. Under more enlightened government the old laws, which practically dictated that the bulk of production should come from the co-operatives, which generally produced strong, mediocre wines, are being dismantled. Individual wine makers are producing outstanding wines from selected grapes. The EU is helping too, trying to bring order into the enormous varieties of grapes being used to make the wine produced by the newly liberated co-ops. What is for sure is that the potential for producing good wine is probably better here than in any other country in Europe. The future looks wildly exciting. We can only hope that the other wine-producing countries of the EU, looking enviously over the fence, will not attempt to stunt growth via Brussels.

For the purposes of this book, suffice to say that in Portugal there are now twelve denominated areas, *Regiões Demarcadas*, now called *Denominação de Origem Controlada*. Originally there were seven. In 1979, Bairrada and four Algarve regions were added to the list. For the record they are as follows:

WINE

Denominação de Origem Controlada

Vinho Verde	Setúbal
Douro	Bairrada
Dão	Lagos
Bucelas	Lagoa
Colares	Portimão
Carcavelos	Tavira

When Portugal joined the EU, the Government created 31 extra areas, called *Vinhos de Qualidade Produzidos em Regiões Determinadas* (VQPRD's), now officially referred to as IPR's, *Indicações de Proveniência Regulamentada.* These wines can always be identified by the VQPRD marking on the label, with or without the *Reserva* designation to mark a good year. If a bottle from a co-operative known to be a VQPRD does not bear this mark, one has to assume that it contains an addition of wine from another source. Borba's *Convento da Vila*, one of the favourite everyday wines in the south, falls into this category.

There's an anomaly here because some of the IPR's are producing very good wine using modern equipment. There is a school of thought which holds that some of the new DOC's should never have been given that rating.

For the record here is a list of IPR's:

Indicações de Proveniência Regulamentada.

Chaves	Planalto-Mirandês	Valpaços
Encostas da Nave	Varosa	Lafões
Castelo Rodrigo	Cova da Beira	Pinhel
Alcobaça	Encostas de Aire	Óbidos
Almeirim	Cartaxo	Chamusca
Coruche	Santarém	Tomar
Alenquer	Arruda	Torres Vedras
Arrábida	Palmela	Borba
Portalegre	Redondo	Reguengos
Vidigueira	Granja-Amareleja	Moura
Évora		

WINE

Buying wine

If you are a wine buff with time to spare, vat-spotting is an interesting pastime. What could be more pleasant than motoring around the wine producing areas, wine book in hand, seeking out progressive little co-operatives, easily recognisable by their stainless steel vats. Go inside for a tasting. Two examples in the Alentejo come to mind: Vidigueira and Reguengos. Another outstanding Alentejo wine is Borba. Some of these IPR's are making really excellent wine which is superior, in our view, to most of the Algarve *Denominação de Origem Controlada* offerings.

If you are not a wine buff, but you enjoy drinking it, shop around in your own area. If you patronise an individual wine merchant, try to see how his wine is stored. There is a national tendency to store wine upright when it ought to be lying on its side to keep the corks wet and swollen. Beware of buying dusty bottles of old wine from establishments which follow this practice; they are likely to be undrinkable. Incidentally, the main co-operative of Borba seem to be aware of this trait. They use oversize, very good quality corks for even their ordinary wines.

Generally, price is an indication of quality - away from the tourist areas in summer, that is. Expect to pay:

200-300 Wine for quaffing
500-800 Good quality VQPRD
1000$ onwards   Individual wine-makers' offerings.

Required reading is Richard Mayson's *Portugal's Wines and Wine Makers*. All we can say is that this is a scholarly book, extremely well written and brimful of information which would be hard to fault. Another good reference book, but a confusing one to read, is Kathryn McWhirter and Charles Metcalfe's *Wines of Spain and Portugal*, published by Sainsbury's.

Both of these contain the information about vintages which are listed with comments on the next page. The comments can only be generalisations. The two sources are sometimes at variance, but what does show up is the consistency of the Alentejo performance. Maybe this is because this area is well away from the sea and less affected by coastal weather than, say, Bairrada, Dão, or Douro.

WINE

Special years

1991 Good or excellent all round.

1990 Good to excellent. Yields were down in the Alentejo and Setúbal but the quality is good. A good year for Port and Arrábida-Palmela.

1989 Good to average due to a very hot summer. Douro, Port and Dão were least good. The best was Alentejo.

1988 A disaster year for output with yields only 20% of normal in the Minho and 50% down in the Alentejo. Not only was the quantity down, but the quality was below the standard of the preceding three years.

1987 Poor to average year all round. Best wines came from Alentejo.

1986 Average to good wines from Alentejo, Arrábida-Palmela and Ribatejo. All the rest poor to middling.

1985 A good to excellent year for all areas. Exceptional Arrábida-Palmela, Bairrada, Douro and Port wines were made. Alentejo wines were a little less so, but still very good.

1984 Poor in the north, especially Dão, Douro and Port. The best were Ribatejo, Alentejo and Arruda.

1983 A very good year for the northern growers. An exceptional year for Alentejo wines.

1982 An excellent year, especially for Arrábida-Palmela, Douro and Alentejo wines. Dão and Bairrada not so good. A good year for Port.

Fortified wines

Fortified wines are those in which fermentation is stopped by the addition of *aguardente*, wine spirit the Portuguese equivalent of French *marc*. Port is the most famous of them, but so far as the mainland is concerned, Madeira is a close second. Another sweet, "pudding" wine is Moscatel de Setúbal which makes a very good first impression. Surprisingly there is dry, sherry-like wine coming from the co-operative at Lagoa in the Algarve. And there is a most interesting moscatel type wine made in the extreme north-east, *Jerupiga*.

Port wine is too big a subject to tackle here. Every variation of it from the cheapest to the most expensive is freely available.

WINE

You will find run-of-the-mill ruby and tawny ports from all the big shippers on the shelves of every village shop, *minimercado* and supermarket throughout Portugal. The better grades and the vintage ports are only to be found in wine merchants' shops, and are mainly for tourists. They are too expensive to be an everyday drink.

The great virtue of port is that all of it is palatable, none of it is undrinkable. Take a bottle of cheap ruby or tawny port by any of the well known names off the shelf of the store. You will be holding in your hand what the majority of expatriates favour as an end-of-dinner drink. It was interesting to find, after settling in Portugal, that there are very few port buffs here. On the other hand, there is a large body of people who like a glass of tawny port at regular intervals.

Of course the low-priced ports, labelled tawny, are deep red in colour and have by no means achieved tawny character. They have to be 10 years old or more for that. Ferreira, who are not well known outside Portugal, are the largest port wine makers. Their ruby and tawny wines are very reliable. There are many others.

AFPOP

WHAT IS AFPOP?

AFPOP is the affectionate acronym for the Associação de Proprietários Estrangeiros em Portugal. It is THE association for property owners or residents in Portugal.

AFPOP is the largest property owners association in Portugal and the only one representing foreign owners at a national level.

AFPOP is a non-commercial, non-political organisation properly constituted in Portuguese law. It is governed and run by an unpaid Management Council and Supervisory Council which counts among its members representatives of the main nations with subjects resident in Portugal.

AFPOP was created in 1987 out of a need for a body which could guide and represent property owners in Portugal at a time when property owning and tax laws were changing daily. There were then, and still are, worries about the energy with which these new regulations might be implemented. The ongoing rapid growth in membership reflects these continuing doubts.

AFPOP aims to further good regulations between foreign residents and their Portuguese hosts by promoting a better understanding of their culture, their history and their way of life.

AFPOP offers membership to all nationalities.

A HELPING HAND

AFPOP

The Association of Foreign Property Owners in Portugal
MEMBERSHIP APPLICATION FORM

Nr.

Last name: ____ Full name for address: Mr, Mrs, Ms etc ____

Mailing address
Line 1 ____ Line 2 ____
City ____ Code ____ Country ____ Tel ____

Other address
Line 1 ____ Line 2 ____
City ____ Code ____ Country ____ Tel ____

Married ☐ Single ☐ Nationality ____ Profession ____ Date of Birth __/__/__

PLEASE USE BLOCK CAPITALS

Joining fee	Esc	1000$00
Annual Membership	Esc	6000$00
Associate Member	Add 2000$00	$00
Foreign Mailing	Add 1000$00	$00
Total Amount paid		$00

Office Use only
Date accepted
Area code
Signature of Council Member

Paid by
Cash ☐
Cheque ☐

ASSOCIATE MEMBER. One only (spouse, or person living under the same roof)
Name (Mr, Mrs, Ms etc) ____
Signature ____ Day / Month / Year

Payment please to: AFPOP (Apartado 23, ALVOR, 8500 Portimão, Portugal)
Associação de Proprietários Estrangeiros em Portugal

AFPOP

TWELVE GOOD REASONS WHY YOU SHOULD JOIN

- Buying, selling, leasing? AFPOP offers help and advice on all stages of domicile from buying the land for your new home to selling the completed house.

- A group insurance scheme with a brokerage organisation of international repute providing massive savings in house and car insurance.

- A weekly free consultancy offering guidance from an experienced, English-speaking Portuguese lawyer.

- UPDATE, a regular newsletter circulated only to members of AFPOP keeping them informed of all the latest developments in legislation affecting residents.

- An accountancy consultancy with a British accountant.

- Guidance on filling-in the whole range of Portuguese official forms.

- A databank of highly qualified nurses from the UK and north European countries.

- Membership of AFPOP Shield offering free registration to Brittany Ferries Property Owners Club and P&O Ferries, with massive discounts on the Plymouth - Santander ferries. Also substantial deductions at many Algarve stores.

- Organised social events bringing members together within their areas.

- Associate membership for spouses or friends.

Rua da Paz 9, Alvor, 8500 Portimão
Tel: (082) 458509   Fax: (082) 458277

SERVICES DIRECTORY

AFPOP	242	
AIRLINE TICKETS	225	*ASAP-Assistência e Serviço Aeroportuário, Lda*
BANKING	17	*ABBEY NATIONAL*
	17	*HAMBROS BANK*
BATHROOMS	113	*IMPORTECO*
B.B.Q.	65	*JORO*
BUILDING	28	*DES TAYLOR*
	28	*ALGARFERRAMENTA*
	28	*HOME*
CENTRAL HEATING	78	*CENTRO DE LAREIRAS*
	78	*R.J. GRUNDWELL*
	78	*JORO*
COMPUTER SERVICES	36	*LERENS INFORMATICA*
	36	*COMPUTECNICA*
		also see Iberian Computer Consultants page 213
DENTISTS	119	DR. NICHOLAS COLE
	119	*DR. ALEX WILSON*
DOCTORS	120	*DR. JOHN PIPER*
	121	*LUZDOC*
	121	*MEDILAGOS*
	121	*MULTICLINICA DO ALGARVE*
	120	*PEREIRA E MOURA, LDA*
EDUCATION	46	*VILAMOURA INTERNATIONAL SCHOOL*
	46	*INTERNATIONAL SCHOOL OF THE ALGARVE*
	45	*BARLAVENTO ENGLISH SCHOOL*
		see also Interlingua page 106
		Centro de Linguas Intergarbe page 106
FINANCIAL SERVICES	59	*BLACKSTONE FRANKS INVESTMENT*
		see also Abbey National page17
		Abacus (Gibraltar) Ltd page 149
		Hambros Bank
GARDEN CENTERS	65	*Q GARDENS*
	65	*GREEN FINGERS*
	65	*JORO*
HEATING	78	*CENTRO DE LAREIRAS*
	78	*REGINALD J. GRUNDWELL*
	78	*JORO, LDA*
INSURANCE	96	*GENERAL ACCIDENT PLC.*
	95	*MEDAL-GESTÃO E MEDIAÇÃO DE SEGUROS*
	95	*BRENDON (PERSONAL INSURNACE)*
INTERIORS	104	*IMPORTECO*
	104	*SETERE*

SERVICES DIRECTORY

IRRIGATION	65	*GREEN FINGERS*
KITCHENS	104	*IMPORTECO*
LANDSCAPE GARDENERS	65	*GREEN FINGERS*
LANGUAGE SCHOOLS	106	*CENTRO DE LINGUAS INTERGARBE*
	106	*INTERLINGUA*
LAWYERS	109	*CARMEN DE ANDRADE E SILVA*
	109	*WILLIAM ODDY, SAMPSON & CO.*
LEGAL DOCUMENTATION	144	*AUTO REGISTOS*
		see also Carmen de Andrade e Silva page 109
		William Oddy, Sampson & Co. page 109
MEDICAL SERVICES		see Dr. Nicholas Cole page 119
		Dr. Alex Wilson page 119
		Dr. John Piper page 120
		Luzdoc page 121
		Medilagos page 121
		Multiclinica do Algarve page 121
		Pereira e Moura page 120
MEDICAL INSURANCE	121	*BRENDON (Personal Insurance)*
MOTOR SERVICES	144	*AUTO REGISTOS LDA*
OFFSHORE COMPANIES SERVICES	149	*INTERNATIONAL COMPANY SERVICES*
	149	*ABACUS (GIBRALTAL) LTD*
PETS & VETS	159	*DR JEFF ALLEN*
	159	*DR DAVID HOGGER*
	159	*CLINICA VETERINÁRIA CANHAM*
POOL HEATING		see Joro page 78
POWER TOOL RENTALS	28	*ALGARFERRAMENTA*
REAL ESTATE AGENTS	179	*STEPHENS, LDA*
		see also Abbey National page 17
RESTAURANTS & FOOD	193	*PIZZA SERVICE*
	193	*SALFINO MEXICAN RESTAURANT*
	194	*RESTAURANTE MESA POSTA*
	193	*RESTAURANTE LOTA*
	193	*RESTAURANTE O CAPACHO*
	194	*RESTAURANTE O BARAFUNDAS*
	194	*NO PATIO - RESTAURANTE E BAR*
	194	*SETERE*
SOLAR ENERGY		see Joro page 78
TELEPHONE ADAPTERS	213	*IBERIAN COMPUTER CONSULTANTS*
TELEVISION	216	*MARC ELECTRONICA PORTUGAL*
	216	*ALGARVE SATELLITE CENTRE*
TRAVEL	225	*ASAP-Assist. e Serviço Aeroportuário, Lda*
WATER TREATMENT	232	*JORO, LDA*